ILLUSIONS OF VICTORY

Illusions of Victory

The Anbar Awakening and the Rise of the Islamic State

CARTER MALKASIAN

OXFORD
UNIVERSITY PRESS

Oxford University Press is a department of the University of Oxford. It furthers the University's objective of excellence in research, scholarship, and education by publishing worldwide. Oxford is a registered trade mark of Oxford University Press in the UK and certain other countries.

Published in the United States of America by Oxford University Press
198 Madison Avenue, New York, NY 10016, United States of America.

CIP data is on file at the Library of Congress
ISBN 978–0–19–065942–4

Dedicated to Corporal Salem Bachar, USMC
April 13, 2006, Karma, Iraq

Contents

Maps

Acknowledgments

This book has taken some time to write. Twelve years have gone by since I first set foot in Anbar. I owe countless people thanks for assistance, advice, and support. Many deserved recognition years ago.

To start, I want to thank Nadia Schadlow and the Smith Richardson Foundation. In 2009, they generously awarded me a grant to complete a book on the war in Anbar province. Without it, I would have been unable to write up the research published herein. I also need to thank Robert Murray and the Center for Naval Analyses. It was through the Center for Naval Analyses that I had the opportunity to work with the Marines as a young academic and go to Anbar. That opportunity provided a perspective on what war really means. Those early years at the Center for Naval Analyses have proven a foundation for all my subsequent work.

Throughout the research and writing of the book, a group of friends from Anbar have been invaluable. They helped me when I was in Anbar and they have now helped in reviewing the text. Ben Connable and Adam Strickland—Marine officers fluent in Arabic—have an intimate understanding of the politics and tribal dynamics of Anbar. Their comments greatly improved the manuscript. So too did those of Ray

Gerber. Ray and I have been talking about Ramadi since 2006, when he was the intelligence officer of 3rd Battalion, 8th Marine Regiment, deployed in the middle of the city. Another steadfast colleague has been Pat Carroll—Marine; student of Islam; speaker of Arabic, Pashto, and Farsi. Few know the Islam of Anbar and Helmand better. In this camp of friends belongs J. Kael Weston. He arrived in Anbar in July 2004 and stayed until 2007. Our debates on policy, writing, and exactly what happened have yet to end. All of us have watched Anbar rise and fall, the war we wish had ended long ago.

Hopefully it goes without saying that I am indebted to the Marine generals who always graciously received my research. Their support has inspired me, whether in the writing of this book or in endeavors in Iraq, Afghanistan, and the halls of the Pentagon.

I would be remiss if I did not mention John Nagl, who hosted me for a week at his battalion's base in Habbaniyah during the grim months between the battles of Fallujah.

In this book and in *War Comes to Garmser*, I have been privileged to work with great publishers. I appreciate the willingness of David McBride and Oxford University Press to publish a book on Anbar. I also thank the three anonymous reviewers. Their constructive criticism led to substantial revisions. I thank Sebastian Ballard for another set of superb maps.

Finally, the teachings of Professor Robert O'Neill, my doctoral supervisor, were fresh in my mind in Anbar. We corresponded throughout my time there on Iraq, insurgency, and the bigger picture. I think he sensed that there would be no escape from the futility of Iraq and Afghanistan much earlier than most observers.

I apologize to those whom I have not named, especially the Marines and soldiers of the battalions that I visited, from the high desert of al-Qa'im to the haunted streets of Karma.

Anbar was a violent place. To my mind, it was worse than Afghanistan. The Marines and soldiers kept me safe. They faced far greater hardship. If memory dulls with time, their accomplishments seem to grow only sharper. The toil and sacrifice of our Marines and soldiers are good reason to care about what happened in Anbar, Garmser, and other corners of the long war.

© S Ballard (2016)
TURKEY
N
0
100
km
Mosul
Tal Afar
Raqqah
Irbil
Dar az Zawr
Kirkuk
Sulaymaniyah
Bayji
SYRIA
Tikrit
Al-Qa'im
Lake Thar Thar
Haditha
Ramadi
Fallujah
IRAN
BAGHDAD
Lake Habbaniyah
JORDAN
Al-Anbar Province
Lake Razazah
Karbala
Tigris R.
Najaf
Euphrates R.
Basra
SAUDI ARABIA
Iraq
KUWAIT
Persian Gulf

Map 1. Iraq

CHAPTER 1

A Decade Later

I have long hoped to write a history of America's war in Iraq's al-Anbar province. I spent eighteen months there as a civilian advisor to the I Marine Expeditionary Force (I MEF), first from February 2004 to February 2005, and then from February to August 2006. These were the times of Fallujah and Ramadi, grinding battles that still define much of America's experience in Iraq, featured in popular books and movies. My job was to carry out research for Marine generals, usually on topics related to strategy, culture, and society. I studied the insurgency, our tactics, and Iraqi politics and tribes. I was lucky enough to get to see Marines and soldiers throughout the province and to speak with plenty of Iraqis. When I left Iraq, I planned to write a full history of the campaign. Alas, in 2009, I went to Afghanistan. The Anbar book fell by the wayside. Two detailed chapters on Ramadi and the Anbar awakening were all that were completed. I have since come to doubt that I will ever have time to return to the project. In an attempt to salvage years of research and writing, I have decided to tell only the story of the battle of Ramadi and the accompanying tribal awakening. Few events have stood out so starkly in America's wars in Iraq and Afghanistan. Few events offer better insight into what difference our sacrifices ultimately made.

Ramadi was one of America's greatest successes in Iraq. From 2003 to 2006, the United States struggled to defeat the Iraqi insurgency, led by the extremist organization al-Qa'eda in Iraq (AQI). During those years, the United States launched a series of violent offensives against insurgents in the cities of Fallujah, Najaf, al-Qa'im, Tal Afar, and Ramadi. The insurgency nevertheless raged on. By early 2006, fighting wracked Baghdad, Iraq's capital. US leaders began to consider whether defeat was looming. Then, in the autumn of 2006, tribes in Ramadi formed a movement—Sahawa al-Anbar, or the "Anbar awakening." Over the course of seven months of heavy fighting, the tribes and the United States inflicted a stunning defeat upon AQI in Ramadi. The movement spread to the rest of Anbar and then to vital areas elsewhere in Iraq. Tribes and communities stood up throughout the country. Eventually, AQI was pushed back, insurgent attacks decreased, and Iraq witnessed an uneasy stability. Ramadi was thus a turning point of the Iraq war, the battle from which wider successes originated.

In the years that followed, Anbar became a model for how to defeat insurgents and terrorists. The US officers of the time—astute Colonel Sean MacFarland, fluent Captain Travis Patriquin, down-to-earth Lieutenant Colonel Bill Jurney, General David Petraeus above them all—earned well-deserved acclaim. Abdul Sittar al-Rishawi, charismatic leader of the awakening, was featured in newspaper and magazine articles. President George W. Bush even met him. Candidate Barack Obama visited Anbar a year later. In terms of strategy, officers, analysts, and policymakers hailed surging troops and empowering tribes as a means of countering insurgents.[1] There were widespread calls to attempt an "awakening" with the Pashtun tribes of Afghanistan, eventually resulting in the formation of "Afghan local police."[2] Later still, the idea of working with tribes influenced US policy debates over how to handle the Syrian civil war.

A decade after the awakening, things looked none so bright. In January 2014, after years of preparation and growth, AQI, re-named the Islamic State, conquered most of Anbar. The tribes that had formed the awakening movement were too divided and isolated to mount an effective resistance. The Islamic State then struck beyond Anbar, capturing Mosul and the rest of Sunni Iraq. For three years, war engulfed Anbar. Almost everything we had fought for from 2003 to 2007 was lost. With Baghdad in danger, the United States was forced to return to war in Iraq. US Marines, soldiers, and special operations forces found themselves back in Anbar trying to help the Iraqi government recapture the province.

This book re-examines the battle of Ramadi and the Anbar awakening from the perspective of a decade later. With almost exactly ten years' distance from the events of 2006 and 2007, we are now better placed to understand the meaning of old successes. The book aims to provide a more rigorous treatment of Anbar than earlier works by using primary source research collected during my time in the province. It tries to determine exactly what we should draw from Anbar and the campaign after its accomplishments have washed away. Is Anbar worth remembering? I think it is. Study of what happened helps explain why the highly regarded successes of 2006 and 2007 ultimately proved fragile. In doing so, the book should help us understand why the successes of military interventions can be so fragile in general. It should help us make more realistic decisions in wars today and in the future.

OLD DEBATES

In the years following the battle of Ramadi, discourse on the Iraq war was tinted by what then appeared to have been a great victory. The big question was: Why did the United

States succeed, defeating AQI and bringing stability to most of Iraq? Why the awakening prevailed in Anbar, specifically in Ramadi, was a pivotal part of the question.

There were two main schools of thought when it came to Anbar. One was that new troops and innovative US tactics made the difference.[3] Take the following excerpt from an influential article by Colonel Sean MacFarland in *Military Review*:

> The "Anbar Awakening" of Sunni tribal leaders and their supporters that began in September 2006 near Ramadi seemed to come out of nowhere. But the change that led to the defeat of Al-Qaeda in Ramadi—what some have called the "Gettysburg of Iraq"—was not a random event. It was the result of a concerted plan executed by U.S. forces in Ramadi.[4]

In this school of thought, additional US Marines and soldiers were deemed to have been necessary to suppress AQI and set the conditions for the tribes to rise up. Equally important were new tactics that US commanders introduced. George W. Bush's 2007 surge was sometimes credited with the new troops and tactics that made the difference in Anbar, not to mention in Iraq as a whole.[5]

The other school of thought was that the tide turned because Iraqis rose up against AQI's brutality and cruelty. Bob Woodward, for example, wrote that the decision of the tribes to turn had little to do with US actions:

> Al-Qaeda in Iraq had made a strategic mistake in the province, overplaying its hand. Its members had performed forced marriages with women from local tribes, taken over hospitals, used mosques for beheading operations, mortared playgrounds and executed citizens, leaving headless bodies with signs that read, "Don't remove this body or the same thing will happen to you." The sheer brutality eroded much of the local support for Al-Qaeda in Iraq.[6]

These two schools of thought played into US policy debates from 2007 onward. Anbar became a point of contention in the 2008 presidential elections. John McCain held up the surge as evidence of how bold US policies had turned around a failing war. He used it to justify an interventionist foreign policy. The Obama camp countered that the success in Anbar had preceded the surge and was the product of AQI brutality, rather than anything the United States had done. Later, proponents of a US surge into Afghanistan used Anbar as part of their case that US troops could turn the tide in that war. Opponents again argued that US troops had been immaterial to success in Anbar. It is worth reiterating that both schools of thought hailed Anbar as an impressive success. Anbar's role in policy debates was defined through that prism.

This book's take on this old debate is that both American troops and tribal rejection of AQI were necessary for success. Without either, the awakening would have failed. The awakening tribes depended on US Marines and soldiers to do the vast majority of the fighting and prevent AQI from overrunning them outright. US Marines and soldiers depended on the decision of the tribes to deny AQI the shelter and anonymity it needed to survive. The presence of US troops did not guarantee that the tribes would do so. After all, Marines and soldiers, using fairly innovative tactics, had been in Ramadi and most of Anbar for years before the awakening. The tribes had to decide to stand up on their own.

The fashion in which these factors played a role differs slightly from the schools of thought outlined above. In particular, the role of AQI is misunderstood. Too much emphasis has been placed on the notion that AQI brutality and cruelty was so bad that it prompted tribes to rise up en masse. The notion paints AQI as far less popular and the tribal leaders as far more popular than was actually the case. No, this was more about a few tribal leaders and their followers pursuing power and avenging blood feuds. Brutality and cruelty had something to do with why they stood up, but in the context of other dynamics. Very early in the war in Anbar, competition emerged between the tribes and AQI. As AQI grew, it marginalized tribal leaders and curtailed their influence and livelihoods. Eventually, a few of these tribal leaders decided to stand up and regain their power. In certain cases, AQI's uncompromising position and brutality inflamed the reaction, but the underlying cause lay elsewhere. Indeed, AQI's worst cruelties largely came after, not before, the tribes stood up, in the violent mafia-esque struggle that followed.

Moreover, American troops and the struggle for power with AQI are only two necessary conditions. The role of those Iraqis on the front line ought to be accentuated. An overlooked condition is the esprit de corps and cohesion within the tribes opposing AQI. Until this condition was present, *the tide did not turn, regardless of the presence of US troops or expansion of AQI's power.* The tribesmen at the forefront of the awakening demonstrated resolve and determination, enduring losses that had broken others. Within their individual tribes, they were more cohesive and less prone to infighting. This enabled them to persevere against AQI where others before had failed. Without them, the tide may never have turned. They were the spearhead. The nature of the man on the ground and his social bonds mattered in this civil war, along with American troops and the power struggle with AQI.

I owe something here to John Keegan's *The Face of Battle*. In that classic military history, he wrote: "The behavior of a group of soldiers on any part of the battlefield ought to be understood in terms of their corporate mood, or of the conditions prevailing at the time."[7] If their mood is to run, then the battle may be lost, depending on their location and other conditions on the battlefield. Social and cultural factors deeply affect that corporate mood. Resilience, cohesion, and willingness to bear loss can derive from kinship, geography, tribal culture, and a variety of other deep factors, often considered anthropological and outside the purview of the study of the war. A wide body of scholarship on the Middle East parallels Keegan and ties such factors directly to military success. The scholarship traces back to fourteenth-century Arab scholar Muhammad ibn Khaldun, who was one of the first to associate group feeling with military capability.[8] In the case of the Anbar awakening—and, I would argue, in others as well—social and cultural factors underlay the outcome. The larger meaning, to which we will return shortly, is that the course of an insurgency, an internal conflict, or a civil war may be determined by unmalleable internal dynamics more than the actions of an outside power such as the United States.

A SOBER DISTANCE

All this discussion of bygone glory is somewhat out of step with the perspective of 2017. After the rise of the Islamic State and its conquest of Sunni Iraq, the bigger question is: Why did success prove fragile? Root problems can be detected in Ramadi in 2006 and 2007. In fact, many policymakers, officers, and observers noted them at the time, their writings later overshadowed by the bright success of the awakening. Through new study of the past, we can see fundamental weaknesses that led to breakdown in 2014, when the Islamic State attacked with remarkable force. Three specifically come into relief.

First, between 2009 and 2014, the government marginalized the Sunnis, undermining the cooperation between the tribes and the state that held the Islamic State at bay. The tribal leaders were Sunni and wanted greater Sunni political power. The government was largely Shi'a and did not. Violence eventually ensued as Anbar Sunnis protested against the government. When the Islamic State attacked in January 2014, the Sunni tribes and the government were fighting with each other instead of standing together to face the onslaught. It is well known that the government's distrust of the Sunnis pre-dated 2011. During the battle for Ramadi, the democratically elected Shi'a majority government was already marginalizing the minority Sunnis. Only the dire threat posed by AQI and American lobbying got the government to help the tribes. Otherwise, the government viewed the Sunnis as the problem. Once AQI receded, the danger of Sunni political consolidation outweighed the security benefit of cooperation.

Second, the tribes could neither sustain themselves nor hold themselves together. Without the United States, they could not generate the resources to field the military forces and deliver goods and services necessary to control the people of Anbar and keep out the Islamic State. The problem was compounded by the tendency of the tribes to compete with each other rather than work toward the common good. When confronted by the Islamic State, the tribes went their own ways. These weaknesses too were apparent in 2006 and 2007. At no point was the awakening movement self-sustaining. The tribe's rise in power was based on US and government funding and military support. Before that, AQI had been able to defeat the tribes quite handily on a number of occasions. Furthermore, Sunni tribes had long suffered from infighting. The cohesion of the families and clans that spearheaded the awakening was largely absent in the rest of the movement. Until months into the actual awakening, Sunni tribes were broken up, with many supporting AQI. In the worst cases, parts of one tribe sided with the awakening while other parts sided with AQI. In other words, tribal dominance was artificial, not natural. On their own, the tribes lacked the necessary unity and wherewithal to defeat the Islamic State.

Third, the Islamic State held the sympathies of many Sunnis, as had AQI before it. After the awakening, tribal and government control of Anbar rested on the military power of a small elite rather than popular mandate. The tribal leaders and the government could cut AQI supporters out of politics but could not smother some degree of popular sympathy. As government and tribal cooperation wavered, AQI, whose members were vastly Iraqi, was able to return as the Islamic State and regain wide Sunni support. Again, in 2006 and 2007, AQI had already demonstrated a resilience and natural momentum—a sustainability that the tribes lacked. By 2006, AQI was deeply embedded in Anbar society and enjoyed popular support, partly because of its espousal of Islam and stand against occupation. AQI's message was clear and simple, and resonated among many people at least as much as tribalism, nationalism, or democracy. After the awakening was declared, AQI carried on a grinding seven-month battle in Ramadi against the full force of the US military and increasing numbers of tribes, a strong indication of the depths of its support.

We missed these signposts. Success over-wrote them. The tribal movement's success was so militarily impressive that we mistook it as irreversible, rather than as a momentary break in tribal infighting. AQI looked so badly beaten and was cast as so brutal that we discounted earlier evidence of popular support. In this regard, the overemphasis placed on the role of AQI's brutality is more than academic curiosity. By understating AQI's popularity, we may have lost sight of the chance they could return. Within months of US withdrawal from Iraq in 2011, the situation was badly regressing. Natural dynamics reasserted themselves. Without US funding and presence, the changes wrought by the awakening and years of US effort slipped away.

REINTERPRETING THE AWAKENING

What happened in Anbar should influence how we think about war. After 2001, the United States fought against insurgents and terrorists in Iraq, Afghanistan, Syria, Libya, Yemen, the Philippines, and many other countries. The wars dominated our foreign policy. Fundamental questions arose as to whether wars in weakly governed or broken countries serve our interests and how we should go about them: Can military intervention bring any stability to the country at hand? How many troops should the United States send and how long should they stay? Can improvements last after the United States departs?

From 2003 to 2011, great effort was put into the idea that the United States could go to war in Iraq and Afghanistan, get out within a few years, and leave lasting stability behind. In his speech that announced the 2007 surge, President George W. Bush set forth:

> Victory in Iraq will bring . . . a functioning democracy that polices its territory, upholds the rule of law, respects fundamental human liberties, and answers to its people . . . it will be a country that fights terrorists instead of harboring them . . . If we increase our support at this crucial moment, and help the Iraqis break the current cycle of violence, we can hasten the day our troops begin coming home.[9]

Over time, as Iraq appeared to calm and Afghanistan dragged on, enthusiasm for intervention waned. Secretary of Defense Bob Gates famously quipped: "In my opinion, any future defense secretary who advises the president to again send a big American land army into Asia or into the Middle East or

Africa should have his head examined."[10] After the United States withdrew from Iraq in 2011, conventional wisdom was that the United States should get out of the intervention business.[11] Before that could happen, renewed conflict in Iraq and the rise of the Islamic State brought war in broken countries back to the center of US foreign policy. The old questions remained, as potent as ever.

For seven years after 2006, Anbar was the foremost example of how US intervention could succeed. It became a model for how to conduct operations. In his September 2007 testimony to Congress on the success of the Iraq surge, General David Petraeus stated that Anbar "is a model of what happens when local leaders and citizens decide to oppose al Qaeda and reject its Taliban-like ideology. While Anbar is unique and the model it provides cannot be replicated everywhere in Iraq, it does demonstrate the dramatic change in security that is possible with the support and participation of local citizens."[12] Along this line of thought, various policymakers, military officers, and commentators suggested Anbar might show how the right numbers and methods could defeat an insurgency in a few years.[13] I myself examined its potential intently.

Today, Anbar is an example of the opposite. The collapse of the leading model of success discredits the idea that the United States can send the military to a country for a few years and create lasting peace. Even the leading model was bound to deeper social, sectarian, and religious forces insensitive to a temporary US presence. Rather than decisive success, Anbar exemplifies how intervention itself is a costly, long-term project. The most brilliant achievement did not escape this wisdom. This reinterpretation endows Anbar with an even greater meaning. If the most successful case of intervention and counterinsurgency was trapped by these forces, why should we expect anything different elsewhere?

The view of Anbar from a distance questions the fundamentals of American foreign policy thinking. Chief among them is the idea that intervention can strengthen stability and bring good. Few Americans doubt that invading Iraq was a bad idea, regardless of Saddam's oppressive dictatorship and atrocities. Toppling over order and letting sectarian, tribal, and religious dynamics run their course harmed the people of Iraq and raised the terrorist threat to the United States. But the problems of intervention run deeper than the initial ill-advised invasion. The pursuit of democracy after Saddam's downfall certainly brought no stability and may have worsened things by empowering vengeful Shi'a before Sunnis could be convinced to join the political process. The military forces that we built fared little better, falling apart after US departure. There is a serious question of whether democracy and nationally configured militaries are sustainable against an Islamic movement without outside assistance. If they are not sustainable on their own, does real change require a military and political presence that verges on colonialism? A study on Anbar alone cannot answer all these questions. They are the troubling heritage of over a decade in Iraq.

What is clear is that the idea the United States can intervene in a country for a few years and enable a government to stand on its own is wrong. The United States can certainly effect tremendous political change and quash violence, but there is a good chance it will be temporary. Political, social, and cultural dynamics are too powerful. Once the United States departs, those dynamics can reassert themselves. Instead of quick departure, the United States probably needs to countenance a long commitment, with boots on the ground. Tens of thousands of boots may not be necessary. Thousands is probably a good guess, staying for decades. Even then change might still reverse itself once the United States departs. Any sober discussion of intervention must recognize the possibility of a long commitment and the uncertainty of any kind of sustainable change. This is the biggest strategic lesson of Anbar.

The lesson should give generals and presidents pause when thinking about future intervention. Expectation of a long commitment should raise the expected cost of any endeavor. If Iraq and Afghanistan are any example, the American people and politicians with domestic priorities may have little interest in carrying that burden for years. The cost should discourage intervention itself. Living with instability may be more bearable than the financial and human expenses of addressing it. Where the risk of terrorism is too dangerous and intervention unavoidable, strategies should be designed that are affordable enough to be executed for decades. On its own, the host nation is unlikely to maintain what we accomplish. Though only one case, Anbar forces us to consider the unproductiveness of intervention writ large.

For students of US strategy, the Iraq war, and Anbar, four texts are essential reading. A good starting point is *The Strongest Tribe* by Bing West. It is based on West's repeated visits to Iraq and observation of front-line combat. He details the tactical prowess of US Marines and soldiers and their bottom-up partnerships with Iraqis.[14] A deeply erudite explanation of the role of tribal customs and AQI's brutality is David Kilcullen's *The Accidental Guerrilla*.[15] For a piece specifically on Anbar, Austin Long's "The Anbar Awakening" is useful.[16] Long warns against putting too much emphasis on the role of the United States versus dynamics between the tribes and AQI. The most quantitative study is "Testing the Surge," an article by Stephen Biddle, Jeffrey Friedman, and Jacob Shapiro. Through analysis of data on insurgent attacks, they assess that the surge and the willingness of tribes to rise up were both essential to success; if the two had not been present together at nearly the same moment, violence would not have declined in Iraq.[17]

There is also a growing literature on the perspective of the Iraqis. Anthony Shadid published his classic *Night Draws Near: Iraq's People in the Shadow of America's War* in 2005. More recent is Mark Kukis's *Voices from Iraq*. It features stories about the war from over fifty Iraqis. For Anbar, Kael Weston's *The Mirror Test* offers good insight. Widely cited is the Marine Corps' wonderful set of original-source interviews with the Iraqi leaders of the awakening, *Al-Anbar Awakening: Iraqi Perspectives*.[18] Finally, Sterling Jensen, an Arabic-speaking American who was in Ramadi from 2006 to 2008, wrote his doctoral dissertation on Iraqi narratives of the awakening. Once published, it will surely be an essential text on both the Iraq war and the Anbar campaign.[19] Appreciating what has been written to date, whether on the Iraq war as a whole or Anbar in particular, the causal role of Iraqis in the outcome of war warrants still greater study. It will hopefully span beyond this slim book.

The book is organized into seven chapters. The first is this introduction. The second describes al-Anbar province and the US war there from 2003 to 2006. The chapter is meant to provide an understanding of the role of the tribal system and religion in Anbar and then the US campaign up to the battle of Ramadi. During this time, the Marines arrived in Anbar, the insurgency broke out, the two battles of Fallujah occurred, and elections were held. The third and fourth chapters look at the fighting in Ramadi from late 2005 to mid-2006. Ramadi was then the hub of the insurgency. The US command reinforced the city in a bid for success. This was a dire time, too often neglected by writers and journalists, when AQI was expanding, the tribes were losing power, and the United States was struggling to gain the upper hand. The beginning of the awakening movement lies here. The fifth chapter examines the awakening and how the tide turned in Anbar. The battle raged from

September 2006 to March 2007. US Marines and soldiers worked closely with the awakening tribes, which endured defeats and casualties to push out AQI. The sixth chapter explains what happened in Anbar from the end of 2007 to 2016. It focuses on the Islamic State and the breakdown of the awakening movement in Anbar. The seventh chapter concludes and re-examines the significance of Anbar and the awakening after the rise of the Islamic State.

The expert on Iraq or the Middle East will note I simplify a great many things. I have done so to ease the task of the reader. I have tried (less than successfully) to do away with military acronyms. I have also tried to use English instead of Arabic words. The plain practicality of "religious leaders," "Islamic law," and "tribal leaders" has replaced the romance of "imams," "shari'a," and "shaykhs." Most egregiously, tribes are often treated as more uniform than in fact. I expect many of my friends to object to tribes marked on maps as if they own clean-cut territory when in fact boundaries blur. I believe the reader needs a rough map to understand the lay of the land. When and where to simplify is the art of the historian.

This is a short book burdened with details. It is a story of what happened on the ground. It errs on the side of the Iraqi point of view—though I am not satisfied that their story has been fully told. I wish I could have learned more about Iraqi lives and society. I came to Iraq ill-prepared. I could not speak Arabic and, regrettably, only acquired a bit during my time there. I put as much detail into this book as I could without losing the clarity of the story. It follows a habit of trying to capture the deep inner workings of society and explain what happened from the ground up. I am biased. I think those inner workings explain a lot about war.

The analysis within this book is my own, and does not represent the position of the US government, Department of Defense, or any other organization.

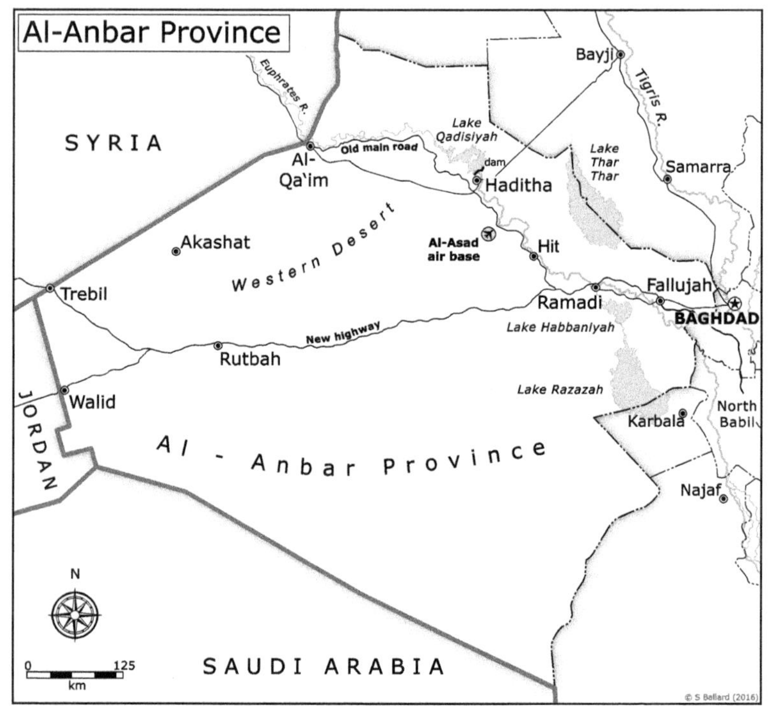

Map 2. Al-Anbar Province

CHAPTER 2

The War in Anbar, 2003–2005

Al-Anbar is Iraq's western province. It begins just west of Baghdad, the capital, and ends on the borders of Syria, Jordan, and Saudi Arabia. The Euphrates River flows out of Syria from one end of Anbar to the other, a distance of over four hundred kilometers. It is the mainstream of life and commerce. Almost all the people in the province live along the river, mostly in the cities and towns, although a substantial number still tend the fertile soil close to the water's edge. Deserts span out hundreds of kilometers from the Euphrates and its thin strip of farmland to the edges of the province. In 2004, Anbar's population was roughly 1.5 million (a small fraction of Iraq's 26 million total, nearly half of whom lived in and around the major cities of Baghdad, Mosul, and Basra).

Anbar is sparse in population and poor in resources, yet strategic in location, linking Baghdad to Jordan and Syria. From Baghdad, Anbar's old main road (known by the US military as "Route Michigan") and a new highway (Route One or, to the US military, "Route Mobile") lead west, shadowing the course of the Euphrates. Both are paved, the former narrow and clogged, the latter wide and modern, with off-ramps and overpasses. After about seventy kilometers, the two come to Fallujah, long known as the city of mosques. Built up over the Saddam years, the city has a square perimeter, a perpendicular street grid, and a skyline of domes and minarets amid modernish gray and tan buildings. The old main road cuts directly through the city and thence through the rich Euphrates farmland of Habbaniyah and Khalidiyah toward Ramadi. The new highway bypasses Fallujah to the north, and heads sixty kilometers through the outskirts of the desert to Ramadi.

Ramadi, the provincial capital, has 450,000 people. It has existed since at least the mid-nineteenth century, starting out as the main market and administrative point for the tribes of Anbar. Today, the Euphrates and adjacent waterways divide Ramadi into three parts: an elongated downtown center, a northern well-populated farmland, and a western urban industrial and residential zone. Saddam Hussein built grand palaces on the riverfronts where the three parts meet. The old main road goes directly through downtown and then the western zone until it again meets the new highway, which skirts central Ramadi to the north, as it does Fallujah.

West of Ramadi, the population thins and the elevation rises by a few hundred feet. The new highway turns southwest and heads through hours of desert to Jordan. A branch of the main road peels off and proceeds along the Euphrates toward the Syrian border. Here the farmland and palm groves cling to the Euphrates. The people concentrate in a string of towns along the river—Hit, Haditha, and al-Qa'im. Compared to Ramadi or Fallujah, these towns are small; 110,000, 65,000, and 120,000 live in each. In Haditha, a dam holds back the Euphrates River and controls its flow southward. Electricity from the dam powers much of the province. Between the west's towns lie smaller towns and villages—Zuwayyah, Tal Aswad, Muhammadi, Baghdadi, Anah, and Rawah. This is the western desert, where the tribes are strong and Baghdad is far.

Anbar has few natural resources and none of the oil wealth of southern Iraq, Mosul, or Kurdistan. Phosphate is mined at Akashat, in the west near the Syrian border. Nearby, an unexplored natural gas field, known as the "Akkaz," is rumored to be substantial and lucrative. Saddam Hussein built a few state-owned factories to process local resources. Old cement and glass factories stand near the big cities and towns. There is a phosphate plant near al-Qa'im. From Baghdad to Hit, significant farming survives a few kilometers out from either bank of the Euphrates before the desert takes over. Agriculture employs a quarter of Anbar's workers.[1] Commerce is also a traditional occupation in Anbar. Tribesmen still herd livestock and other goods across the desert, often shadowing the Euphrates. Many of the towns started as waypoints between Damascus, Aleppo, or Amman and Baghdad. Goods flow to and fro on the roads and highway to Syria and Jordan, with accompanying customs fees. In turn comes smuggling, hijacking, and black-market trade, activities that have sustained Anbar's tribes for centuries. The most important income for Anbar from 1970 onward, however, was government salaries and transfers from the profits of the oil coming from the south and the north. Anbar depended on Baghdad for their services, livelihood, and standard of living.[2]

The people of Anbar are overwhelmingly Sunni Arab. Iraq is divided into three major groups, differentiated by ethnicity, sect, or both: Kurds, Shi'a Arabs, and Sunni Arabs. All are Muslim. The Kurds, who are Sunni but not Arab, make up roughly 20 percent of the population and live primarily in the north. Shi'a Arabs are the majority. They make up 50–60 percent of the population and live in southern

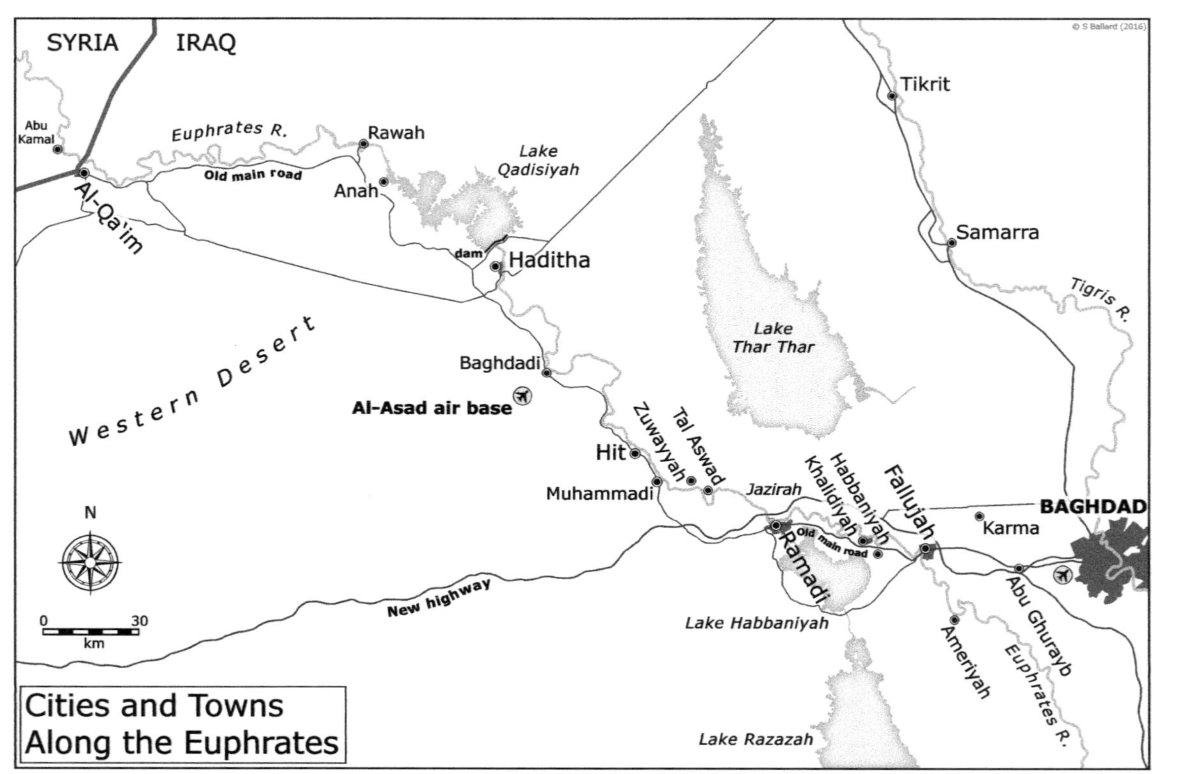

Map 3. Cities and Towns along the Euphrates River

and central Iraq. In 2003, most of Baghdad was Shi'a. Two of the holiest sites in Shi'a Islam—Najaf and Karbala—are in Iraq. Ayatollah Ali al-Sistani, who lived in Najaf, was one of Shi'a Islam's revered leaders. Sunni Arabs are a minority, roughly 20–30 percent of the population. They live in northern and western Iraq. Until 2006, a substantial minority was also in Baghdad. Sunni Arabs ruled Iraq for centuries, under the Ottomans, the British, and finally Saddam. That is why Saddam distributed jobs and oil profits to the Sunni people of Anbar. Loss of power and the rise of the Shi'a, whom the Sunni Arab governments had kept down, was a shock. For the sake of simplicity, I refer to Iraqi Sunni Arabs as "Sunnis" even though Kurds are also Sunni.

Tribes play a significant role in Anbar even though true Bedouin—"people of the camel"—are few and the locus of power is in the cities. Most of the Anbar tribes gave up the Bedouin lifestyle roughly two hundred years ago for farming along the Euphrates. Certain segments still herd and smuggle back and forth from Syria, Jordan, and Saudi Arabia.[3] Tribal leaders, known as shaykhs, meet with their tribesmen in large villas in the countryside or, more likely, in a house or office in one of the cities.

Nearly every person in Anbar is a member of a tribe. It is a source of group identity and belonging. The degree of affinity varies. Plenty of townspeople distanced themselves from their tribes decades ago. Nevertheless, very few shed tribal ties altogether. Tribe as a source of identity pervades the province. It both complements and competes with nationalism and Islam.[4]

Roughly two dozen tribes live in Anbar. Theoretically, nineteen fall under the Dulaymi tribal confederation.[5] In 2003, the old principal tribe of confederation—its former political leaders—was the aristocratic Albu Assaf, who lived just west of Ramadi. In the western desert, the large

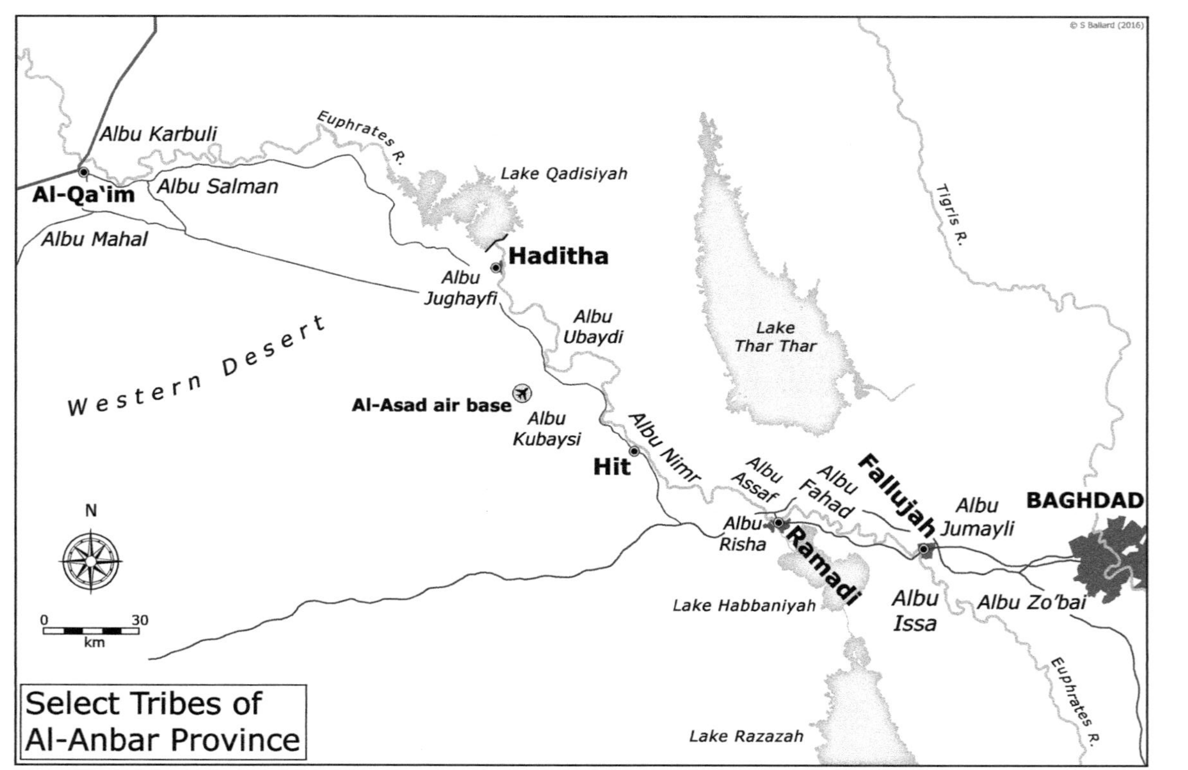

Map 4. Select Tribes of Al-Anbar Province

Albu Mahal near al-Qa'im and Albu Nimr near Hit held their own baronies. Around Ramadi, a large yet fragmented tribe, the Albu Fahad, was influential. It was one of ten in the area, including the Albu Alwan, Albu Thiyab, and Albu Risha. Fallujah had its own set of tribes. Of them, the Albu Issa were notable for both their size and political stature in the province and Baghdad. Further east, and closest to Baghdad were the Albu Zo'bai, notorious smugglers, bandits, and rebels.[6]

Tribes are segmented, meaning that no strict hierarchy exists in which all tribesmen obey a single leader. The Dulaymi confederation had an appointed leader, the "shaykh of shaykhs," since 1920 a descendant of Ali al-Sulayman of the Albu Assaf tribe. The British had empowered Ali Sulayman to run Anbar in the 1920s. The historical record is foggy as to who had been the previous shaykh of shaykhs; the British may have re-created the position. The power of the shaykh of shaykhs waned over the years. Individual tribal leaders often made decisions on their own, irrespective of his wishes. By the end of the twentieth century, each tribe had become an independent actor and could cooperate or disregard the confederation at will. In the competition for power, rivals undermined and fought the leading tribes of the confederation as suited their interests. Indeed, Ali al-Sulayman himself had been unable to control the entire Dulaymi without British help.[7]

The same dynamic existed within the tribes themselves. A tribal leader (shaykh) could not always control his entire tribe. Tribesmen were not bound to listen to him. There was often competition with lesser sub-tribes and their leaders (who, by tribal custom, also called themselves "shaykh"). Younger leaders looked to advance at the expense of the head tribal leader. Tribes existed in this state of perpetual competition and fragmentation.[8]

Nevertheless, a head tribal leader with prestige, land, guns, or money could dominate his tribe and influence the leaders of other tribes. Iraqi tribal leaders (shaykhs) held more authority than tribal leaders (khans) in Afghanistan. Iraqi tribes generally had a single head tribal leader with at least nominal authority over the tribe, which was rarely the case in Afghanistan. If conditions were right, an Iraqi tribal leader could get the tribe to take common action. The power of a tribal leader was not the only factor in tribal power or unity. Certain tribes, because of individual culture, history, or location, had particularly strong "asabiyya"—an Arabic term that connotes tribal cohesion or solidarity.[9]

Tribes were only one source of authority in Anbar. The state was another. Since 1920, successive Sunni-run governments had attempted to instill a sense of nationalism in Iraq. It was a nationalism meant to justify the existence of the state and mask Sunni rule. Over the decades, nationalism gained influence, hiding the enduring authority of tribalism and Islam within Iraqi society.[10]

Until the fall of Saddam Hussein, a government structure of a governor for the province and mayors for the cities and towns administered Anbar. The tribes had autonomy, but the state ruled. The state tried to dominate the tribal system while working within it to enhance its own power. The Ba'ath hierarchy of the state attempted to weaken tribes and prevent the rise of political competitors. It used its military power and access to resources to tie members of tribes directly to it, thus circumventing and marginalizing the tribal structure. At the same time, the state relied on the tribes. The Ba'ath Party was itself based on an elite network of Sunni tribes. During Saddam's later years, the state delivered patronage to the tribes to maintain their allegiance and to keep order within their territory. After

1991, Saddam allowed tribes to be armed and gave them land and money.[11]

The army was the main tool of the Sunni-run state. It was a source of authority and a symbol of nationalism. The Sunnis of Anbar were close to the army and the government. They held many of the officers' posts within the army and made up many of the Ba'athists working in Baghdad. The generals and officers from Anbar gained power and stature through the army. In the wake of the 1991 Gulf War, Anbar had stayed loyal to the Sunni regime and had not joined the intifada against the government. Units composed of Anbar tribesmen harshly suppressed the Shi'a that rose up in the south.[12]

Segments of society were partially detribalized, particularly in the cities of Ramadi and Fallujah, where businessmen, shop owners, civil servants, the officer class, and professionals resided. Tribal leaders often lived there too, administering their land from afar and tending to the requests of tribesmen. Urbanization interrupted tribal territorial solidarity. Farmers had migrated to the towns. Towns had expanded into cities. Tribesmen were often dispersed across a city instead of concentrated in single neighborhoods where a tribal leader could easily exert his authority. Within the cities, the growth of state authority since Iraqi independence helped segments of society live a life less tribal. The oil-rich central government favored Anbar Sunnis for civil service and military jobs. The government also directed revenues toward Anbar for education, health care, and state-run industries. The state allowed certain businessmen to access land, contracts, and control of industries, on which they grew rich. In return, they obeyed the state.[13] Thus, during the Saddam era, authority within the city derived as much from the state and Iraqi army and security services as from the tribes.[14]

The other social structure and organizing principle within Iraqi society was Islam. Even though Saddam's rule had been largely secular, Islam was a foundation of identity for the people of Anbar. Through the strongest periods of Ba'ath secularism, religious leaders had maintained an enduring influence. Islam could inspire, organize, and discipline. Its influence transcended tribes, governments, and regimes. Compared to the fragmented nature of tribes, Islam was unifying. Compared to secular strongmen and nationalism, Islam was permanent.

The various types of Sunni religious leaders (ulema) had independent authority over the interpretation of Islam. Imams, scholars, judges (qazi), and members of religious families related to the Prophet (sadah) influenced Anbar society. Sunnis have no central religious leaders, unlike Shi'a. Certain cities had a senior scholar, known as a mufti, but he could not issue orders to the other religious leaders. The people tended to see religious leaders as legitimate sources of knowledge of Islam. This knowledge allowed religious leaders to shape the views of Sunnis.[15] Their influence was particularly strong in the cities, where a respected imam could lead thousands in prayer. In a city, individual tribal leaders could rarely summon comparable numbers. With such an audience, religious leaders could overshadow the divided tribal leaders and hold their own against the state. During the first decades of the Saddam era, the authoritarian state could keep the religious leaders in line. As was the case with tribalism, the state's temporary dominance masked the deeper enduring authority of Islam.

Religious leaders gained influence in the 1990s. As a means of shoring up his power, Saddam re-emphasized Islam. He eased the Ba'athist secularism and nationalism of the 1970s and 1980s. He distributed salaries to more religious leaders and refurbished more mosques. Thus, when the

United States invaded, religious leaders had a solid base of power from which to guide resistance.

Imams were the commonest type of religious leader in Anbar. They led prayers at mosques and guided people in following the Qur'an and customs of the Prophet Mohammed. They usually worked out of a mosque and had been educated either by another, older, imam or at a religious university. Every mosque had at least one imam. Hundreds of imams lived in Ramadi and Fallujah. The more educated imams, sometimes known as scholars (alim), could issue religious edicts, known as fatwas, that carried weight among the general population and across tribes.[16]

Well-known imams or members of religious families managed endowments (waqf), which were funds or property devoted to charitable purposes. The funds or property were inherited or provided by tribal leaders, the government, or other outsiders. Certain endowments had been around for decades and were a source of influence for the religious leaders. In Anbar, the most important was the government-run Sunni Endowment. It provided salaries to the majority of the imams. Under Saddam, it was a way of exerting government control.[17]

Religious leaders also interpreted the law. Religious scholars and judges (qazis) explained Islamic law (shari'a). Muftis were acknowledged authorities on Islamic law and could issue fatwas pertaining to legal matters.[18] Governors, officials, and even Saddam could be challenged by a fatwa. Partly for that reason, the Saddam regime had taken over the justice system and monitored religion closely. The state appointed the judges. Those who offered opinions contrary to state policy could be jailed.[19]

Many of the imams and judges that had been paid by the state chose to accept the Saddam regime. But it would be wrong to think all were bought off. Religious leaders could be a thorn in Saddam's side. Money was a surprisingly ineffective bribery tactic. The power of religious leaders derived from more than the state. Plenty of imams spoke out against the state and did not cooperate. Historically, religious leaders in Iraq led dissent or rebellion. It was also religious leaders who rallied the people against invaders in defense of Islam, as they had in the 1920 revolt against the British.[20] Fallujah exemplified this tradition. It had been a center of Islamic unrest. During the 1990s, its religious leaders refused to eulogize Saddam in prayers. In response, Saddam supposedly persecuted them.

Certain Anbar religious leaders affiliated themselves with the Iraqi Islamic Party. An offshoot of the Muslim Brotherhood, this political party included teachers, engineers, lawyers, and professionals. Its goal was to restore the values and morals of Islam in order to reverse corruption and discontent within society. The organization had started in the 1940s, with strong support in Ramadi, where one of its first offices opened. In 1962, six of the party's twelve official leaders hailed from Ramadi. Two of those were religious leaders (an imam and a scholar). The persecution of the Ba'ath regime later forced the party out of politics. The party focused on education and social work until 2003, when it returned to politics and competed for provincial council and parliamentary spots in Anbar and Baghdad.[21] In spite of its admirable goals, the political bent and wide secular membership circumscribed the Iraqi Islamic Party's religious legitimacy. As the US occupation began, the party's power in the religious space was limited compared to that of the imams and muftis in the cities and towns.

In 2003, with the end of the Saddam regime, the state fell apart as a source of authority. In Anbar, a delegation of tribal leaders and Saddam's military commander for Anbar negotiated a ceasefire with US forces. The standing military formations in the province dissolved. Attempting to keep order, tribal and religious leaders met and selected a governor and mayors and police chiefs in each city. Without a state to back them up, these "officials" had no real authority.[22] A skeleton justice system and police force remained in the cities. Neither was fully functional. West of Ramadi no courts functioned at all.[23] The delivery of other forms of goods and services was better. Bureaucrats kept the schools, hospitals, and power running. Throughout Anbar, the tribes (weakened by the loss of their government patron), religious leaders, US forces, and budding insurgent leaders were the only sources of authority left.

THE BEGINNING OF THE INSURGENCY

The Iraqi insurgency broke out after the United States' lightning victory over Saddam Hussein's standing forces in March and April 2003.[24] Sunnis represented the overwhelming majority of the insurgents. A combination of nationalism, sectarianism, and Islamic belief influenced the Sunnis to take up arms. An Oxford Research International poll in March 2004 found that 66 percent of the people in central Iraq, which included Anbar, viewed the invasion as humiliation for Iraqis rather than liberation. Fifty-seven percent opposed the presence of US forces.[25] In general, Sunnis thought of the United States as an occupier. They also tended to believe that US destruction of the Saddam regime had stolen Sunni political power and economic benefits and given them to the Shi'a Arabs. US plans for democracy promised to place the Shi'a, representing 60 percent of the population, in the most powerful political position. The large role played by exiled Shi'a leaders in the newly constructed Iraqi Governing Council (an interim advisory body), the dissolution of the old Iraqi army (which Sunnis had largely officered), and the prohibition of former members of the Ba'ath Party from working in the government (de-Ba'athification) exacerbated the Sunni feeling of marginalization.

After the fall of the Saddam regime, the US Army outposted Anbar. Battalions went to Fallujah, Ramadi, and the western desert. The 82nd Airborne Division eventually took responsibility for these areas and Anbar overall. The insurgency began in May 2003 when people started protesting US presence and organizing for insurgent activity. Key tribal and religious leaders opposed US activity within cities and towns. Those who chose to cooperate with the Americans lost influence. The shaykh of shaykhs of the Dulaymi confederation fled to Jordan. Insurgent groups began small and conducted mortar attacks and laid improvised explosive devices (IEDs)—homemade mines that could be set off by pressure, a command wire, or remote control. IEDs would become the ubiquitous weapon of the insurgency. By the time the Marines arrived at the beginning of 2004, insurgents had already proliferated throughout the province. They called themselves the "resistance."

In early 2004, the resistance formed the heart of the insurgency. Men from the villages, towns, and farms along the Euphrates—in their own words the "sons of al-Anbar"—filled its ranks. Religious leaders, former military officers, Ba'athists, tribal leaders, and young men angered by the occupation led groups of fighters. The groups often paralleled tribal or family lines. The tribal system facilitated meetings between different groups.[26] Each resistance group contained a variety of smaller groups, which the US military often called "cells," in keeping with counterinsurgency parlance. The exact size of a cell has never been determined, but it is probably safe to say that one could number anywhere from two to forty men. The networks of former Iraqi Intelligence Service agents and other members of the former regime's security apparatus provided ways for intelligence and money to flow to insurgents. The Association of Muslim Scholars, a network of Sunni religious leaders, enhanced the resistance's legitimacy through the vociferous endorsements of its head, Harith al-Dhari. Many of the religious leaders within the association commanded resistance groups.

The resistance had no centralized command-and-control structure. The different resistance groups operated relatively autonomously, cooperating with one another but answering to no single leader. Differentiating between the groups was confusing, to say the least. A few of the major groups were the 1920 Revolutionary Brigade, Jaysh Islami ("Islamic Army"), Jaysh Mohammed ("Army of Mohammed"), and Harakat Islami (Islamic Movement"). For the sake of simplicity, I refer to all these groups as the resistance.

The Sunni resistance lacked a unified set of aims. Almost all Sunni insurgents opposed the United States. They wanted the United States, viewed as an occupying power and impediment to Sunni security, to withdraw from Iraq. Heavy-handed US actions and collateral damage helped generate a willingness to fight. Most notably, popular mobilization in Fallujah had been spurred by two unfortunate incidents in 2003, shortly after US forces occupied the city. On April 28 and 30 2003, US soldiers, feeling threatened, fired into mass gatherings protesting US occupation of a school, killing thirteen civilians and wounding ninety-one. In May and June, smaller incidents, such as aggressive cordon and search missions and demolition of homes, followed. Partly because of these incidents, the people of Fallujah rejected the Americans. Many joined the insurgency.[27]

Additionally, Sunni insurgents often wanted greater political power and economic benefits. The fall of the

Saddam regime curtailed Sunni political influence. That Iran, the Saddam regime's longtime enemy, could gain power via the Shi'a magnified their concern. The loss was institutionalized by de-Ba'athification and then compounded by the dissolution of the Iraqi army. These three events denied many Sunnis their livelihood, as well as political power. Sunnis lost jobs in the military and bureaucracy. They also lost subsidies the Saddam regime had given to agriculture and industries. Estimates of unemployment in Anbar in early 2004 range from 40 to 60 percent. A truly accurate count is missing. The remaining Sunnis were underemployed, surviving off part-time jobs in the towns and cities.

Members of the Sunni resistance differed as to the extent of political power and economic benefits they sought. Many desired a return to Sunni dominance over the central government and the armed forces.[28] Others—especially those tribal leaders, civic leaders, and politicians only tacitly supporting the insurgency—did not go so far. They wanted executive positions in the Iraqi government, greater representation in legislative bodies, a greater Sunni role within the Iraqi armed forces, and substantial economic assistance to Sunni areas.

Alongside the resistance, a more dangerous movement was coalescing in Anbar under Abu Musab al-Zarqawi, the terrorist from Jordan. As a young man, Zarqawi had been a disgruntled criminal from the town of Zarqa. In 1989, he went to Afghanistan and worked with the mujahedin. Experiences there and then in prison in Jordan in the early 1990s inspired him to form a relationship with al-Qa'eda. After being released from prison in 1999, Zarqawi returned to Afghanistan. In 2000, Osama bin Laden gave him money to start an organization anywhere in the Middle East. With the US invasion, Zarqawi chose Iraq as his location. He went there in early 2003 and started building his network.[29] Sheer aggression complemented by angry looks—his penchant for black clothes, long black hair, and a black beard—drew foreign fighters and Iraqis to his cause.

At first, Zarqawi's budding network was one of several extremist groups, such as Ansar al-Sunna and Ansar al-Islam. Iraqis and Americans alike often referred to these groups collectively as "terrorists," because of their proclivity toward suicide bombings. Terrorist groups were more likely than the resistance to contain foreign fighters. These men from around the Middle East regularly transited from the Syrian border to Ramadi and Fallujah. Some continued on to Mosul or Baghdad. Foreign fighters occasionally were captured by US units. Based on detainee numbers, US analysts estimated that, at best, 10 percent of the insurgency were foreigners.[30]

Zarqawi's network did not officially join al-Qa'eda until October 2004, when Zarqawi announced the formation of al-Qa'eda in Iraq (AQI). Nonetheless, for simplicity's sake, I will call Zarqawi's network AQI from 2003 to 2013. Most terrorist (extremist, jihadist, takfiri) groups would eventually tie themselves to AQI. Zarqawi and other like-minded insurgent leaders aimed to expel the United States and establish an Islamic state in Iraq. In provinces with mixed populations such as Baghdad, Zarqawi purposefully targeted Shi'a in order to draw reprisals upon the Sunnis and instigate a civil war that could eventually lead to the formation of a Sunni Islamic state.[31]

In February 2004, US forces discovered the "Zarqawi letter." Written by Zarqawi, the letter set forth his aims to the al-Qa'eda leadership. The strategic goal was to establish an Islamic state. The operational goal was to outlast the United States. Zarqawi sought to raise the cost of the US presence to a level that would shake US resolve.[32] He believed that the United States would back down before a prolonged conflict. He wrote: "The enemy [the United States] is apparent, his back is exposed, and he does not know the land or the current situation of the mujahidin because his intelligence information is weak. We know for certain that these Crusader forces will disappear tomorrow or the day after."[33]

More ominously, the letter called for targeting Shi'a in order to trigger a Sunni backlash and instigate a civil war. A bloody civil war would create an anarchical environment where Zarqawi's network would flourish.[34] Once an Islamic state was established in Iraq, Zarqawi may have intended to carry out terrorist attacks elsewhere in the Middle East (indeed, he dispatched a suicide bomber against a Jordanian hotel in 2005).

In 2004, Zarqawi's command-and-control structure was already far more centralized than that of the resistance. As early as mid-2003, he had established cells in key cities and was conducting operations. That year, he masterminded the bombings of the International Committee of the Red Cross, the United Nations headquarters, and the Jordanian embassy in Baghdad. The majority of Zarqawi's network consisted of Iraqis, but it had a larger percentage of foreigners than the resistance (no exact figure on the number of foreigners is available). AQI held the allegiance of the foreign fighters and Iraqi terrorists of greatest concern to the United States.

Throughout 2004, the resistance and AQI worked together. AQI took root in Anbar. Zarqawi frequently operated out of Fallujah. Resistance leaders viewed extremist foreign fighters and Zarqawi as a useful ally that brought dedication, organization, and funding into the fight against the common enemy—the American occupiers and Iraq's new Shi'a leaders. Differences over Islam and the use of terrorism were put aside. Only as AQI grew in power would the resistance change its position.

THE MARINES IN ANBAR

In 2004, the I Marine Expeditionary Force (I MEF) came to al-Anbar province. Lieutenant General James Conway was in command. He had led the Marine ground and air forces during the initial invasion of Iraq. The ground combat element of I Marine Expeditionary Force, which would be conducting the day-to-day operations in the cities and towns, was the 1st Marine Division, under Major General James Mattis. Renowned for his drive and incisive military mind, Mattis had led the division in the 2003 invasion. He had blitzkrieged through the Iraqi army and irregular fighters from the Kuwaiti border to Baghdad. His forward elements had advanced all the way to Tikrit. Conway reported to Combined Joint Task Force 7 (CJTF-7), commanded by Lieutenant General Ricardo Sanchez. CJTF-7 controlled all military forces in Iraq. Conway and Mattis took over from the 82nd Airborne Division on March 24, 2004.

Three regiment-sized formations, each two to five thousand strong, made up the 1st Marine Division. One Marine regimental combat team, with three Marine infantry battalions, held the Fallujah area. Marine infantry battalions contained roughly one thousand Marines. A US Army brigade combat team (the army equivalent of a Marine regimental combat team), with two US Army battalions (of roughly seven hundred soldiers) and a Marine infantry battalion, held Ramadi. Another Marine regimental combat team, with three Marine infantry battalions, spread out across the towns along the Euphrates River in the western desert. That regimental combat team was headquartered out of the large al-Asad airbase, located between Haditha and Hit. This distribution of forces stayed roughly the same throughout the war, with certain formations being reinforced for particular battles.

Conway, Mattis, and the Marines were experienced and felt they understood both straightforward warfighting and nuanced counterinsurgency. Five of the seven Marine infantry battalions and much of the headquarters' staffs had seen combat during the 2003 invasion. After the heavy fighting of 2003, Conway and Mattis had been tasked to stay in the south and keep an eye on law and order. The Marines had embraced a light touch and had enjoyed a friendly relationship with the Shi'a of the south. Careful foot patrols and efforts to build relationships with locals took precedence over using tanks or armored vehicles and raids to capture insurgents. Under Mattis's eye, the Marines had been supremely mindful of the risks of inadvertently creating enemies by using too much force. Success in the south gave the Marines confidence that with the right tactics they could adapt to Anbar and succeed there too.

The Marine Corps has a culture of being able to fight guerrillas and insurgents. During the 1920s and 1930s they fought a series of "small wars" against guerrillas in the Caribbean and Central America. Lessons from those operations were captured in their *Small Wars Manual*, a classic of Marine Corps literature. Marines experimented in fighting insurgents again in Vietnam. Although they saw a great deal of heavy combat along the DMZ, elsewhere the Marines prided themselves on protecting villages and advising Vietnamese forces. They famously developed "combined action platoons," small teams of Marines that embedded with village defense forces—living, eating, and sleeping with Vietnamese day and night. Bing West immortalized the combined action platoon experience in another Marine classic, *The Village*.

While preparing to deploy to Anbar, Conway and Mattis had disseminated lessons from Marine history and their deployment to southern Iraq. At Camp Pendleton, Mattis held a conference on how to fight insurgents. He also trained a platoon in every battalion to operate within an Iraqi unit, patterned after the combined action platoons of the Vietnam War. The platoons received a month of special training in Arabic, Arab culture, and Soviet weapons handling. Across the division, Mattis reiterated the dangers of accidentally killing Iraqi civilians and the benefits of good relationships. Mattis gave the 1st Marine Division the motto "No better friend, no worse enemy."[35]

Years of heavy fighting lay ahead for the Marines. The lack of immediate results would be disappointing. Nevertheless, the training and mindset instilled early on would help lead to adaptations and eventual successes in Fallujah, Ramadi, and Anbar as a whole.

THE BATTLES OF FALLUJAH

With minarets and domes silhouetted on its skyline, Fallujah is known as the "city of mosques." The title personifies the city's religious conservatism. Since the April and May 2003 incidents, Fallujah residents and city leaders had supported the insurgency. Graffiti in the city read: "Fallujah is the heart of the resistance."[36] A large number of army officers and former Ba'athists lived in Fallujah. They disliked seeing Americans providing security and threatened any Iraqis working with US forces.[37] By March 2004, insurgent cells had organized within the city. Foreign fighters massed there to join the jihad against the United States. The city was already a center of activity for AQI. Abdullah al-Janabi, a respected imam, helped coordinate local insurgent activity with Zarqawi's terrorists.[38]

On March 31, 2004, insurgents and Fallujah citizens murdered four American civilian contractors who were driving through the city and then hung their bodies from a bridge over the Euphrates. The Fallujah police stood by and watched while it all happened. The media televised video of the gruesome event. In the aftermath, local universities reportedly supported the violence, and Fallujah imams refused to explicitly condemn the killings. The US government considered the murders an inexcusable affront. Against the advice of Mattis and Conway, the Bush administration ordered an offensive to clear Fallujah.[39]

The ensuing offensive ignited widespread Sunni outrage. Viewing it as an attack on their society, Sunnis poured into Fallujah from other Sunni cities. When the Marines stepped off, they encountered heavy resistance from roughly two thousand insurgents. Insurgents coordinated mortars, volleys of rocket-propelled grenades, and machine-gun fire in defense of their positions. Marine commanders risked prohibitive casualties unless they reverted to artillery, air strikes, and tanks as per their conventional combined arms doctrine. Such firepower was applied selectively. Civilians died nevertheless (the Iraqi Ministry of Health estimated 220 for the first two weeks of fighting).[40] Insurgent propaganda and Arab media exploited these casualties to inflame opposition to the United States. The Iraqi Governing Council came under tremendous pressure from Iraqis to stop the fighting. Sunni members threatened to resign if Bremer did not initiate ceasefire negotiations. With the democratization process in jeopardy, Sanchez, commander of US forces in Iraq, halted the offensive on April 9.[41] Fighting around the Marine bridgehead persisted until April 30, when Conway pulled the Marines out of the city.

The fighting in Fallujah spread to most of Anbar. Battles broke out in the smaller towns surrounding Fallujah. Insurgents ambushed and cut off key roads and the highway. As the Marines moved into Fallujah, insurgents let loose attacks in Ramadi (April 6) that rapidly turned into a popular uprising.[42] As in Fallujah, mosques called men to arms. The people of Ramadi readily rallied against the Marines. The battle raged until April 10. Overall, the Marines estimated killing three hundred insurgents.[43] The Marine battalion in Ramadi—2nd Battalion, 4th Marine Regiment—suffered roughly one hundred casualties. A week later, on April 17, violence reached all the way west to al-Qa'im, when insurgents (mostly affiliated with the Abu Mahal tribe) launched a major attack on the Marines patrolling the town.

As a result of Fallujah and separate Shi'a uprisings in the south, attacks throughout the country jumped from just under two hundred per week in the first three months of 2004 to over five hundred in the summer.[44] Fallujah became an insurgent base of operations and staging ground for attacks elsewhere in the country. Three to six thousand insurgents were ensconced there. The insurgency enjoyed widespread support among the Sunni population. Sunnis perceived that the insurgents had won a great victory by forcing an embarrassing withdrawal upon the United States. A poll in late April found that 89 percent of Iraqis considered the United States and its allies an occupying force.[45]

On June 28, 2004, the United States granted Iraq sovereignty and created the Iraqi Interim Government under Prime Minister Ayad Allawi. Shortly thereafter, Sanchez stepped down and General George Casey became commander of Multi-National Forces, Iraq (the new military headquarters of the United States and its partners). Casey took immediate steps to give the campaign strategic purpose hitherto lacking. His priorities were to ensure the democratic process succeeded and to build up the Iraqi army and police so that they could take the lead for security. Before he addressed these larger goals, he moved to deal with centers of violence, one by one, before the January 2005 elections.

Fallujah was the most important.[46] He and his commanders paid attention to the mistakes of the past year, taking care to tailor military action to political priorities. Casey delayed the Fallujah operation for months as he waited to obtain the full support of the Iraqi Interim Government and for US presidential elections in early November to pass.

New Marine generals, Lieutenant General John Sattler and Major General Richard Natonski, took over in Anbar at the end of the summer. They listened to Conway and Mattis about the lessons of the first battle. Measures were taken to lessen the political impact of the firepower needed to defeat so many insurgents. Civilians were encouraged to leave the city through leaflets, radio announcements, and a whisper campaign. In the event, US soldiers and Marines would find only 5,000 civilians in a city of 250,000 people. To lessen the image of occupation, Sattler and Natonski, in parallel with Allawi, pressed for Iraqi army units to accompany American forces in the assault. The 1st and 3rd Iraqi Brigades joined the 1st Marine Regimental Combat Team, 7th Marine Regimental Combat Team, and US Army Blackjack Brigade Combat Team for the operation.

The battle was the insurgency's largest attempt to stand against a US assault. There had been months of US air strikes on insurgent defenses and command-and-control nodes. While many high-level leaders fled before the battle, others, such as the infamous Omar Hadid (one of Zarqawi's lieutenants), as well as the three to six thousand fighters, stayed. Emboldened by their perceived success in halting the Marine offensive in April, they planned to defend the city. They stocked caches, established strong points, blocked roads, and laid IEDs. Insurgents were arrayed in teams of roughly eight to forty men, assigned to defend different zones. Insurgents prepared ambushes in the staircases, floorboards, and upper stories of homes. Defensive lines were formed along the old main road and on the south east edge of the city.

The offensive, known as Operation al-Fajr, kicked off on November 7, 2004. US tactics within Fallujah were those of a straightforward conventional battle. Four Marine infantry battalions methodically cleared out the insurgent defenders in the wake of two US Army armored battalions that spearheaded the assault. As in the first battle, the strength of insurgent defenses compelled the Marines to call in artillery fire and air strikes. Marines could fight well over one hundred insurgents in any single engagement. Marine squads aggressively cleared buildings, making use of grenades, AT-4 rocket launchers with thermobaric warheads, and well-drilled urban combat tactics. By the end of December, the insurgent resistance had expired. Roughly two thousand insurgents were killed, wounded, or detained in the course of the battle.[47]

After the battle, Marine battalions set up in Fallujah, preventing the insurgency from openly ruling the streets as it had before. The United States initiated an intensive reconstruction effort. The State Department representative, Kael Weston, worked hand in hand with city leaders. They built a municipal government and encouraged the people of Fallujah to participate in the political process. Approximately 65 to 80 percent of the city's population participated in each of the three electoral events of 2005. Over 2005 and 2006, the Iraqi government provided a total of $180 million in compensation for damage to homes, while the United States embarked on major water, sewage, health, and power projects. One to two thousand Marines operated in the city, eventually alongside roughly 1,500 soldiers of the Iraqi army.

Second Fallujah was the swansong of the resistance. Fallujah resistance leaders, including Janabi, fled to Syria and Jordan. Few returned. Outside Fallujah, the resolve of other resistance leaders shuddered. US special operations raids, which captured numerous resistance leaders, worsened their situation. Meanwhile, AQI reorganized itself to continue the war. As resistance leadership fractured, insurgent fighters naturally realigned with the better organized AQI. Over 2005, AQI would become the dominant insurgent group in Anbar.

THE IRAQI ARMY

The United States began building the Iraqi army and police as early as 2003, but they did not receive serious attention within US military strategy until 2005. At the end of 2004, Casey ordered a review of his military strategy. The review concluded that the formation of the Iraqi army was lagging and needed to be accelerated if US forces were eventually to withdraw from Iraq. The Iraqi army and police had always been a priority for Casey. With Najaf settled and Fallujah captured, he now devoted the resources and attention to turn the police and army into a priority in reality as well as in concept.[48]

The United States designed the Iraqi army to be a national force that integrated Kurds, Shi'a, and Sunni. In all, ten divisions (later, thirteen) were planned.[49] Few Sunnis joined, though, and the army became largely Shi'a. A number of battalions, brigades, and divisions had Sunni commanders, but the vast majority of the officers and soldiers were Shi'a. Although the Shi'a spoke Arabic, the Sunnis distrusted them. In order to accelerate Iraqi army development, Casey's headquarters created transition teams—ten to twelve advisors embedded into every Iraqi army unit from battalion to brigade to division.

Table 2.1 Iraqi Army Brigades in Anbar

Name	Abbreviated Name	Initial Location	Arrival
2nd Brigade, 1st Division	2-1 Iraqi Brigade	Fallujah	Spring 2005
3rd Brigade, 1st Division	3-1 Iraqi Brigade	Fallujah	Spring 2005
4th Brigade, 1st Division	4-1 Iraqi Brigade	Vicinity of Fallujah	Spring 2005
1st Brigade, 7th Division	1-7 Iraqi Brigade	Ramadi	Autumn 2005
2nd Brigade, 7th Division	2-7 Iraqi Brigade	Hit, Haditha, Rawah	Winter 2006
3rd Brigade, 7th Division	3-7 Iraqi Brigade	Al-Qa'im	Winter 2006
1st Brigade, 1st Division	1-1 Iraqi Brigade	Ramadi	Spring 2006

The 1st and 7th Iraqi divisions (totaling seven brigades and roughly ten thousand men) deployed to Anbar between January 2005 and April 2006. Table 2.1 gives the name, location, and time of arrival of every brigade.

The Marines put special effort into the 1st and 7th divisions. Although national guardsmen and US Army reservists composed the first advisory teams, the Marine Corps later filled over half the teams with its own personnel. Officers slated for command and key personnel within Marine infantry battalions became advisors. Additionally, Marine and Army battalions partnered with Iraqi battalions, in order to assist in their operations and training. "Partnering" meant that the US battalion had an Iraqi battalion in its battlespace and would mentor and involve the Iraqi battalion in its operations. Usually, the partnership process entailed the

Iraqi companies working with the US companies and Iraqi battalion leadership working with the US battalion leadership. The idea was that eventually the companies would operate independently, followed by the battalion, and ultimately the entire brigade. The process would take years. By March 2006, the Iraqi army was providing 40–50 percent of the manpower for operations in Anbar but rarely in independent operations.

THE WESTERN DESERT

As the Iraqi army developed, the Marines shifted their attention to Anbar's borders. The clearing of Fallujah had been a major blow to the insurgency, but much of Anbar was still with them. Ramadi was a battleground. Marines tried to hold the center of the city against insurgents who moved freely in the surrounding neighborhoods. Farther west, the towns dotting the Euphrates flowing down from Syria were a line of insurgent safe havens: Hit, Haditha, Rawah, and al-Qa'im. After the Second Battle of Fallujah, insurgents affiliated with AQI displaced to al-Qa'im, a cluster of five towns (Husaybah, Karabilah, Old Ubaydi, New Ubaydi, and al-Qa'im) along the Euphrates River at the Syrian border. Roughly 120,000 people lived in the area. AQI turned it into a base of operations. Foreign fighters from Syria flowed over the Syrian border, through al-Qa'im, often staying several days for processing, and thence toward Baghdad.

In July and August 2005, General Casey decided that the foreign fighters executing suicide bombings in Baghdad had to be stopped, especially with the constitutional referendum and national elections looming. After personal visits to western Anbar, Casey chose to intensify operations there. He wanted to close down the "rat lines" of foreign fighters entering Iraq from Syria.

As operations kicked off in the western desert, the Marines acquired unexpected allies among the tribes. The tribes of the western desert covered more territory than their counterparts in Ramadi and Fallujah and were more cohesive. Living in the desert, they also retained more of the romance of the old tribal life. Shaykh Sabah al-Mahalawi, the influential head of the Albu Mahal, once boasted: "The tribes out west are stronger because they have traditionally been warriors. They like to fight."[50]

One of the largest and best-known western tribes was the Albu Nimr. The tribe resided north of the Euphrates near Hit. "Nimr" means tiger. Fittingly, the tribe had a reputation for violence. The Albu Nimr had been powerful throughout Anbar, enjoying influence in Ramadi, until they rose up against Saddam Hussein during 1994 and 1995. Saddam quashed the rebellion and oppressed the tribe. Consequently, there was no love lost between the Albu Nimr and the Saddam-friendly resistance. In 2004, US forces started working with the Albu Nimr. For a variety of reasons, cooperation did not take off until summer 2005 when the United States cleared the nearby town of Hit. Special Forces formed a high-quality Albu Nimr "scout platoon" that worked with the local Iraqi army battalion and conducted independent operations of their own against insurgents. The tribe manned the newly formed Hit police as well. Of the recruits for the Hit police, 150 came from the Albu Nimr. Three came from other tribes.

One hundred miles west of the Albu Nimr lived the Albu Mahal, the largest tribe in al-Qa'im. Their territory astride the border of Iraq and Syria, right next to one of Anbar's three major crossing points, placed the tribe to profit off customs and smuggling. They traditionally controlled al-Qa'im. They dominated two smaller tribes—the Albu Karbuli and Albu Salman—who resented their weaker position. The Albu

Mahal had been insurgents in 2004. In 2005, AQI came to al-Qa'im. The Albu Karbuli and Albu Salman sided with AQI, upending Albu Mahal dominance. The Albu Mahal disliked AQI's marginalization of their power, killing of their tribesmen, importation of foreign fighters, and encroachment upon their control of the black market. Shaykh Sabah, the head tribal leader, later explained: "al-Qa'eda tried to isolate and to humiliate the tribals in the areas ... We started to understand their mission was to destroy our tribe."[51] Sabah moved to Jordan to run the tribe from the ends of AQI's reach.

In spring 2005, the Albu Mahal tribe turned against AQI. The spark was AQI's assassination of the al-Qa'im police chief, who was Albu Mahal, and the kidnapping of the provincial governor, another Albu Mahal tribesman.[52] The tribe formed the "Hamza battalion," a tribal militia that actively defended al-Qa'im against AQI and initiated a unilateral ceasefire with US forces. Unfortunately, absent from the center of town, the Marines could not ensure the survival of the militia. In August, AQI (possibly led by Zarqawi himself) assembled six to eight hundred fighters for a large converging attack. AQI fielded sniper teams, medium machine guns mounted on pickup trucks, car bombs, and mortars. The Albu Mahal put up a well-organized defense. Sabah went through intermediaries to the Marines and requested air support. The Marines conducted a set of select air strikes in support of the tribesmen. Nevertheless, the Albu Mahal eventually succumbed to AQI's numbers and ample supply of ammunition. Albu Mahal fighters were hunted down and Islamic law was enforced in the city.[53] By September 5, AQI had taken over al-Qa'im, posting a sign that read: "Welcome to the Islamic Republic of Qa'im."[54]

The battle was a lesson for the Albu Mahal and the Marines. For the Albu Mahal, it showed the importance of cooperation; for the Marines, the importance of fully backing the Albu Mahal. Speaking with Marine leadership shortly afterward, Sabah warned: "It is difficult for one tribe to act unless all the others do because otherwise all the other tribes oppose it."[55] He advised: "Tribes align against any tribe that sides with the United States. Once there is more security, more tribes will side with the United States. The United States should put advisors with the tribes to work with them."[56]

Thereafter, the Albu Mahal openly helped the United States and the Iraqi government. The United States formed a set of "desert protector" platoons, composed of Albu Mahal and advised by US special operations forces. The Iraqi Ministry of Defense made special allowance for the formation of these militia-like units. The desert protector platoons proved especially useful collecting intelligence. Fellow tribesmen readily provided information on AQI sleeper agents, safe houses, ammunition caches, and bomb-making workshops.[57]

The big Marine operation of 2005 was Operation Steel Curtain, the military offensive to capture al-Qa'im. Two reinforced Marine infantry battalions (2,500 Marines) and one Iraqi battalion (roughly 500 soldiers) cleared the city from November 5–16, killing roughly 100 insurgents.[58] In the aftermath of the battle, Lieutenant Colonel Dale Alford, commander of 3rd Battalion, 6th Marine Regiment, dispersed his Marines into platoons and squads, integrating them thoroughly with Iraqi army units. Every platoon lived and worked with an Iraqi platoon in one of twelve outposts. The platoons conducted intensive satellite patrolling both day and night. Living close to the population generated intelligence and forced the Marines to learn how to interact with the locals.[59]

The Iraqi government rewarded the Albu Mahal for their support of Operation Steel Curtain. The Ministry of Defense allowed tribesmen to serve in 3rd Brigade, 7th Iraqi Division, the new army brigade that garrisoned al-Qa'im, breaking the standard rule that brigades in Anbar could not be composed of local Sunnis. An Albu Mahal tribal leader, Colonel Ishmael, became the brigade's commander. Two battalion commanders and several staff officers were also Albu Mahal. Roughly 20–40 percent of the brigade came from the tribe.[60] The same thing happened with the police. Colonel Ishmael's brother commanded the police force, largely made up of the Albu Mahal. Within three months of the completion of Operation Steel Curtain, the Albu Mahal had devoted seven hundred tribesmen to 3rd Brigade, 7th Iraqi Division and four hundred tribesmen to a newly established police force.[61] To top it all, the Ministry of Defense appointed Major General Murthi, from the tribe, to command the entire 7th Iraqi Division.

The Albu Mahal received other forms of rewards besides influence over the Iraqi army brigade and the police. Another tribal leader became mayor of al-Qa'im. In terms of money, the tribe now had freedom to retake control of the black market and run smuggling operations into Syria. Control over phosphate mines in the desert granted the tribe a lucrative commodity to trade through al-Qa'im.[62] These rewards meant the Albu Mahal had the interest and power to better ensure AQI could not return to al-Qa'im.

As the Albu Mahal reasserted themselves, the lesser tribes—the Albu Karbuli and Albu Salman—again lost power. Fearing they would be targeted by vengeful Albu Mahal tribesmen, many fled to Syria. The Marine policy was actually to include these two tribes in the new order and prevent any abuse. Alford refused to attend meetings short of representation of all the tribes. Nevertheless, the Albu

Salman and Albu Karbuli still distrusted the Albu Mahal. Indeed, Albu Mahal police often targeted their tribal rivals instead of AQI. A large number of Albu Salman and Karbuli tribesmen stayed in Syria or hid ties with AQI that would make themselves evident eight years later.[63]

Al-Qa'im was the largest battle yet in which a tribe turned against AQI. In the future, Iraqis and US officers would sometimes refer to it as the first stage of the Anbar awakening. In reality, it was a forerunner, not directly connected to later events but a useful example of how AQI might be defeated.

ELECTIONS

In parallel to developing the Iraqi army, General Casey and Ambassador Zalmay Khalilzad pushed democratization forward. The Coalition Provisional Authority's transitional administrative law had scheduled three electoral events for 2005: in January, the election of a transitional government responsible for drafting the constitution; in October, a referendum on the constitution; in December, the election of a permanent government. US leaders considered the establishment of a legitimate democratic government central to cutting support for the insurgents and building cooperation across sectarian communities.[64]

In January, the Iraqis elected their new transitional government. Sunni political parties boycotted the election. Turnout in Anbar was low, as it was throughout Sunni Iraq. Just under thirteen thousand people voted in Anbar. Sunnis found themselves almost cut out of the new government. The electoral system of proportional representation meant that there were no electoral districts. Representation was tied to turnout, not districts. If few people from a city or province voted, that city or province would have no representation.

Thus the Sunnis ended up with very low representation in the new transitional government.

In mid-2005, the transitional government set to their task of drafting a constitution. Ibrahim Ja'aferi, a Shi'a from the Da'wa Party, had been chosen as the transitional prime minister. Constitutional debate was divisive. The Sunnis had some representation in constitutional deliberations, but their own boycott of the January elections limited their access. Sunnis felt they lacked a voice at the table. The fact that the draft constitution allowed for federalism, which threatened to deny Sunni provinces (including Anbar) a share of oil profits, upset them. A last-minute deal negotiated by Ambassador Khalilzad averted a Sunni boycott of the referendum but did not create consensus. While the constitution passed nationwide, the roughly 260,000 Sunnis who voted in the October 2005 referendum in Anbar rejected it by an overwhelming majority. The referendum widened the polarization of the Sunni and Shi'a communities.

The election of the permanent government followed in December. Sunnis voted en masse in order to maximize political representation rather than support a system that promised power to the Shi'a majority. In Anbar, roughly 500,000 Sunnis voted. They were determined to prevent the Shi'a from controlling Iraq. To their disbelief, a Shi'a majority was elected into the parliament (the Council of Representatives). The Sunnis simply rejected the fact that the Shi'a were the majority. Polls found that the majority of Sunnis considered the new democratic government illegitimate and preferred that a strong leader take charge of Iraq.[65]

The members of the newly elected legislature had to select a prime minister who could establish the new permanent government. After months of political wrangling, the various political parties came to agreement in May 2006. The new prime minister would be Nuri al-Maliki, from the Shi'a Da'wa Party. Maliki had been chosen because he was acceptable to all parties. He had been the spokesman of the Da'wa Party, ranking beneath other party leaders. Da'wa itself was not the most powerful Shi'a Party. That rank fell to the Supreme Council for the Islamic Revolution in Iraq (SCIRI), which opposed important reconciliation initiatives, including review of de-Ba'athification and granting amnesty to Sunni insurgents. Maliki owed his position to a coalition between Da'wa and other Shi'a parties. The coalition gave Maliki the critical bloc of seats in the legislature to become prime minister. The divided Shi'a political environment and Maliki's own personal biases would constrain any attempt to address Sunni grievances.

AN EMBATTLED PROVINCE

At the end of 2005, al-Anbar province had been the scene of over three years of intense warfare. The Marines had made progress. Fallujah and al-Qa'im had been cleared and held. Yet high levels of violence persisted province-wide. After August 2005, violence rose precipitously, often exceeding 2004 levels. The Albu Mahal and Albu Nimr notwithstanding, most Sunnis were still unwilling to fight for the government. Police forces were scarce and poorly motivated. The army was made up of outside Shi'a and distrusted. War marched on. At its heart was Ramadi. The provincial capital was a battleground, increasingly controlled by AQI.

© S Ballard (2016)
Euphrates River
"C-Lake"
New highway (MSR mobile)
Jazirah region
Euphrates River
Camp Blue Diamond
Camp Hurricane Point
Sufiya
Camp Ramadi
First officers' district
General Hospital
Combat Outpost
Old main road (Route Michigan)
Government center
Milaab district
Tam'eem district
Second officers' district
Railway line
Camp Corregidor
Railway station
Railway line
Al-Anbar University
N
Habbaniyah canal
Ramadi
0
1500
meters

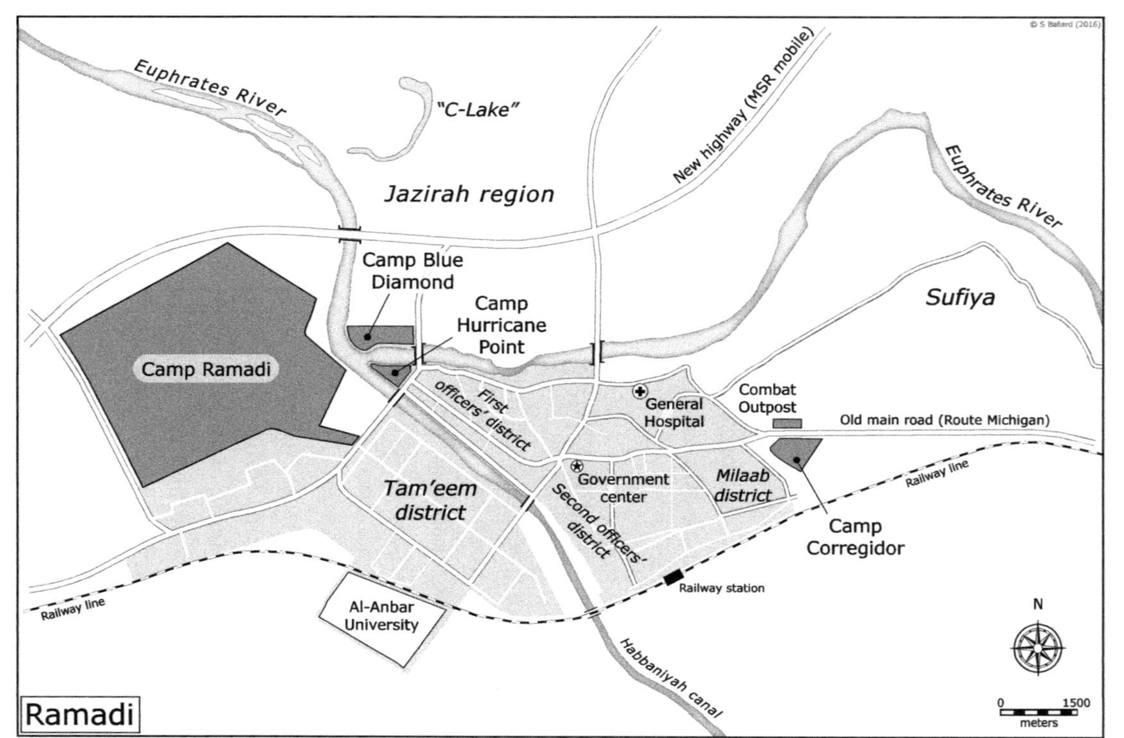

Map 5. Ramadi

CHAPTER 3

The Battle for Ramadi

From Washington, DC, the situation in Iraq looked relatively good at the end of 2005. The United States had won a string of victories. AQI had been pushed out of their safe havens in the western desert and farther north in Tal Afar. The October referendum and the December national election had passed successfully, with resounding turnouts. Meanwhile, the Iraqi army had grown and begun to operate. These successes heartened US military staffs and the US government. General George Casey, Secretary of Defense Donald Rumsfeld, and the White House thought that the strategy and number of forces in Iraq were right—large enough to train, equip, and turn over operations to the Iraqis. Although casualties persisted and attacks had dropped only slightly, in their view, the Iraqi government appeared able to defeat the insurgency. Particularly optimistic, Casey ordered his forces to defeat AQI in six months and set a schedule for reducing the number of US brigades in Iraq from fifteen to twelve by the end of the year. In early 2006, Casey actually sent one brigade home and another to Kuwait.[1]

The rosy picture quickly shattered. On February 22, 2006, AQI bombed the Askariya (golden) mosque in Samarra, a Shi'a holy site. Shi'a militias, Jaysh al-Mahdi in particular, responded with attacks on Sunni neighborhoods in Baghdad. Sunni resistance groups and AQI retaliated with their own attacks and suicide car bombs. Sectarian violence would escalate over the coming months. The United Nations reported that 5,818 civilians died in Iraq in May and June.[2] By June, the United Nations estimated that 150,000 Iraqis had fled Baghdad. Zarqawi's plan to ignite a civil war had succeeded.

With few Shi'a residents, Anbar was spared sectarian violence, but the civil war's effects could still be felt. Anbar Sunnis had strong links to Baghdad through employment or family members. They heard stories of Shi'a atrocities. Refugees from Baghdad, friction with the predominantly Shi'a Iraqi army, and the deaths of family members living in Baghdad brought the civil war home to the Sunnis of Anbar.

Before the latter half of 2005, the people of Anbar had not worried much about the potential for civil war. Credible surveys in March and September 2005 showed that only a small minority of respondents thought civil war likely. The percentage jumped to over 50 percent in October 2005, seemingly because of the referendum and its institution of federalism. In May 2006, in the wake of the bombing, the percentage struck nearly 80 percent.[3] Sunnis spoke of "the long war" or "the next war," by which they meant that the war with the Iranian-backed Shi'a would outlast or follow the jihad against the United States. It was this war that the Sunni minority feared.

Of the cities of Anbar, Fallujah—less than an hour's drive from Baghdad—felt the impact of the civil war the most. Residents traveled to Baghdad regularly, some to work, some to see family. There, they witnessed the repression of the Shi'a militias and Shi'a-dominated special police commandos firsthand. Rumors abounded of special police commandos entering Fallujah by night to murder and kidnap.[4] Anxiety rose as the Shi'a militias drove the outnumbered Sunnis in Baghdad out of their own neighborhoods. Thousands fled to Fallujah and its environs. The International Organization on Migration estimated that thirty thousand people fled between March and August. They came to Fallujah because the city was relatively secure and protected from Shi'a militias.[5] The Fallujah city council relayed stories of sectarian violence in Baghdad, of family members kidnapped or killed, and disparaged the government for leaving Sunnis unprotected.[6] "We want to participate in government but what are the results? What are the benefits?" asked one city leader in the summer. "We know the results. It is total failure. We still see the killing in the streets. Baghdad is in chaos. Iran's hands are everywhere."[7] Concerns over sectarian violence prompted certain Fallujah leaders to demand that the United States withhold withdrawal. One religious leader said, "Even for Fallujans, Baghdad is too dangerous. The new government is too weak to solve the problems. The problems are sectarian. These are very old problems for Iraq. The United States came here and caused disorder. The United States cannot leave the situation as it is—chaotic."[8]

The people of Ramadi also knew what was happening in Baghdad, though distance reduced their exposure. Their concerns were hard for Americans to miss. At the government center, a young and upset religious leader told Kael Weston, the State Department's representative in Anbar: "People do not oppose the terrorists because the national government does not serve the people. Ja'aferi is Shi'a. The government is killing the leaders of the Sunni community. The security situation is worsening in Ramadi. The biggest reason is Iranian interference in Iraq."[9] Provincial bureaucrats, shaykhs, shop-owners, and lowly tribesmen told the same story. Ubaydi tribesmen at a gas station remarked: "There is sectarian violence in Baghdad. Sunnis are getting killed by the Shi'a."[10] A religious student at the government center asked me: "Jaysh al-Mahdi killed fifty Sunnis yesterday. Jaysh al-Mahdi is just as bad as al-Qa'eda. Why does the United States do nothing?"[11] "Sunnis believe you will leave soon," he said. "Your departure will leave the government, the Iraqi army, and the police under Iranian control. It will be very bad."[12]

The climactic events of the war in Anbar would take place in this context of sectarian strife. As Zarqawi had hoped, the civil war rallied many Sunnis to fight harder, lest the Shi'a take over.[13] For others, the possibility of Shi'a victory and control over the government caused them to reconsider the wisdom of expending their energy in a war against the United States, especially once Sunni defeats in Baghdad became evident. Raising local Sunni forces for self-defense gained all the more importance, especially for the tribal and former military elite. A few Sunni leaders argued that Iran was the real enemy, not the United States. The civil war weakened the logic of uncompromising resistance to the United States.

RAMADI

Ramadi is the heart of Anbar: the largest city, the provincial capital, the crossroads between Baghdad and Jordan and Syria, and the seat of the Dulaymi tribal confederation. Roughly a third of the province's population live there, an estimated 450,000 people. The city proper—mazes of two-story homes and shops overlooked by five- to ten-story apartment and government buildings—is wedged between Lake Habbaniyah to the south, the Euphrates to the north, and a canal to the west (leading to Lake Habbaniyah). To the east, the city proper opens up into homes divided by orchards and palm groves (Ramadi's version of suburbs). To the north, across the Euphrates, spans farmland—a region known as the Jazirah—to the edge of the desert.[14] Here also runs the highway from Baghdad, Route One, to the Jordanian border (known to the US military as "Route Mobile"). The defining feature of Ramadi is the old main road (known by the US military as "Route Michigan"). Running east to west down the center of city, it is downtown Ramadi's main thoroughfare. Along it stand the provincial government center, the city's largest mosque, the market, and the entryways into the city. Many Americans died for Route Michigan.

In 2005, the tribes that traditionally led the Dulaymi confederation lived in the countryside outside the city. To the west were the Albu Assaf, the tribe of the shaykh of shaykhs of the Dulaymi confederation. Shaykh Ali al-Sulayman, the great pillar of British rule in Iraq in the 1920s, had been Assafi. To the east were the Albu Fahad, renowned bandits, and the Albu Khalifa, wealthy supporters of the Saddam regime. Smaller tribes of lesser standing circled the city, moving clockwise from eleven o'clock: the Albu Ali Jassim, Albu Thiyab, Albu Faraj, Albu Aetha, Albu Soda, Albu Ghanem, Albu Mar'ai, Albu Chulayb, and Albu Risha. Every tribe is not named here. In all, because of its size and urban mix, Ramadi included substantial numbers of approximately fifteen of Anbar's tribes.

Within the city itself, no tribe held set territory, other than an enclave of the Albu Alwan, in the western downtown corner, between the Euphrates and the canal to Lake Habbaniyah. Everywhere else, people from different tribes

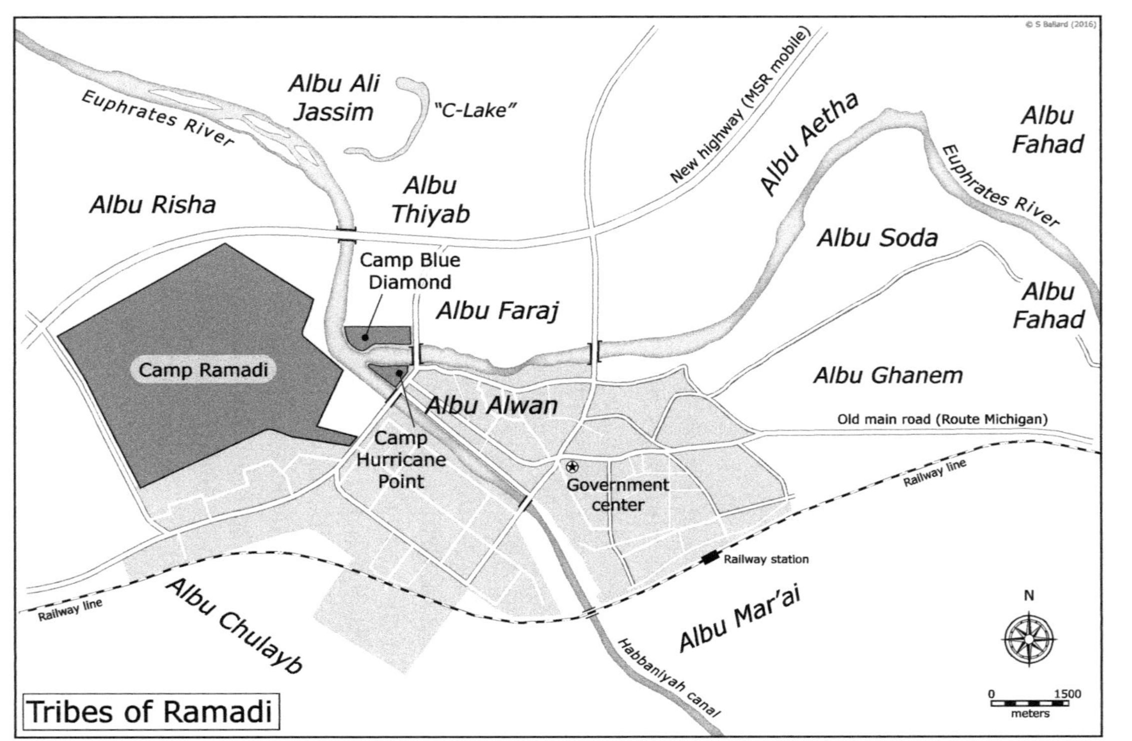

Map 6. Tribes of Ramadi

mixed. The provincial government, the religious leaders, the businessmen, and the apartments and shops (stacked on top of one another in objection to tribal contiguity) short-circuited tribal control. Neighborhoods had mukhtars, managers elected to organize community activities and help report on crime. Often short on tribal kinsmen and funds, their ability and willingness to actually undertake these roles was minimal. A professional upper class of politicians, bureaucrats, lawyers, businessmen, and former military dominated city life. They still belonged to a tribe but were less reliant upon it than Iraqis in the countryside. They had their own sources of income and, during times of peace, recourse to secular rather than tribal rule of law.

In this heterogeneous environment, the religious leaders held an edge over the tribal leaders. Tribal identity did not limit a religious leader's influence; everyone was Muslim. Neighborhoods had at least one mosque and imam, and probably more. The religious leaders were linked into larger networks that enabled them to share their teachings across a broad area. Those networks included the Association of Muslim Scholars and local student associations. Several religious leaders taught at al-Anbar University, where they had access to large numbers of students. The provincial director of Sunni Endowments was also headquartered in Ramadi but his influence was weak without a powerful government. Religious leaders preferred to hold themselves apart from the state.

In the countryside and to a greater extent in the city, tribes tended to be fragmented. They were divided into families, clans, and subtribes. The head tribal leader had to continually buy the loyalty of his tribe; the lesser tribal leaders had to continually buy the loyalty of their subtribes. Traditionally, military prowess and the accumulation and distribution of wealth bought loyalty. The fall of the Saddam regime cut off a source of funding and hence reduced the tribal leaders' support base. As Governor Ma'amoun Sami Rashid al-Alwani described, "The people here belong to tribes, guided by shaykhs [tribal leaders]. Everyone knows that no tribe is 100 percent controlled by the shaykh. Maybe the shaykh controls 50 percent. Perhaps even less since the money for their activity has decreased by 50 percent."[15]

At the onset of the occupation, many tribes joined the resistance. Indeed, several tribal leaders took on leadership roles. The tribal leaders of the Albu Assaf, including the shaykh of shaykhs of the Dulaymi, sided with the United States. When the resistance took off in Ramadi, they fled to Jordan. The tribe most affiliated with the resistance was the Albu Fahad. Before they settled on the banks of the Euphrates and joined the Dulaymi, the Albu Fahad had been part of the Shammari tribal confederation. Unlike the sedentary Dulaymi, the Shammari are supposedly "true" Bedouins, people of the camel, who in decades past took pleasure in raiding the Dulaymi, which may account for the Albu Fahad's reputation for banditry. Albu Fahad territory in the rural farmland east of downtown Ramadi straddled the Euphrates, dividing the tribe in two—politically as well as physically. Historically, the two sections of the tribe often pursued their own policies. Indeed, they sometimes pledged their allegiance to two different shaykhs of shakyhs of the Dulaymi confederation. The river was only one rift. Twenty subtribes and numerous landowners further diluted tribal cohesion. In the 1800s, the Ottomans had dealt with each landowner within the tribe and bypassed the head tribal leader, legitimizing sub-tribal divisions. These divisions and the absence of strong tribal leaders probably made it easier for those at the bottom of the tribal hierarchy to stand up and mobilize various tribal subgroups to fight.[16]

The Insurgency in Ramadi

For the United States, since the beginning of operations in 2003, the situation in Ramadi had never been good. In 2004, Ramadi had been a secondary front while the Marines had dealt with Fallujah and then al-Qa'im. The thousand Marines of the single battalion posted there, strung out along the old main road, endured the popular uprising in April and then attacks orchestrated by scores of insurgents in the summer and autumn of 2004. The addition of 1st Battalion, 503rd Infantry Regiment in November 2004 and Iraqi forces in the spring of 2005 temporarily reduced insurgent activity. The situation regressed in October. Violence reached new heights. By then, two years of war had dimmed Ramadi's fortunes. The glass factory and railroad, two major sources of employment, had become inoperable. The market (*souk*) was empty and the bureaucrats and provincial council members normally present at the government center had run away. Unemployment was estimated to exceed 35 percent.[17] Once a thriving commercial avenue so clogged with cars, donkeys, and people that Marines had to walk alongside their Humvees, the old main road was now empty and cratered, lined by pockmarked abandoned buildings.

Outside the Iraqi army, the only Iraqi leader who worked with the Americans was Governor Ma'amoun Sami Rashid al-Alwani, an engineer elected by the provincial council in early 2005. He was from the Albu Alwan tribe and a member of the Iraqi Islamic Party, the offshoot of the Muslim Brotherhood that sought political dominance over Sunni Iraq. The tribal leaders disliked the Iraqi Islamic Party, viewing it as a rival. Scarcity of friends did not faze Ma'amoun. A great bear of a man, he reputedly once crushed the carpals of a backstabbing rival with his handshake. He never faltered. He kept the government center—the object of weekly, almost daily, attacks—open as his concrete redoubt in the center of the city.

The increase in violence in Ramadi occurred because AQI took on a larger role organizing insurgent activity in 2005. In early 2005, the resistance dominated Ramadi. It was led by religious leaders, tribal leaders, former military, and young men. They had proven themselves in 2003 and 2004. The major resistance groups in Ramadi were the 1920 Revolutionary Brigade, Nu'aman Brigade, Harakat Islami, and Jaysh Islami. The foremost resistance leader was Mohammed Mahmoud Latif, of the Albu Fahad tribe. Latif was a religious scholar and part of the Association of Muslim Scholars. He commanded the 1920 Revolutionary Brigade in Ramadi.[18]

Over time, more and more AQI cells arrived in Ramadi: first after the Second Battle of Fallujah in 2004; then after the battles in Hit, Haditha, and al-Qa'im in 2005; and then again after Ramadi became one of the cities that Zarqawi sought to control. Ramadi was important enough that AQI senior leadership issued many of the orders for operations there.[19] One of AQI's main strongholds was located in the semi-rural area of dispersed homes, orchards, and palm groves on the city's eastern outskirts. Few US or Iraqi troops were there. Access to the city and the rest of the AQI cells was easy. AQI reputedly ran training classes and a prison in the area. Suicide bombers staged there before executing their missions.[20]

AQI brought a steady flow of foreign fighters into Ramadi. They came from a variety of countries: Algeria, Morocco, Syria, Lebanon, Egypt, and even Italy and Canada. They were usually young men eager to fight. In spite of the victory in al-Qa'im, foreign fighters still found their way over the border to AQI rendezvous points. AQI coordinators sent them forward to join existing cadres in Ramadi or other locations. Because of their unfamiliarity with Anbar, they were usually assigned to cells of Iraqi fighters.[21]

Most insurgents that worked with AQI were not foreign fighters. Estimates of the number of AQI coming from outside Anbar were low—twenty to one hundred financiers, facilitators, foreign fighters, and suicide bombers. According to Colonel Fadhil, the provincial director general of internal security, "attacks on the Iraqi security forces are by locals, not foreign fighters, [who are] a small group of young disgruntled men who threaten and intimidate others."[22] What AQI's leadership did was gather resistance cells under their umbrella. The same insurgents US forces had been fighting since 2004 joined AQI. Sometimes insurgents would fight with AQI at the same time they were still part of a resistance group.[23] An entire AQI subgroup existed out of locally based cells with locally based leadership. Cells numbering anywhere from two to fifty gathered under certain commanders, who were connected to the AQI leadership. It is unlikely that many of the fighters espoused AQI's most extreme ideological goals. They fought nonetheless.[24]

Nor were AQI's supporters simply angry young men. A wider section of society, including women, sympathized with them. More than a few women joined AQI and helped provide supplies and information.[25]

In terms of leadership in Anbar, AQI had a set of commanders, known as "emirs." Emirs were responsible for geographic areas and groups of cells. Under high-ranking emirs could be other emirs with functional responsibilities, such as security, intelligence, or management. The exact number of emirs that were in Ramadi is not really known. There were Abu Khattab, Abu Mustafa, and Mullah Kattan, all from Anbar. There was also an administrative emir for Anbar as a whole who was responsible for all incoming revenue from the province and expenditures. Each emir's group worked independently. The cells under an emir were largely kept unaware of the operations of other groups. Even emirs themselves were often unaware of the operations of other emirs.[26]

How did AQI attract followers? For one, the group offered social mobility. Successful attacks brought prestige and promotion. A young man could go from laying IEDs, to leading an IED cell, to commanding a direct-action cell, to perhaps becoming an emir in control of scores of insurgent cells. Many key AQI leaders had once been working class—repairmen, mechanics, or taxi drivers. As insurgent leaders, they held the foremost positions in society, dominant over the tribal leaders, religious leaders, and businessmen who had tried to control their old lives. Mullah Kattan, for example, one of the AQI emirs in Ramadi, had been a petty criminal during the Saddam regime, dismissed by tribal leaders as a lowlife.[27] No one fit the description better than Abu Khattab, a repairman from the Albu Fahad tribe, who fought with the resistance in 2004, was detained, released, and then joined AQI. He became an emir, commanded hundreds in battle, and tirelessly opposed Ramadi's tribal leadership. In two years, he had gone from being nobody to being the most feared insurgent leader in Ramadi.[28]

It was more than just social mobility that won AQI followers. Resources mattered too. The funding sources of the tribal leaders and the resistance proved less robust than AQI's criminal enterprises and international financing. Tribal leaders and the resistance depended upon black-market activities and former regime money. By 2005, former regime money was running dry and AQI was competing with them for control of protection rackets, smuggling, and black-market fuel sales. Without regime resources and taxed by the war with the United States, tribal leaders lacked the wherewithal to defend their old share of the illegal pie against this fairly new and organized competitor.[29]

Interpreters at the government center in early 2006 said that tribal leaders could give the people barely any money (let alone buy weapons and equipment), whereas cell leaders could pay for IEDs to be laid or for someone to be killed.[30] More money meant more fighters. Governor Ma'amoun said, "The people who want to be mujahedin are the people who want money. They do not know where the money comes from and they do not care. They will kill people for money."[31]

AQI probably made millions on black-market oil sales and other criminal activity. They stole the oil by hijacking tanker trucks coming from the refinery at Bayji or bribing officials to give it to them directly at the refinery. The oil could then be sold in Syria, Anbar, or Ramadi, where AQI ran gas stations.[32] Additionally, AQI, in cooperation with other criminal gangs, interdicted the new highway through Rutbah to Jordan and Syria. They took money from travelers or confiscated goods and vehicles and then sold them.[33] I suspect AQI could outperform the tribes on the black market partly because their network allowed them to operate better in Ramadi and other cities and over a wider area. For example, if one tribe could control a highway within its territory, AQI could interdict the highway across its length, interfere with distribution points, and control gas stations within the cities. Thus they had a broader base of revenue than any single tribe or even group of tribes. On top of this, AQI received some amount of international terrorist financing.[34] The combination of internal and international financing gave AQI an edge in recruiting.[35]

Religion should be noted as well. AQI was well resourced, but their wages were hardly generous (probably lower than a paying job in the private sector) and certainly did not compensate for the risk of death that their fighters faced.[36] Deeper ideas may have encouraged Sunnis to fight.

An AQI emir wrote in 2007: "My brothers al-Ansar [Iraqi "supporters" or members of AQI] and al-Mujahidin should know the truth about our fight that is ideological and not tribal nor national and they should learn about the ideology matters since it's the foundation of standing fast on this path."[37] Sunnis may or may not have wanted to institute AQI's interpretation of Islam, but by all indications jihad against the infidel was quite inspiring. Tellingly, Brigadier General David Reist, one of the deputy commanders of I Marine Expeditionary Force in 2006, had a meeting with a prominent Anbar religious leader in the summer of 2006. The religious leader told Reist that the problem in Anbar was the 5 percent of the people who were hard-core terrorists. Reist asked: "Why do 5 percent fight us?" The religious leader replied: "You think 95 percent like Americans?"

On this score, AQI, with its unrelenting commitment to jihad and young angry religious leaders preaching jihad, could outbid the more secular resistance and the tribal leaders, who were hardly known for their piety. AQI's message was simple and clear. It resonated and applied to all, unlike squabbling tribes or the Shi'a government.

One thing I have left unaddressed in examining AQI's rise in Ramadi is intimidation. AQI, as we shall see, excelled at intimidation and brutality. They targeted anyone who worked with the United States or the government. Those who joined the police or the army probably suffered the worst. On the other hand, AQI left those who remained neutral alone. The logic was unassailable: oppose violence and be killed or stay quiet and be left alone.[38] But we need to be careful here. The resistance intimidated too, if without AQI's penchant for beheadings. It had similar tools at its disposal—and used them. Moreover, it is not at all clear that intimidation *motivated* insurgents to fight. It was only on occasion that AQI recruited fighters at gunpoint. We heard of such events very rarely. To motivate people to join them and risk their lives for them, AQI had to rely on tools other than intimidation. In this respect, social mobility, money, and religion get to the heart of the matter.

In Ramadi, AQI's leadership followed the same policies as elsewhere. They pursued jihad against the occupation relentlessly; brooked no compromise; and opposed Ba'athism, tribalism, and other secular forms of governing. They sought to enforce Islamic law (shari'a). Ultimately, Ramadi would become part of the Islamic state they planned to establish in Iraq.[39] There are many stories of AQI brutalizing Sunnis in the name of Islam: killing women, cutting off the fingers of smokers, forcing marriages, and beheading schoolteachers. To be honest, I question how much of this is true. Anyone collaborating with the US military or Iraqi government was brutally intimidated, but that is different from indiscriminate murder. It was remarkable how few Sunni civilians were killed by AQI suicide car bombs. My strong feeling is that, until late 2006, much of their reputed killing and abuse of civilians unconnected to the government or US military was rumor that American ears anxiously accepted.[40] In 2006, Reist asked Governor Ma'amoun whether the rapes and forced marriages were true. The governor shrugged, as if to say, "Who knows?"[41]

US Forces in Ramadi

In 2005, Major General Stephen Johnson and Major General Richard Huck succeeded Lieutenant General Sattler and Major General Natonski in command of the US military forces in Anbar. They knew that Ramadi needed to be secured. The violence, Ramadi's status as provincial capital, and the size of the population made this clear. Operations in the western desert prevented them from sending reinforcements to Ramadi other than new Iraqi army units.

By late 2005, three US battalions and six under-strength and predominantly Shi'a Iraqi army battalions were operating in Ramadi. All fell under the 2nd Brigade of the 28th National Guard Division (2-28 Brigade Combat Team), commanded by Colonel John Gronski. Of the three US battalions, one Marine battalion (roughly one thousand Marines) held the center of downtown Ramadi, one army infantry battalion (roughly nine hundred regular soldiers) held the eastern part of downtown and the Sufiya district, and one National Guard battalion (roughly four hundred soldiers) held the wide swath across the farmlands north of the city to the southern edge of Tam'eem. Three of the Iraqi battalions belonged to 1st Brigade, 7th Iraqi Division (1-7 Iraqi Brigade). They operated in Tam'eem, the western part of downtown Ramadi, and the Jazirah. Out of an authorized strength of 759, each battalion had roughly 400 men on hand for operations. Another Iraqi battalion had transferred from the 2nd Brigade, 1st Iraqi Division (2-1 Iraqi Brigade) in Fallujah to the center of Ramadi. The two remaining Iraqi battalions were special police units from the Ministry of Interior (they would be called away in early 2006). The four Iraqi army battalions were able to conduct basic operations, if at a low tempo. They did not want for bravery.[42]

The US and Iraqi main bases bookended the old main road. On the western end, they occupied a former Iraqi army base (Camp Ramadi) and two of Saddam's palaces (Hurricane Point and Blue Diamond). On the eastern end, they occupied the agricultural college (Camp Corregidor) and a plot of warehouses across the old main road (Combat Outpost). From west to east, a series of smaller outposts dotted the main road: Snake Pit, "OP VA" ("OP" stands for observation post), the government center, and "OP Huriya." The southern and northern neighborhoods of the city had no posts and had become insurgent safe havens. Patrols into the southern neighborhoods encountered makeshift road barriers, ambushes, and layers of IEDs. Patrols into northern Ramadi (the location of the hospital, which was under the control of AQI) risked being immobilized or cut off by sophisticated ambushes and IEDs.[43] Similarly, scarcity of manpower precluded the placement of entry control points on every route into the city.[44] Insurgents transported large quantities of munitions through the expanse of homes and farms (known as the Sufiya) abutting the eastern downtown, circumventing the entry control point on the main road. The entry control points themselves withheld from inspecting every car and purposefully let trucks go uninspected in order to avert massive traffic backups.[45]

THE DEFEAT OF THE RESISTANCE

In November 2005, a unique opportunity arose to secure Ramadi without vast numbers of American reinforcements. National elections, set for December 15, were pending. Former regime and tribal leaders in Ramadi realized that boycotting the January elections had worsened their political position. Sunnis now stood to lose national political influence to the Shi'a.[46] Several tribal leaders and former military officers were open to negotiations if some of their grievances with the Shi'a government could be addressed and if US withdrawal could be expedited. After two years of fighting with little to show, support for violent resistance to the occupation—their raison d'être—had weakened.

AQI had preempted an early attempt at negotiations in the summer. Mohammed Mahmoud Latif, the resistance leader and respected Islamic scholar from the Albu Fahad, secretly met with Major General Huck.[47] What was discussed is unknown. After the meeting, certain high-ranking tribal and religious leaders became interested in reducing violence. AQI attacked them while they met in a mosque.[48] The attackers shot and killed the head of the Sunni Endowment. The other leaders were intimidated into silence. Brigadier General Jim Williams, deputy commander of the 2nd Marine Division, and Lane Bahl of the US State Department rekindled the opportunity in November by releasing a respected religious leader from a detention center. Subsequently, a few senior religious leaders agreed to meet. At the meeting, they told Williams and Bahl that the United States should "show an open hand," implying that the resistance would respond favorably if the United States offered to negotiate.

Williams followed their advice. He was one in a line of Marine generals who saw the resistance as a potential ally. He strove over the next months to turn the resistance and the tribal leaders. He worked hand in hand with Colonel Gronski, commander of the army brigade in Ramadi, who also committed himself to trying to win over the resistance and tribal leaders. It has been too often overlooked that it was Gronski who set up the first US outposts and sent the first Iraqi army battalion into the Jazirah farming region of northwest Ramadi—the area that would later become the heart of the awakening movement. Coincidentally, Williams was a reserve Marine officer and Gronski was a national guardsman. After 2006, Williams and Gronski would be neglected in histories of the awakening.[49]

Williams convened a "reconciliation conference" in Ramadi on November 28, 2005. Over two hundred tribal leaders, prominent religious leaders, and former military officers attended. Williams promised that the United States would eventually leave Anbar. His statement made an impression. After much debate and repeated calls for US withdrawal from Ramadi, the conference ended with the formation of a "provincial security council," composed of the key religious leaders, tribal leaders, and former army officers from Ramadi.[50] The US promise to replace its forces with Iraqi forces, and to eventually withdraw from Ramadi convinced the leaders of the council to support the upcoming national elections and encourage their tribesmen to join the police. This quid pro quo became the basis for continued discussions with US leaders.

The key figures in the council were Anwar Abdul Razzaq Kharbite al-Khalifawi (of the Albu Khalifa tribe), General Sa'ab Manfi Muhammad al-Rawi (of the Albu Rawi tribe), and Shaykh Nasr Karim Mukhlif al-Fahadawi (of the Albu Fahad tribe). Anwar was a leading member of the wealthy Kharbite family, longtime financiers of the resistance. Sa'ab was a former general in Saddam's army and very outspoken. He oversaw an initiative to recruit Sunnis from Anbar into the Iraqi army. Nasr was the real heavyweight. A high-ranking Ba'athist, professor at al-Anbar University, business owner, and the leader of the Albu Fahad, he had wealth, power, and reputation.[51] All had been involved in the resistance. Governor Ma'amoun was not an official member of the council but would work closely with it.

The council decided to talk with the United States out of a combination of concern about the future of the Sunnis and concern about AQI. Securing Sunni power against the rising Shi'a strongly compelled them to act. They particularly wanted to use the election to regain a Sunni voice. Fear of Shi'a aggression against the Sunnis weighed heavily on their minds. Anwar Kharbite warned: "As much as we achieve, there are dark forces that work to undermine everything we achieve. I hear of people coming in the night with Shi'a militia."[52] A Shi'a Iraqi army greatly worried them. The council wanted Sunni military formations to secure Anbar instead of Shi'a ones. Sunni military formations would guarantee

Sunni control of Anbar and political weight vis-à-vis the Shi'a. As Tariq al-Halbusi, a powerful Anbar businessmen in Amman, said, "The Shi'a have the army and militias. We just want a Sunni army to balance them."[53]

The council also disliked AQI's influence in Ramadi. They told their people to help stop the terrorists. AQI's rise weakened the power of the already fragmented tribes. The council said the terrorists leaders were from outside Iraq and paid Iraqis to carry out their attacks. AQI stole tribesmen out of the very tribes supposedly run by prominent resistance leaders. In certain cases, tribal leaders of subtribes turned against the head tribal leader because of a dispute or a bid for power. More often, recruits were members of lower families and clans who suffered less status, power, or money than the tribal elites. Tribal loyalty was not guaranteed, especially in times when the patronage available to tribal leaders had greatly diminished. The council told US officers they would gain greater influence through working with the government than with AQI.

The council wanted to get rid of both AQI and the United States. Shaykh Khamis, the brother of Nasr, later explained the council's view on this point:

> The situation in Ramadi is bad. There is a great deal of violence . . . The violence has been caused by the United States and the terrorists. The United States raids homes. The United States kills people too . . . The United States should withdraw gradually . . . The situation can be solved by giving Sunnis our own forces. We should form units of men from Ramadi. They would work for the Ministry of Defense, not work for the United States.[54]

Anwar Kharbite expressed a similar distaste for both the United States and AQI: "I work with the United States but also let insurgents nearby . . . just because I oppose the occupation does not mean I work with terrorists."[55]

On December 12, the council met with General Casey and Minister of Defense Sa'adun Dulaymi. At the meeting, the council rejected AQI. The participants agreed that the council, the Iraqi Transitional Government, and the United States would work toward ending violence. The agreement centered on the principle that US forces would pull out as Iraqi forces, recruited in Anbar, established security.

After the meeting, the council sent a petition to Prime Minister Ja'aferi asking his government to: release all detainees not proven guilty; place two Iraqi Army divisions in Anbar; and recruit a division's worth of men from Anbar for the Iraqi army. The petition then listed actions that the council would take, which included advocating for Sunni political participation, arguing against foreign influence in Iraq, refuting fanaticism, and encouraging young men to join the army and police. The petition expected US forces to conduct a phased withdrawal once violence decreased, leaving the army and police in their stead. The council accepted that, even thereafter, some US forces would continue to operate alongside Iraqi forces against foreign fighters and terrorists.[56]

The petition represented a shift from previous resistance negotiating demands. Usually, resistance interlocutors had demanded that the United States immediately withdraw from Sunni cities, that all detainees be released regardless of guilt, that Sunnis be allowed to form their own military units, that de-Ba'athification be reversed, and that former high-ranking officers be allowed into the Iraqi army. Casey accepted the petition and set his staff to formulating a response.

For their part, Williams and Gronski, who wanted nothing more than to get police on the streets of Ramadi, did their best to back the members of the council. It goes without saying that they held meeting after meeting with them. They tried to build the council's power by encouraging the Iraqi government to endorse it and endow it with funding. Another source of funding was the US commanders' emergency response program (CERP). Williams and Gronski used projects to show the people that the council was delivering public goods. Projects were contracted via both the Provincial Reconstruction and Development Council and US civil affairs teams, who interacted directly with the tribal leaders. Certain civil affairs teams went a step further. They tried to use projects not simply as a public good but as a means of empowering certain leaders, such as Shaykh Adnan of the Albu Alwan and Shaykh Mahmud of the Albu Soda. Any project represented potential jobs that a tribal leader could give to his tribesmen. Shaykh Abdul Sittar of the Albu Risha, one of the most vocal in his willingness to fight AQI, received a multimillion-dollar project to gravel Camp Ramadi.[57] Unfortunately, the Provincial Reconstruction and Development Council hardly expended funds quickly and there was no common policy of using CERP to empower the tribal leaders. Thus the effect of CERP spending was less than it could have been.[58]

To further help the Anbar security council, Williams decided to allow the tribal leaders to patrol and protect their own territory—an important concession, given Sunni dislike of occupiers and the tribal leaders' need for legitimacy.[59] The tribal leaders then openly fielded militias (sometimes resistance cells by another name). By and large, US forces abstained from interacting with the tribal militias. They withheld advisors and even training. This was not out of reluctance on the part of Williams, Gronski, or any other American. The tribal leaders did not want advisors or training, let alone US outposts sitting next to their homes. Even rudimentary coordination with US commanders to avoid friendly-fire accidents was rejected. In their eyes, such contact would taint the movement and challenge their control of their territory. They wanted the Marines and soldiers to stand back and let them police themselves. A few tribal leaders asked for guns, which Gronski refused, but this was not a mainstream request of the movement or its major leaders.[60]

Positive results manifested themselves over the following month. Tribal leaders convinced their tribesmen to join the police. Furthermore, substantial intelligence reporting and a few US eyewitness accounts revealed that the tribal militias were setting up checkpoints, barricading neighborhoods, and even detaining AQI fighters.[61] Latif, the key leader of the resistance, aligned with the security council and organized resistance cadres behind it.[62] Gunfights broke out between tribal militias and AQI. On one occasion, Marines battling insurgents watched their attackers take fire from a separate location, unaffiliated with friendly forces. The attacks of the militias may have driven a few AQI leaders from the city. On December 9, Albu Risha tribesmen turned in Amir Khalaf Fanus, an AQI leader known as "the Butcher of Ramadi," to Camp Ramadi. Thereafter, the US forces started working with the tribesmen's notably aggressive tribal leader, Abdul Sittar, who became a good source of intelligence.

Tribal leaders, tribal militias, and resistance groups (such as 1920 Revolutionary Brigade and Jaysh Islami) clamped down on Ramadi for the December 15 national elections.[63] They told AQI to get out of the city. Insurgent activity was completely suppressed. There is a famous story that Nasr held several AQI fighters in his basement at gunpoint until the election was over. He supposedly would have shot them if their colleagues had started anything.[64] US and Iraqi army units stayed in their outposts. Marines watched hundreds play football on the main road. Following the instructions of their tribal and religious leaders, between fifty thousand and one hundred thousand people voted that day. Barely anyone had voted in January or October.[65]

Success was misleading. Back in November, a school teacher, Haifa Omar, had looked skeptically upon the new people's council:

> I don't think today's meeting will lead to any good results . . . The Ramadi residents meeting here have no authority, nor any control over the situation in the city, because the real authority is in the hands of al-Qaeda, who are running the city as they wish . . . They are looking for fighting and death like we are looking for our daily livelihood.[66]

Indeed, AQI had not been defeated. It had backed off to take stock of the situation. After the elections, with the blessing of Zarqawi, Abu Khattab, Abu Mustafa, and other AQI leaders planned a series of attacks and assassinations. "After we took a look at the situation," an AQI commander would later write to his superiors, "we found that the best solution to stop thousands of people from renouncing their religion is to cut off the heads of the Shaykhs."[67] To justify the killing of traditional leaders, he asked: "What's more important? Religion or honor and land?"[68]

Abu Khattab and Abu Mustafa had their men post leaflets declaring tribal leaders working with the security council to be targets.[69] They gathered a list of people on the security council—a simple task considering that most of the meetings were public—and then had cells observe the targets for a prolonged period in preparation for a hit.[70] AQI had plenty of fighters from the lower echelons of the Ramadi tribes, including Abu Khattab and Abu Mustafa themselves, who had no issue with betraying their tribal leader—a ready-made informant network. Indeed, the hit cells were often made up of members of the same tribe as their targets. It was easy for them to gather information. In the words of an influential Anbar tribal leader and businessman, "AQI took advantage of the weak of al-Anbar to hit at the province's leadership."[71]

It began on January 5, 2006, at a police recruitment drive at the glass factory. Over one thousand applicants had reported to the glass factory that morning. Soldiers and working dogs were inspecting the men standing in a long line along a concrete wall. Suddenly the dogs started barking aggressively. Before anyone could react, a suicide bomber blew himself up. The explosion killed forty people and injured sixty. Screening continued—one thousand recruits were sent to police academies in Jordan and Baghdad that day. The leaders of the security council were worried, but their will held.

The body blow came eleven days later. Shaykh Nasr, Governor Ma'amoun, and the security council had a well-publicized meeting with Prime Minister Ja'aferi, General Casey, and Ambassador Khalilzad on January 15. The next day, insurgents gunned down Nasr as he was driving alone in Ramadi. The letter from the AQI commander later explained the reasons for the killing: "This man worked so hard fighting the (Tanzim) organization [AQI] with all he's got, from money to power, and reputation in Ramadi . . . he protects with his soldiers the election centers, and encourages people to volunteers [*sic*] in the police force and the Iraqi army."[72] The assassin was allegedly from the Albu Fahad.

News of Nasr's death, coming so soon after the glass factory, shook the security council's resolve. The council stopped meeting. Many members lost heart. AQI never gave the council a chance to recover. Shortly after Nasr's murder, two lesser tribal leaders of the Albu Fahad living north of the Euphrates were assassinated.[73] Next, on January 18, Shaykh Muhammad Sadaq al-Battah, head of the Albu Chulayb, was killed in Baghdad. And on January 23, insurgents blew up Anwar Kharbite's house (located in the city and thus surrounded by other tribes—hardly a defensible position).[74]

The Albu Fahad tribe, already fragmented, splintered into opposing groups. Tribesmen loyal to Nasr initially retaliated against tribesmen who had aligned with AQI. Unfortunately for the council, the effort was half-hearted. Within two months almost all Nasr's loyalists had either submitted to AQI or resumed fighting US forces as the resistance. Fragmentation probably obstructed tribesmen loyal to Nasr from accessing an informant network comparable to that of AQI. The new head tribal leader, Nasr's brother, Khamis, fled to Jordan. The tribe was broken. According to the letter of the AQI commander, "there was a complete change of events . . . cousins of Sheik Nasr came to the Mujahidin begging, announcing their repentance and innocence, saying we're with you, we'll do whatever you want. The turmoil is over, our brothers now are roaming the streets of Albu Fahd without any checkpoints."[75] Cowed, tribal leaders from the Albu Ubaydi, Albu Chulayb, and many other tribes realigned with AQI as well.[76]

The final stroke was the murder of Major General Sa'ab. Insurgents shot him dead on the morning of February 26, as he stepped alone out of his home. He was the second-to-last of the council to fall—the head shaykh of the Albu Alwan was killed in March. But after Sa'ab's assassination, the movement was dead. Remaining members fled or went to ground. Anwar Kharbite could not be found. Latif disappeared. Other council members told US officers that they would only step forward again when Sunni Iraqi police and army had saturated Ramadi. The morale of the security council had cracked. Other than Governor Ma'amoun, who continued to brave gunfire at the beleaguered government center, only remnants continued to fight AQI. On the eastern side of the city, a few Albu Fahad resistance fighters skirmished with AQI in the farmland and homes to the east of the city in occasional if persistent bursts.[77] On the other side of the city, Abdul Sittar and a set of tribal leaders from the Albu Thiyab and Albu Risha quietly took steps to regain control of their tribal territory. A civil war simmered between these tribal leaders and AQI.[78]

The effectiveness of assassination and intimidation impressed AQI's leaders. In just over two months, AQI had gutted the leadership of the Sunni resistance and the tribes in Ramadi. The intensity, tactical sophistication, and scope of the assassination and intimidation campaign were unprecedented. The letter of the AQI commander to his superiors noted how the campaign had compelled tribal leader after tribal leader to come to AQI in fear to offer homage, with scarce popular outcry over the brutality of the tactic.[79]

The defeat of the security council allowed AQI to consolidate its hold over Ramadi. The traditional tribal leadership was in disarray. The old tribal leaders were gone. Large numbers of their tribesmen willingly worked with AQI for money, credibility, and power. Shaykh Sabah, patriarch of the Albu Mahal, bemoaned the situation to his east: "I am very sad because the tribes are broken. Every tribe should be like the Albu Mahal. They are not."[80] In the words of Hamid Rashid, the new head of the Albu Alwan, "People don't listen as much to the tribal leader. They don't respect him. They follow their own cause."[81] Shaykh Khamis of the Albu Fahad said, "Young and angry males support AQI. They do this because of money or because they want to fight."[82] The traditional authority of the tribal leaders could only buy so much. Alone, it could compel few to turn away from AQI's money, brave AQI's intimidation, and take sides with the infidel occupier. The defeated tribal and religious leaders had little to give. One of Anbar's senior religious leaders proclaimed: "Fitna [civil war] has overturned traditional society."[83]

Elsewhere in the province, AQI was gaining influence as well. AQI managed a minor resurgence in Fallujah. Because the city was firmly in the grasp of the Marines, insurgents never had a chance of massing for Ramadi-style street battles. Instead, they assassinated nonviolent religious leaders and police officers. In November 2005, AQI gunned down Shaykh Hamza Abass Muhna al-Issawi, the mufti of Fallujah, the highest religious legal authority in the city. Two months later, insurgents got Shaykh Kamal Shakir al-Nazal, the imam who chaired the Fallujah city council. The city council stopped meeting. The mayor went into hiding. After that, insurgents killed the deputy police chief and approximately twenty policemen between June and August. Seemingly overwhelmed, the police chief took long stretches of leave and eventually arranged for a new posting in Baghdad. Police morale teetered on the edge of breakdown. For Marine leaders and Kael Weston, who had seen Fallujah go from insurgent safe haven to an island of some sort of calm, the hits were deeply concerning.

So far, I have written little about the perceptions of the people. If counterinsurgency is about hearts and minds, their perceptions would seem to matter a great deal. Did the people support violence against the occupation? Did they oppose AQI?

The most rigorous understanding of popular perceptions comes from a set of surveys the Marines commissioned for Anbar. Iraqi pollsters asked the interview questions. Between November 2005 and August 2006, a small minority of respondents in Anbar and Ramadi supported the Iraqi government, while a substantial majority opposed it. Substantial majorities also supported attacks on the US military.[84] The surveys did find that a majority of Sunnis opposed the foreign fighters affiliated with AQI and viewed them as a significant threat.[85] A small minority of AQI, however, were foreigners. The feelings of the people toward Iraqis fighting for AQI were never clear—regardless of what the tribal leaders and former generals thought of them. In August, for instance, locals took to the streets in western Ramadi to protest the detention of a local religious leader, even though he was connected to AQI.

While certain older religious leaders and Latif had been willing to cooperate with the Anbar security council, the numerous mosque imams and students could be antagonistic. Religious scholars as well as other teachers at al-Anbar University were close to the insurgency. They encouraged their students to oppose occupation and labeled Governor Ma'amoun a collaborator.[86] One intelligent young religious leader and teacher at al-Anbar University heavily criticized the United States and the Iraqi army. Iraqi soldiers sometimes stopped him at checkpoints on his daily trip back and forth from downtown Ramadi to the university. He despised them for it: "The Iraqi army are ignorant. They do not know how to read or write. They do not know how to act."[87] One day, the soldiers learned the young man was an imam. They then cursed: "All mosques are like the sole of a shoe."[88] References to feet are highly insulting in Iraqi culture, even more so in reference to Islam. By telling the story, the young religious leader was impugning the Iraqi army's legitimacy as Muslims. One of his colleagues was more caustic. He said, "The United States makes things worse by killing and detaining innocents. It turns the hearts of the people against the United States. It opens an opportunity for terrorists to recruit people to kill Americans. Without a doubt, people now want to kill Americans."[89]

Deputy Prime Minister for Security Khalef al-Aliyan, who was from Ramadi and had supported the resistance, described deep popular antipathy to the United States in meetings with American and British generals in 2006: "Every nation that is attacked has the right to resist. There are two types of resistance. The first is on the basis of religion. It is a duty to undertake jihad. The second is on the basis of patriotism. We must fight to get our country back ... The tribes and people fight the United States. People sympathize with them. They give assistance and funds ... Some resistance groups do not want to work with the United States because of Islam."[90]

Sunnis told Marines and US civilians again and again that acts Americans labeled as terrorist were actually legitimate resistance. One tribal leader said that "the resistance cloaks the terrorists."[91] On another occasion, Lieutenant Colonel Daniel Walrath, commander of 1st Battalion, 6th Infantry Regiment (which would arrive in June), was on foot patrol in the northern agricultural outskirts of Ramadi. He ran into three Albu Fahad tribesmen sitting oddly in the grass, as if they had been expecting him and his soldiers. The tribesmen's words, their body language, their age (late twenties), their physical fitness, and their coolness implied that they were insurgents. Walrath asked them about the difference between the resistance and the terrorists. The Albu Fahad, after all, were known for their ties to the resistance. One of them replied: "We cannot tell the difference between the *muqamwa* [resistance] and the *irhabiyeen* [terrorists]. Who can?"[92]

None of this necessarily points to popular Sunni commitment to violence above all else. Widespread popular support for insurgent activity must be balanced against dislike of foreign fighters and growing concerns about civil war. Nevertheless, it was hardly an environment in which a tribal leader could turn against the insurgency, work with the occupier, kill fellow Sunni Iraqis, and expect to be carried forward by waves of popular enthusiasm. Rather, a tribal leader needed to build a movement that could survive amid antipathy toward the United States and the government. That demanded solid organization and the means to retain the loyalty of his following.

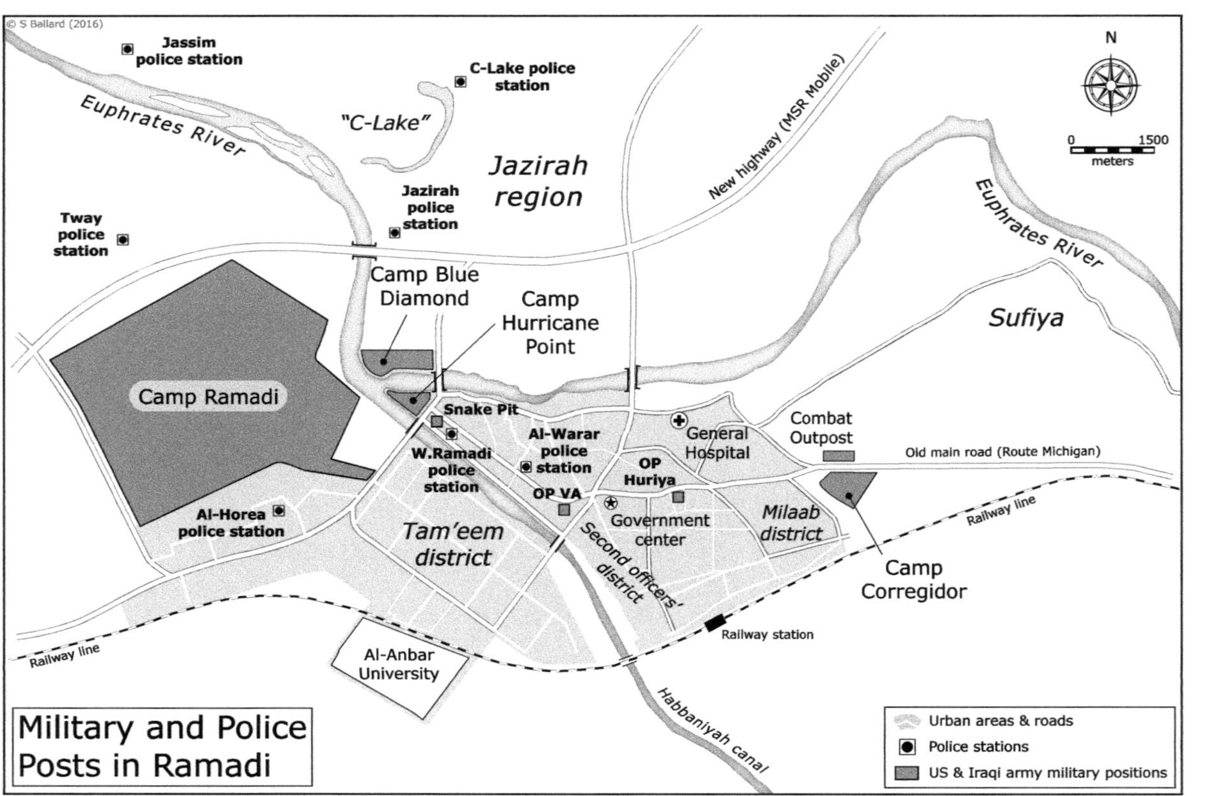

Map 7. Military and Police Posts in Ramadi

CHAPTER 4

Before the Surge: The US Offensive in Ramadi

I Marine Expeditionary Force (I MEF), commanded by Major General Richard Zilmer, replaced II Marine Expeditionary Force (II MEF) in al-Anbar in late February 2006. Major General Johnson, Major General Huck, and Brigadier General Williams returned home. Zilmer and his team came to Iraq knowing that Ramadi would be their problem to address. An impressively calm and reasoning general, Zilmer was well suited to the adversity of Ramadi. Two deputy commanders backed him up. Brigadier General David Reist would take over Williams's role of handling economic and governance issues and working with the Iraqi government, tribal leaders, and other officials. Brigadier General Robert Neller would oversee day-to-day aspects of military operations and the advising and training of the Iraqi army and police. Neller was the definition of gruff. A grimace of intense displeasure was permanently imprinted on his face. He was also intensely practical, analytic, and close with the Marines and soldiers on the ground. Many of the best solutions to the most intractable problems would come out of his mind.

With the demise of the provincial security council, Zilmer and the I Marine Expeditionary Force staff began planning for a major operation in Ramadi. Casey visited Zilmer and his staff at Camp Fallujah on March 18. He confirmed that their main goal would be to secure the city. Zilmer's goal was to reduce the violence in Ramadi to a level that Iraqi forces could manage, as had occurred in Fallujah and al-Qa'im. He wanted, however, to avoid a Fallujah-style battle, in which bombs and artillery wrecked neighborhoods and risked civilian casualties.[1] Marines and soldiers already held positions deep in the city, so Zilmer dismissed with a set-piece assault. Rather, he wanted US soldiers and Marines, and Iraqi soldiers and police, to expand out from their preexisting positions into new outposts until the entire city had been saturated.

Lieutenant Colonel Alford's successes in al-Qa'im in late 2005 strongly influenced the thinking within Zilmer's headquarters about how to handle Ramadi. His planning team, under the guidance of Colonel Michael Marletto (the operations officer), planned for US and Iraqi army units to establish outposts throughout the city, manned by twenty to one hundred men. They would execute dismounted patrolling from those outposts. Additionally, population control measures—checkpoints and barriers—would be set up in order to cordon off the city and block the movement of arms and insurgents.

The planning team estimated that one additional US brigade and two additional Iraqi brigades would be needed. I Marine Expeditionary Force had no US battalions, let alone a brigade, free for Ramadi. Regarding the two Iraqi brigades, the 1st Brigade of the 1st Iraqi Division (1-1 Iraqi Brigade) was due to come to Ramadi already. Lieutenant General Peter Chiarelli, commander of I MEF's higher headquarters—Multi-National Corps Iraq (MNC-I)—needed the permission of the Iraqi government to deploy a second brigade.

Minister of Defense Sa'adun Dulaymi refused. The moment was politically inopportune. Iraqi politicians were in the midst of debating the composition of the permanent government. The lame-duck transitional government was in no position to support a major operation in Ramadi. The Iraqi government had asked General Casey to refrain from any battalion-size operations during the formation of the new government.[2] Moreover, rising sectarian violence in Baghdad absorbed the attention of Iraqi politicians. In March, Chiarelli launched Operation Scales of Justice, meant to secure Baghdad through more patrols and more checkpoints. Rather than receive reinforcements, Zilmer lost two rifle companies, a light armored reconnaissance company, two special police battalions (taken from Ramadi), and the 3rd battalion of 1-1 Iraqi Brigade (slated to go to Ramadi) to Baghdad. The forces would return after the government had formed.

Realizing that they might never have the forces to saturate Ramadi, the Marine planners fell back on what was an oil-spot strategy. Brigadier General Neller advocated a concept in which US and Iraqi forces would secure neighborhoods in the city one by one. US and Iraqi forces would only move into a new neighborhood after the preceding one had been cleared. Civil affairs projects, intense dismounted patrolling, and the establishment of small outposts would facilitate the clearance. Most importantly, local police would provide security in the wake of the US and Iraqi army operations. The plan depended upon development of effective police to "backfill" US units as they expanded the oil spot.

Consequently, Neller focused on recruiting, training, and advising the police. Casey had dubbed 2006 the "year of the police." He wanted 11,330 police recruited in Anbar by the end of the year. Unfortunately, police recruitment slowed dramatically after January. Nevertheless, Neller proceeded on other fronts. To build the best police force, the police advisory teams would need to be improved. At the beginning of 2006, there were fewer than seven advisory teams, all understaffed and made up of National Guard. None lived with the Iraqis. Neller worked to increase the number of teams. They would eventually grew to over twenty. In the summer, he would strip out law enforcement professionals from 1st Battalion, 24th Marine Regiment—a reserve battalion with plenty of cops—and move them into advisory teams. Still unsatisfied, he then took ten Marines from every other Marine battalion to give the teams enough men to run convoys and patrol with the police. Slowly but surely, the teams left the US bases to live and work with the Iraqis. These reforms would not fully take effect until September, but early on in his tour Neller pressed to get the process started.[3]

Zilmer and Neller also wanted to expand the Iraqi army. Its deployment and recruitment policies were preventing many Sunnis from joining. In late 2005, the Ministry of Defense had granted that 5,000 Sunnis from Anbar could be recruited into the army. In early 2006, the figure was raised to 6,500. However, the ministry did not want all of the Sunnis serving in the 1st or 7th Divisions. Rather, the Sunni recruits would be deployed throughout the armed forces, lest the Sunni elements of the two divisions become de facto Sunni militias resistant to the Iraqi government.[4]

The first recruiting effort occurred at the end of March. It aimed for 1,000 recruits. Ultimately, I Marine Expeditionary Force sent 1,017 recruits, largely from Fallujah, to training. Unfortunately, success had been built on false pretenses. The Sunni recruits believed they would be serving near their homes. The mayor of Fallujah, in fact, had reassured the Fallujah recruits that they would serve in Fallujah. The recruits were unaware that they could be deployed anywhere in Iraq or anywhere in Anbar.

On April 30, the new soldiers graduated from training. During the ceremony, replete with US and Iraqi generals, it was announced that many would be deployed outside Anbar. Yelling and throwing their uniforms to the ground, six hundred of the newly trained soldiers refused to deploy. The main reason was a desire to stay close to home, but this was connected to a fear that they would face Shi'a militias and sectarian retribution if they joined predominantly Shi'a units deployed outside Anbar. The mayor of Fallujah supported the recruits, telling US officers: "As long as I am receiving corpses from Baghdad, I will not send soldiers there!"[5] In the end, more than six hundred of the one thousand recruits deserted.[6] The mutiny deterred Sunnis from volunteering in subsequent recruiting efforts. Building police became all the more essential for success in Ramadi.

Neller encountered further resistance from the Ministry of Defense just getting the existing Sunni soldiers paid. These were the seven hundred or so Albu Mahal soldiers out in al-Qa'im. High-level officials in the Ministry of Defense delayed distributing salaries. They also turned away over one hundred former army officers who wanted to join the brigade in al-Qa'im or other units in the western desert. According to Sunni government leaders, the defense officials did these things partly because they feared a Sunni military force could assist in violence against the state.[7]

Brigadier General Reist, who oversaw economic and governance issues for Zilmer, tried to accelerate the flow of US military funds. The commanders' emergency response program (CERP) had been a powerful carrot in 2005. Unfortunately, Congress had yet to approve funding for the program for 2006. As the program was the primary source of money for US commanders to use to provide economic assistance to the Sunnis, US forces in Anbar found themselves short on cash. Reist and US commanders in Anbar had to rely on the less than $1 million left over from 2005 and allotments from Chiarelli's pot of reserve CERP. With the onset of sectarian violence, Baghdad, Basra, and Diyala provinces were Chiarelli's priorities.[8] In lieu of US money, Reist tried to get economic assistance from the Iraqi government, but this too was not forthcoming. The new CERP funds would only be approved and available for disbursement in June.

In the spring, Reist started traveling to Amman to speak with Sunni tribal, religious, and business leaders who had fled Anbar. Included were several of the richest and highest-ranking men of the province. Several had been part of the security council or the resistance. They wanted to get Anbar in order. Reist spoke with them about how to improve economic investment in Anbar and how to get more people to turn against violence, particularly in Ramadi. They warned Reist repeatedly of the threat that Iran posed and of the need to build Sunni armed forces to defend against it. Several economic conferences were convened, during which the tribal, religious, and business leaders discussed the future of the province. Partly on the basis of these discussions, Reist laid out his plans to use the commanders' emergency response program to assist economic development. Paul Brinkley, assistant secretary of defense for business transformation, helped Reist by examining ways to restart Anbar's state-owned factories. Additionally, Reist used his engagement efforts in Amman to garner greater support from the Sunni leaders for operations in Ramadi and elsewhere in the province.

As Zilmer's plan for Ramadi took shape, violence in the city escalated dramatically. Captain Andrew Del Gaudio, a company commander in 3rd Battalion, 8th Marine Regiment (3/8), spoke with only slight hyperbole of battling one hundred insurgents per day.[9] Fighters rallied from inside and outside Ramadi. The one thousand Marines of 3rd Battalion, 8th Marine Regiment fought in the western half of the city. They held most of the outposts on the main road (Route Michigan), where insurgents concentrated their attacks. The nine hundred soldiers of 1st Battalion, 506th Parachute Infantry Regiment (1-506) fought in the eastern half of the city. Besides covering the eastern section of the old main road, they patrolled the dangerous Milaab neighborhood in the southeast quarter of the city. Both battalions faced constant attacks. Soldiers in 1-506 said that any patrol out for more than thirty minutes was guaranteed to get shot at.

One of the largest attacks took place on April 17. On that day, over one hundred insurgents simultaneously struck twelve US and Iraqi positions from western Ramadi to Khalidiyah at precisely 1:00 p.m. Abu Khattab, the well-known AQI emir in the city, quarterbacked the operation. Zarqawi may have planned it. The main effort was against Observation Post VA, in the center of the city. A suicide truck bomb drove into the compound and detonated, leaving an eight-foot-deep crater and flinging a Humvee fifty feet. Luckily, no one was hurt. The insurgents nevertheless used video of the truck bomb attack to claim that they had won the day. Heavy fighting continued until 5:45 p.m. At one point, mortar rounds were falling on the government center every thirty seconds. The insurgents never assaulted, let alone captured, a position. That was not the point. What mattered to them was that they could mass for a resounding attack in the heart of the provincial capital and then withdraw sufficiently unscathed to go at it again another day. Indeed, Zarqawi publicized it as a great victory in a video televised in late April (which also featured him planning attacks in Ramadi); irrefutable evidence that the US military was not in control.[10]

War frightened people into fleeing the city. Of the roughly 450,000 people in and around Ramadi, Marines estimated that 100,000–200,000 fled. Stretches of the main road were abandoned. So were the multi-story buildings surrounding the government center. Buildings within one hundred meters of it had been shot to pieces. The water main had busted and flooded the street. Other battlegrounds in the Milaab and around OP VA were similarly abandoned. Off the main road and in quieter pockets, Iraqis lived in between the violence. Workers went to their jobs, if they were lucky enough to have one. Iraqis in cars and trucks filed in and out of the entry control points that tried to screen insurgents from entering the city. Children went to the few remaining schools. Lonely women wove through barricades to buy goods. Shops were still open. Where necessary, shop owners made deals with the insurgents, either to survive or because they sympathized. One battered father whose son had been injured by an IED told Iraqi army and US officers: "We can't do anything. I blame you Americans. You came to our country. You do not fix anything and cause destruction. I do not blame the insurgents for laying the IED."[11]

During April, Colonel Gronski started implementing the oil-spot strategy. First was the deployment of 1st Brigade, 1st Iraqi Division, which had arrived in east Ramadi in late March. A hard core of veterans from the battles in Najaf, Fallujah, and al-Qa'im made the brigade the best in the Iraqi army. In late April, working with 1-506, they established two outposts on the eastern edge of the Milaab district of southeast Ramadi.[12] Heavy fighting immediately followed.

Next was the new set of population control measures. Gronski placed a new entry control point on the road into the northeast area of the city, obstacles in the western first officers' district (meant to limit insurgent vehicular movement), and a checkpoint to inspect trucks entering the city from the west. These measures constrained insurgent movement into Ramadi and complicated the organization of mass attacks. Most impressively, no suicide car bombs went off for months within downtown Ramadi.

Finally, Gronski brought the first police into Ramadi. In late April, the thousand police recruited at the Glass Factory completed their training. Only four hundred showed for work. These police had largely been recruited from the Albu Thiyab, Albu Ali Jassim, and Albu Risha tribes in the countryside northwest of the city. Gronski assigned part of the police to two stations in the western part of the city—one at an old police station near Camp Ramadi in the Tam'eem neighborhood, the other at a youth center near Camp Snake Pit in the first officer's district.[13] They would respectively be known as the "al-Horea" and "western Ramadi" police stations. The Ministry of Interior was slow in providing the new police with their salaries. Through May none were paid. The Ministry of Finance refused to put money into Anbar because it distrusted Anbar officials. Neller began pressuring Ministry of Interior officials and US generals in Baghdad to pay the police, a process that would repeat itself throughout his tour.[14]

US forces witnessed greatest progress in the first officers' district, the corner of downtown Ramadi where the Euphrates and the canal to Lake Habbaniyah meet. Here, in early May, Lieutenant Colonel Steve Neary, commander of 3rd Battalion, 8th Marine Regiment, approved an initiative by Captain Ray Gerber (his intelligence officer) and Captain Max Barela (one of his four company commanders) to create a safe area as per Neller's oil-spot concept. Attacks had been significantly lower in the first officers' district than elsewhere in Ramadi. The population was wealthier and more educated. The governor and his tribe lived in the area, creating a natural popular support base. Plus, bordered on two sides by water and adjacent to three US bases, first officers' district was relatively easy to control.

Barela's company, shifts of roughly fifty police (three hundred total worked at the police station in various shifts), and two companies of 2nd Battalion, 1st Brigade, 7th Iraqi Division (2-1-7 Iraqi Battalion) secured the district. Barela had his Marines patrol on foot and as much as possible at night. The tactics befuddled the insurgents, who had adapted to daytime patrols in Humvees, and reduced the company's casualties. Barela's Marines patrolled with the Iraqis and independently (roughly five to seven per day). The Marines emplaced barriers on two eastern entrances to the first officers' district, further channeling traffic down the main road, which they kept under observation. Barela also conducted a census in order to be able to better understand, categorize, and control the population. The police were still in the early stages of training and mounted only a handful of patrols near the police station. Nevertheless, locals met the initial patrols with enthusiasm, coming forward to greet them in broad daylight. The governor's personal security detachment defended his residences, serving as a de facto neighborhood watch.[15]

Barela minimized the use of force in his operations. In contrast to other units in Ramadi, his company never used close air support, artillery, or rockets. Barela consciously accepted that he might be increasing the risk to his men. Over the long term, he believed that minimizing the use of force would actually reduce the number of vengeful Sunnis and hence the number of casualties. Furthermore, Barela demanded that his Marines cause as little disturbance as possible during house searches, and he limited the activities of Iraqi units that showed any tendencies toward abusiveness. Barela refused to conduct raids that swept up large numbers of locals and relied upon a single intelligence source. Instead, he built as much intelligence as possible against select individuals or cells before mounting a raid.[16]

An intensive effort to strengthen local leaders accompanied Barela's security measures. Tribal leaders, religious leaders, technocrats, and the former military were targets of his efforts. He met with them regularly. To empower them, Barela executed civil affairs projects, such as giving generators to neighborhoods and running trash pick-up programs.[17]

The oil-spot concept seemed to help. Security improved further in the first officers' district between April and June. Roadside bomb and large attacks decreased. Locals moved in the streets freely and there was some remnant of normalcy.[18]

Amid the efforts to secure the streets of Ramadi, the campaign to capture AQI leadership continued. US forces drew up lists of insurgent leaders and mounted raids to try to capture them. Several such raids occurred weekly, almost nightly. Too many Ramadi targets were dry holes. For whatever reason, accurate intelligence to identify, locate, and capture the AQI leadership in Ramadi was hard to acquire.

THE SUMMER FIGHTING

Zilmer finally received US reinforcements in May. After much wrangling, Lieutenant General Chiarelli had decided to replace Gronski's outgoing 2-28 Brigade with the 1st Brigade, 1st Armored Division (1-1 AD), which would be given an additional US battalion. As important, political constraints eased. The new permanent government formed in late May, allowing Chiarelli to send 1-1 Iraqi Brigade's third battalion and the three Marine companies from Operation Scales of Justice back to Anbar. With the return of the Marine companies, Colonel Marletto, Zilmer's operations officer, could transfer a battalion from the vicinity of Fallujah to Ramadi. Furthermore, the new Iraqi government was willing to countenance major operations in Ramadi. Minister of Defense Abdul Qadr permitted an Iraqi tank company and a battalion from the north to take part. All in all, Zilmer would have an additional two US battalions, two Iraqi battalions, and one Iraqi tank company to devote to Ramadi. He could not saturate Ramadi with men, but he could better implement the oil-spot strategy and clear insurgent-controlled neighborhoods.

Colonel Gronski and 2-28 Brigade Combat Team left Ramadi during the beginning of June and 1st Brigade, 1st Armored Division arrived. Colonel Sean MacFarland commanded the brigade. Sean MacFarland is a signal figure of the battle of Ramadi, the awakening, and the later campaign against the Islamic State. Few other Americans would play an equivalent role. MacFarland was soft-spoken and thoughtful, so much so that his drive could be missed. He was unstoppable in implementing what he—often with unmatched perspicacity—recognized as a promising course of action, regardless of the obstacle. MacFarland and his brigade came straight from four months in Tal Afar, one of the successes of 2005. They had been following a set of counterinsurgency tactics, involving protecting the population. MacFarland was optimistic similar success would be possible in Ramadi.

MacFarland's plan, in accordance with Zilmer's plan, was to set up outposts in the second officers' district in southwestern Ramadi, at the stadium in the Milaab neighborhood of southeastern Ramadi, and at the hospital in northern Ramadi. These operations involved entering areas considered under insurgent control.[19]

Before the operation started, another dramatic event happened outside Anbar. On June 7, a US air strike killed Zarqawi in Baqubah, just north of Baghdad. US special operations forces had been stalking Zarqawi for months. Zarqawi's deputy, Abu Ayyub al-Masri, took his place. He was from Egypt. Hence the nom de guerre "al-Masri." Insurgents often took on names from their homelands. In Arabic, *al-Masri* means "of Egypt." Less apt to televise himself in dramatic acts of violence, al-Masri lacked Zarqawi's charisma. Within I Marine Expeditionary Force, few thought

Zarqawi's long-awaited demise spelled the end of AQI, but many hoped it would at least confuse and slow their command and control in the short term.

Originally, Zilmer had intended to step up operations in Ramadi gradually, allowing time for the new units to conduct thorough preparations. In the event, Zilmer decided to launch into the southern part of the city early. He did this for four reasons. First, a large portion of the population was fleeing Ramadi. Lines of tanks and armored vehicles rolling down the highway into bases, media reporting of the violence in Ramadi, and an unauthorized Iraqi army whisper campaign (they told locals that the Americans would attack and burn down their homes on June 15) convinced the people that a Fallujah-style offensive was imminent.[20] Second, the death of Zarqawi raised the possibility that AQI could be in momentary disarray. Third, special operating forces captured Abu Mustafa, a key AQI leader in Ramadi. Fourth, Colonel Peter Devlin, Zilmer's intelligence officer, was aware that parts of the Albu Risha and Albu Thiyab had been fighting AQI. Discussions with Sunnis from Ramadi suggested that going in quickly might embolden the resistance and tribes to fight AQI and support the police.[21] Devlin told Zilmer that a unique opportunity presented itself to strike while AQI was off balance. Zilmer seized that opportunity.[22]

On June 17, the Ramadi operation began. Over the next two weeks, two additional US battalions and two additional Iraqi battalions deployed: 1st Battalion, 6th Infantry Regiment (1-6 IN) went to the Jazirah area north of the Euphrates; 1st Battalion, 37th Armored Regiment (1-37 AR) headed to the south of the city, along with the Iraqi army battalion from the north (2nd Battalion, 3rd Brigade, 2nd Iraqi Division); and the 3rd battalion of the 1st Iraqi Brigade broke up into detachments and dispersed throughout the city. New outposts were established at the Ramadi general hospital by the Marines of 3/8 and at the stadium in the center of the Milaab by the soldiers of 1-506. The highlight of the operation was 1-37 AR's entry into the second officers' district of southern Ramadi, where insurgents had operated freely for years. The battalion maneuvered into position south of the city, advanced into the second officers' district, and then set up two outposts in the middle of the district.

The soldiers clearing southern Ramadi encountered no insurgent strong points, no ad hoc fortifications, no mutually supporting positions, and no ambushes inside homes. Defeats in Fallujah, Tal Afar, and al-Qa'im had probably taught insurgent leaders the folly of standing and fighting. Each time Marines or soldiers entered a new neighborhood and established an outpost, insurgents in the area dispersed. They did not leave, though. They waited, observing the new outpost, analyzing its strengths and weaknesses, tracking US patrols, and identifying good firing positions. Then, within a few days, complex attacks against the outpost kicked off, designed to pin and wear down US forces. Insurgents would often open fire from multiple directions. Separate insurgent teams might lay down fire with a medium machine gun from a rooftop from one direction, launch a volley of RPGs from an alley, and shoot AK-47s from apartment windows. Sometimes a few mortar rounds or rockets would accompany the attack. A commander on a rooftop or in a mosque would have sufficient rudimentary communications to put the different pieces together. Insurgents rarely attempted any sort of assault. The stand-off battle could go on for hours or until US air strikes and artillery fire became too much. Outside the outposts, US patrols would be carefully monitored and then ambushed at an opportune moment.[23] These attacks could be the most dangerous because insurgents could combine RPGs and IEDs. In this way—dispersing, watching, and attacking at the right moment—the insurgents kept the initiative.

The Ramadi "surge" commenced ten months of bloody attrition. From July 2006 until April 2007, the insurgents killed or wounded four to six hundred American and Iraqi security personnel per month. Never before had so many been killed or wounded for so long a period in Anbar. Equally high casualties had occurred before only briefly, during the first and second battles of Fallujah. In no month during this period did the insurgents lose more in dead and wounded, which varied from two hundred to three hundred per month, than the US and Iraqi forces. The statistics are gruesome but clearly show AQI at its best.

An early setback involved the Iraqi battalion from the north—2nd Battalion, 3rd Brigade, 2nd Iraqi Division (2-3-2 Iraqi Battalion). Predominantly Sunni—a rarity in the Iraqi army—the eight-hundred-man battalion deserted en masse when informed they would be sent to Ramadi. The Iraqi soldiers refused to fight fellow Sunnis. Only 145 reported for duty in late June. A platoon of fewer than thirty remained by the beginning of July, and it soon refused to fight. They returned to northern Iraq. The other Iraqi army units buckled as well. AQI hit 1st Battalion, 1st Brigade, 7th Iraqi Division in Tam'eem with a suicide car bomb, killing a company commander. The battalion's losses from this and other attacks forced MacFarland to assign the battalion a smaller area of operations. The 2nd Battalion of the same brigade wavered after a mortar attack on their base in the first officers' district cost them casualties. Thereafter, the Iraqi soldiers needed to be given more time in Camp Ramadi, which was in a safer location.

In any case, the Iraqi army was no substitute for the police. Besides the fact that there were too few of them, the population disliked the Iraqi soldiers (*jundi*) because of their Shi'a identity. From the locals' perspective, the Iraqi army was little more than a Shi'a militia out to oppress them. Polls confirmed that the majority of Sunnis in Anbar viewed the Iraqi army as a threat.[24] Virtually no Iraqi army formation could gain the support of a critical mass of the local population. First Brigade, 1st Iraqi Division probably held the best record in collecting intelligence, but this never sufficed to decapitate insurgent command and control or regularly warn of insurgent attacks. Few people wanted to interact with the brigade's soldiers. They refused to take handouts of water offered at the height of the summer (some angrily poured it onto the superheated asphalt). Nor did they stop insurgents from bombing the brigade's mobile clinics devised to render medical care to the people. A battalion commander said he felt little sympathy from them. One of his officers estimated that 25–30 percent of locals were insurgents. In the battalion's experience (which ranged throughout the province), no other area of Anbar was so irreconcilable.[25]

The battalions of 1st Brigade, 7th Iraqi Division, operating on the other side of Ramadi, also could never get enough intelligence to take out significant numbers of insurgent leaders. One battalion commander, Colonel Mustafa, a Sunni, complained that the people, mukhtars, and city leaders were uncooperative. They provided him scant worthwhile information. Another battalion commander said that his men got little of value from the locals. Some were openly hostile. They refused to talk or provide information.[26]

The Iraqi army fed Sunni sectarian fears by occasionally mistreating the population. At times, Iraqi soldiers cursed at Sunnis, stole from them, and occupied their homes as observation posts.[27] If under stress, Iraqi soldiers could be physically brutal. Usually, though, Iraqi officers intervened and re-enforced discipline.[28] Overall, brutality was the exception rather than the rule. Plenty of soldiers and officers had ties to Shi'a militia and admired Sadr, but in spite of some Sunni propaganda, no entire army unit in Anbar pursued a sectarian agenda during these years. Sunnis resented them regardless of their behavior, good or ill.

By August, it was clear that the Ramadi surge had stalled. A commanders' conference on August 8 between Zilmer, Neller, MacFarland, and the two Marine regiment commanders (Colonel Blake Crowe and Colonel Larry Nicholson) recognized that operations in Ramadi were in trouble.[29] After the initial push, outpost construction now required more police to proceed. The new outposts expanded into previously untouched neighborhoods but could only provide partial surveillance. Insurgents walked openly in the city between US patrols, maintaining control over the population. Marines and soldiers became tied down in the protection of their new outposts. With a few exceptions, the new units were surrounded by insurgents.[30] Even in the first officers' district, where the Marines continued to keep things fairly calm, sufficient police never materialized to allow Captain Barela and his company to expand their oil spot beyond a few new neighborhoods to the east. Throughout Ramadi, expansion depended on the growth of the police. It is to that topic that we now turn.

THE TRIBAL MOVEMENT

When the new police first started walking the streets of Ramadi, the AQI killing machine kicked into gear. In spite of the death of Zarqawi, AQI moved swiftly to hamstring the nascent force and its tribal backers before it could get off the ground. Tribal leaders and police immediately became targets for an assassination and intimidation campaign modeled after the one that had defeated the Anbar security council. Forty police were killed in June alone. The new campaign was every bit as sophisticated as its predecessor. AQI infiltrated tribes, collected precise intelligence, set up checkpoints to intercept the police on their way home from work, drove suicide car bombs into police stations, and propagandized their efforts. Most US commanders and intelligence analysts, including myself, thought that the police would not last long.

In October, *Time* magazine printed "The Secret Letter from Iraq," penned earlier in the year. The author, an anonymous officer in Anbar, was surprised by the fortitude of the handful of police (*shurta*):

> I never figured that we'd get a police force established in the cities in al-Anbar. I estimated that insurgents would kill the first few, scaring off the rest. Well, insurgents did kill the first few, but the cops kept on coming. The insurgents continue to target the police, killing them in their homes and on the streets, but the cops won't give up. Absolutely incredible tenacity. The insurgents know that the police are far better at finding them than we are—and they are finding them. Now, if we could just get them out of the habit of beating prisoners to a pulp.[31]

The police impressed other Americans as well. Lieutenant Colonel Jim Lechner, MacFarland's deputy, noted the resilience of the police posted at the Ramadi general hospital. Several shifts had taken casualties, yet they still came back to work.[32] Amid the devastation of Ramadi, we could see the first signs of a police force: a policeman manning a machine gun at the bullet-hole-ridden Rafidain Bank, a thin line of bright blue shirts staggered out on a lonely patrol through pockmarked apartment buildings. They were not much, but they were there.

Police recruitment in Ramadi, slow from April to June (50 in May and 35 in June), picked up in July. Over 330 men stepped forward, followed by 150 in August. Most hailed from the Albu Thiyab, Albu Ali Jassim, and Albu Risha tribes from the countryside northwest of Ramadi, with a small number from the Albu Assaf and the Albu Alwan.[33]

After the fall of the Anbar security council, the set of leaders from the Albu Ali Jassim, Albu Thiyab, and Albu

Risha had continued to resist AQI within their tribes' territory. These leaders were not necessarily the heads of their tribes.[34] Nor did they have the support of their entire tribes, which were themselves small in number and down in the hierarchy of the Dulaymi confederation. AQI had influenced some tribesmen. Nevertheless, they enjoyed the following of a cohesive and loyal cadre of tribesmen from their clans and sub-tribes. From the Albu Ali Jassim there was Khalid Arak Ehtami and his son, Tahir Bedawi.[35] From the Albu Thiyab, there was Hamid Farhan al-Hais and Colonel Tariq Yusef Muhammad, two men who welcomed combat. In the early summer, Hais was in a running gun battle down the new highway (Route Mobile) with AQI. He approached a US checkpoint too quickly and was shot and wounded. In spite of this untoward incident, he kept on fighting AQI. Tariq—an efficient and intelligent former border police commander—led his crew against superior numbers of insurgents in the Albu Thiyab area for months.[36] And from the Albu Risha were Shaykh Abdul Sittar Bezia Ftikhan al-Rishawi and his brother, Ahmed Bezia Ftikhan al-Rishawi. Together, these leaders refused to submit to AQI.[37]

Of them, Abdul Sittar was ascendant. It was Sittar whom US forces had noted for aggressiveness back in the beginning of the year. In his mid-30s, Sittar was headstrong and self-centered. He read and wrote poorly. Religious leaders disliked him because he was far from pious.[38] His elder brother, Ahmed, was his superior in intellect, patience, and diplomacy. But Sittar was also an intrepid and experienced commander who led from the front.[39] US officers would later talk about his tendency to drop out of a meeting to lead a raid against AQI. Sittar had run smuggling out of Ramadi to Jordan and Syria for years (the Albu Risha were known for this). Since 2003, he had expanded the tribes' smuggling and legitimate trucking enterprises. And Sittar had charisma.

Wiry and goateed, with an AK-47 and a shaykh's headdress, he looked the part of a warlike Bedouin chieftain.

Sittar and his allies skirmished with AQI in the rural outskirts of Ramadi. They were careful to conceal their activities. They wished to avoid the Anbar security council's mistake of exposing itself too early. They initially focused on organizing and building support. The leaders commanded their own militias, which filled a neighborhood watch function, running checkpoints and patrolling their tribal areas. They set up checkpoints on the streets in an attempt to block AQI infiltration. AQI fighters ran their own patrols and set their own checkpoints.[40] Gunfights with AQI often broke out near the opposing checkpoints. Early on, the total size of the militias, before the police returned from training, probably exceeded one hundred but fell under three hundred. Sittar and his allies also tried to kill or capture AQI leaders. For Sittar, this was a priority. Hais later described the fighting in an interview in 2009:

> Al-Qa'eda began targeting my family, abducting and killing people related to me. And we began doing the same toward them in retaliation . . . It kept going like this for months . . . The killing just seemed to go on and on. There was no end in sight. Finally we decided to get more organized and form a proper armed group . . . We managed to form a group of about fifty people willing to fight . . . we were able to secure our homes. Gradually we were able to start establishing checkpoints on some of the roads, just as al-Qa'eda did in areas they controlled.[41]

In the past, one of the most effective insurgent intimidation tactics had been to kill police while at home or to threaten their families there. AQI used this same tactic in Ramadi. The Albu Risha, Albu Thiyab, and Albu Ali Jassim tribesmen serving as police had to commute from their homes in order to serve in downtown Ramadi. The tribal structure afforded some protection against such intimidation. Fellow tribesmen would defend the police and their families. Many police also lived next to each other, and their families tended to look out for one another.[42] Where present, the tribal militias also helped protect the police and their families. Thus, tribal solidarity strengthened the police against intimidation.

In May 2006, Sittar allegedly met individually with leaders from eighteen Anbar tribes to rally them against AQI. They were lesser tribal leaders (or simply tribesmen) rather than the heads of the tribes. It was the number that was symbolic. There are nineteen lineal tribes in the Dulaymi tribal confederation. Eighteen plus Sittar himself made the nineteen.[43] Sittar later claimed that fifteen decided to work with him at this early date. If Sittar's story is true, their involvement was nominal. For months, Sittar and the core of the Albu Risha, Albu Thiyab, and Albu Ali Jassim would be the vast majority of the tribesmen fighting AQI.[44]

Sittar's family and most of his tribal allies had never adamantly opposed the United States. In 2003, his family had helped negotiate the initial US entry into Ramadi. By the best US military accounts, once violence broke out, Sittar fought in the resistance. At the same time, he and his family cooperated with the government and the United States. They worked with the early provincial governors that preceded Ma'amoun. The family dealt with US forces from 2003 onward, even after insurgents labeled them stooges and marshaled the people against them.[45] To whatever extent Sittar was fighting the United States, it ended by late 2005 when he aligned with the Anbar provincial security council movement.[46] A similar pattern pertains to Sittar's allies. Hais had been quarreling with AQI and working with the United States since at least 2005. Colonel Tariq had been a border policeman before returning to Ramadi to defend his villages against AQI. The Saddam regime had tried to arrest him throughout the 1990s, which probably deterred him from joining the resistance in 2003.[47] The point is that very early in the war Sittar and his allies were at odds with AQI.

What made these leaders decide to actually go to war against AQI? Publicly, they spoke of the need to bring peace to Ramadi and that they had tired of AQI's violence. For instance, Sittar said in an interview in September 2006: "Terrorists claimed that they were fighters working on liberating Iraq, but they turned out to be killers. Now all the people are fed up and have turned against them."[48] In meetings, Sittar and his allies often conveyed to US officers that they were tired of AQI's murder and intimidation and viewed the organization as truly evil.[49]

The reality was less idealistic. Other factors played a larger role, especially power and honor. AQI's rise threatened the power of Sittar and his allies. Tribesmen were joining AQI and opposing their own tribal leaders. Sittar and the rest were losing control over their territory. His brother Ahmed would later explain how the enmity with AQI had to do with influence over the people: "They [the resistance] marshaled the people against us, so we left them . . . And then . . . al-Qaeda came in. And . . . the foreign Arabs, the emirs, came in place."[50] Hais explicitly told US officers that he wanted to regain control over "his" tribal territory.[51] As their power grew, AQI commanders disregarded tribal law and called for greater adherence to Islamic law. This further upset Sittar and his allies. Colonel Tariq, known for detesting extremists, often remarked that he disliked being told how to pray.[52] In Sittar's words, "We began to see what they [AQI] were actually doing in Anbar province. They were not *respecting us* or *honoring us* in any way . . . their tactics were not acceptable" [italics added].[53]

As it expanded, AQI threatened the economic foundation of these tribal leaders' power. AQI started to creep in on tribal fuel smuggling and hijacking rackets.[54] The main highway to Jordan and Syria was controlled by AQI operating out of Rutbah and south of Ramadi, impinging on Sittar's smuggling and extortion profits. As early as March 2006, Sittar complained to the national guardsmen of 1st Battalion, 172nd Armored Regiment that AQI was hijacking his trucks and selling his goods. This friction point had been one reason he had kept fighting AQI after the fall of the people's council. As long as AQI threatened his sizable smuggling and other businesses, it was difficult for Sittar to settle.[55] Securing the highways and maintaining the finances of tribal leaders would be ranking points on the future movement's official agenda.[56]

On top of competition for political power were blood feuds. Hais told US officers that he was fighting, among other reasons, because AQI had blown up his house and killed his brother. They had also shot him back in 2005, accusing him of being a collaborator. More famously, insurgents had killed Sittar's father, Bezia, in November 2005. Bezia had been working with the provincial government, calling for an al-Qa'im-like desert protector program for Ramadi, and criticizing AQI leaders.[57] One of Sittar's brothers had been killed earlier in the year. The obligation to exact vengeance for the death of a family member is one of the most important tribal customs. The average tribesman could ignore tribal custom; less so a tribal leader, whose authority depended partly upon adherence to traditions. Whether out of tradition or love for his father, Sittar's war with AQI had something to do with revenge. What made Sittar, his allies, and their tribesmen special is that they carried out the duty for vengeance, whereas other tribes of the Anbar security council did not. Perhaps because they were small and close-knit, living outside the city in a traditional setting, and low-ranking and hungry for promotion, the Albu Risha, Albu Thiyab, and Albu Ali Jassim displayed especially strong tribal bonds and customs. It is important to stress here that Sittar and his allies were not reacting to indiscriminate brutality. They were reacting to brutality selectively targeted against them for working against AQI. Brutality and revenge were more functions of the power struggle between tribal leaders and AQI (and other insurgents) than the other way around.

Fighting also offered Sittar and his allies a chance to move up within the tribal structure and Iraqi politics. As lesser tribal leaders, they were hungry for rank. If successful against AQI, the standing of Sittar, his allies, and their tribes in the Dulaymi confederation would rise. The traditional Dulaymi leadership had fled. The door was open for Sittar and his allies. Their ambition spanned beyond tribal leadership. Fighting AQI offered a route to curry political favor with the United States and the government. By aligning with the United States and demonstrating military effectiveness, they hoped to sideline the governor and take over the governorship and the provincial council.[58] Tribal leadership and provincial political leadership would put them in position for greater things, such as national political status and influence over the economic development of Anbar. Therein lay the greatest prize of all: the exploitation of the Akkaz natural gas fields. Gas had been identified there but had yet to be fully explored, let alone tapped. No one knows if, in 2006, Ahmed and Sittar had their eyes on the Akkaz, in the far west of Anbar near the Syrian border. But the notion is hardly far-fetched. Most Anbar tribal elites knew of its existence. In the following years, Ahmed would be involved in the business deals surrounding its exploitation.

All this took form in the context of the unfolding civil war in Baghdad. The sense of rising Shi'a power and Iranian interference was widespread among Anbar Sunnis. Tribal leaders and former military had long been eager to deploy legitimate Sunni military forces that could defend Anbar. Fighting AQI with the blessing of the United States opened an avenue to do so. Securing political power against the Shi'a had been a major reason that the Anbar security council had formed in 2005. Sunni reverses in Baghdad and a desire to secure Sunni influence writ large were important to Sittar and his allies too. They often complained to US officers that the Iranians were assassinating Sunni leaders. Sometimes they asserted that Iran was behind AQI.[59] Sittar and his allies realized their chances of securing Sunni political power were greater working with the United States than following AQI down the path of civil war. They could shore up Anbar against the Shi'a in the process of prevailing in their power struggle with AQI.

The activity of Sittar and his allies was northwest of the city. A smaller degree of anti-AQI activity, more secretive, went on to the east, in Albu Fahad territory. After the collapse of the Anbar security council and disappearance of Mohammed Mahmoud Latif, the respected resistance leader, the Albu Fahad had largely submitted to AQI. Only a few of the tribe's resistance fighters carried on. They waged a desultory guerrilla campaign against AQI. It was a mysterious thing to US observers. US soldiers from 1-506 IN standing post in Ramadi sometimes heard gunfire or even mortar fire at night from farmland and homes out to the east. Iraqi army officers reported that AQI was trying to subdue the last of the independent resistance. Locals told one of Razzaq's deputies in 1st Brigade, 1st Iraqi Division a story of a father and two sons fighting for hours until killed, and another of a lesser tribal leader fielding armed men to defend his family. Rumors filtered in of resistance fighters who were former military watching over certain villages. Supposedly the fighters disappeared whenever a US patrol came near. The sounds and rumors were consistent in substance if sporadic in occurrence from spring 2006 onward.[60]

Since 2006, various Iraqis have said that these resistance cells were tracking down and killing AQI fighters and leaders in their strongholds east of the city. It has also been confirmed that the Iraqi military and intelligence sponsored secret hit squads from the Albu Fahad starting early in 2006. In June 2006, Khalef al-Aliyan, deputy prime minister for security, met with Brigadier General Reist and Lieutenant General Robert Fry, Casey's British deputy. Khalaf, who was from Ramadi and had very strong ties to the resistance, detailed how he had mobilized a roving cell of seventeen fighters. He claimed they had killed twenty-four AQI fighters over the previous three months.[61] Three Albu Fahad military officers, one of whom was Nasr's brother, ran the effort. To this day, it is unclear how much of the anti-AQI activity east of the city was the work of independent resistance cells and how much was the work of government-funded hit squads.[62]

While the Albu Fahad resistance was a mystery, Zilmer, Neller, and MacFarland and his battalion commanders knew of the activities of Sittar and his allies. They kept it quiet in order to limit the leadership's exposure to retribution. During June, MacFarland and his battalion commanders started dealing with Sittar, Hais, and Khalid, who had maintained relationships with Colonel Gronski and 2-28 Brigade Combat Team.[63] Because tribesmen preferred to police their own neighborhoods, MacFarland decided to let the new recruits serve locally. The decision increased recruitment and the prestige of the movement's leaders in their own territory. MacFarland opened new police stations in the Albu Thiyab tribal territory and new substations (manned largely by militia waiting to become police) in the Albu Risha and Albu Ali Jassim territory (see Table 4.1).[64] On July 15, 260 police were assigned to the new Jazirah police station, near a critical road junction between the city and where their tribes lived. US police advisory teams (known as police transition teams) worked in each station. Unlike the Anbar security council, the leaders of this new movement had no problem

Table 4.1 Police Stations in Ramadi

Police Station	Tribal Territory	Month Opened	Number of Police
Western Ramadi	Albu Alwan	May 2006	300
Tam'eem (al-Horea)	NA	May 2006	250
Jazirah	Albu Thiyab	July 2006	260
Jassim	Albu Ali Jassim	August 2006	(militia)
C-Lake	Albu Thiyab	August 2006	(militia)
Tway	Albu Risha	August 2006	(militia)

working side by side with Americans. In August, a company from 1st Battalion, 6th Infantry Regiment, which operated north of Ramadi, and an Iraqi army company occupied the new "C-Lake" substation, on the border between the Albu Ali Jassim and Albu Thiyab.[65] Finally, in July and August, MacFarland and his battalion commanders started contracting civil affairs projects to the leaders of the movement as a means of increasing their influence within their tribes.

Meanwhile, AQI kept up its intimidation campaign, confident that fear would deter any backlash against their brutality. This time they were wrong. On August 21, AQI hit the Jazirah police station with a truck bomb and assassinated Khalid of the Albu Ali Jassim. The truck bomb wounded twelve police and killed two. Yet the police continued to work, even if frightened. Officers from the Albu Thiyab rallied the police. Operations resumed by the end of the day. Khalid was killed separately. He was driving home, along with two of his children, when AQI gunned him down. The killers included Albu Aethea tribesmen with AQI. AQI broke Islamic tradition by not returning the shaykh's body. A few days later his tribesmen launched a raid and recovered his body.[66]

Sittar, Hais, and Tariq exploited the death of Khalid. According to one of Sittar's advisors, "they severed his head, they left him out in the open . . . We used that as a pretense to start the revolution."[67] The day after Khalid's death, Sittar met with US officers and asked for greater US financial assistance and more raids against insurgents. About a week later, Lieutenant Colonel Anthony Deane, MacFarland's battalion commander who usually met with Sittar, went to Sittar's house and found him and several other Iraqis writing a manifesto for a tribal movement, to be known as Sahawa al-Anbar, or the "Anbar awakening."[68] The manifesto's first point was to bring tribal sons into the army and police. The second point was to declare war on al-Qa'eda. The third point, tellingly, was to restore the respect due to tribal leaders.[69] MacFarland himself met with Sittar and the key tribal leaders of the movement a week later. Sittar and the other leaders pledged to fight AQI.[70]

On September 14, Sittar publicly announced the formation of Sahawa al-Anbar, a tribal movement opposed to AQI and other foreign-backed terrorists. He claimed that twenty-five Anbar tribes and thirty thousand armed men (a mild exaggeration) stood ready to confront the terrorists that had, in his words, damaged tribal life in Anbar. The movement sent a letter with these points to Maliki, replete with the signatures of twenty-five tribal leaders, asking for support.[71] Again, in reality, the movement was essentially just a core of certain families and clans from the Albu Risha, Albu Thiyab, and Albu Ali Jassim tribes. Signatures from other tribes brought few, if any, fighting men.

On September 26 and 27, a "Re-awakening of al-Anbar" conference was convened near Ramadi that enunciated an eleven-point platform, based on Sittar's original manifesto:

1. Election of a new Provincial Congress.
2. Formation of Anbar Province Shaykhs Congress, with the condition that none was or will be a terrorist supporter or collaborator.

3. Begin an open dialogue with Ba'ath Party members, except those involved in criminal/terrorist acts in order to quell all insurgent activities with all popular groups.
4. Review the formation of the Iraqi Security Forces and the Iraqi Army, with tribal shaykhs vouching for those recruited.
5. Provide security for highway travelers in Anbar Province.
6. Stand against terrorism wherever and whenever it occurs, condemn attacks against Coalition forces, and maintain presence of Coalition forces as long as needed or until stability and security are established in Anbar Province.
7. No one shall bear arms except government-authorized Iraqi Security Forces and the Iraqi Army.
8. Condemn all actions taken by individuals, families, and tribes that give safe haven to terrorists and foreign fighters, and commend immediate legal and/or military remedies to rectify such acts.
9. Recommend measures to rebuild the economy, to entice industrial prosperity, and bolster the agricultural economy. Also find funds and resources to reopen existing manufacturing facilities. The main objective is to fight for welfare and deny the insurgents any grounds for recruitment.
10. Strengthen shaykhdom authorities, help tribal leaders adjust to democratic changes in social behavior, and maintain shaykhs financially and ideologically so they can continue this drive.
11. Respect the law and Constitution of the land, and support justice and its magistrates so no power will be above the law.[72]

The difference from the provincial security council's position was notable. Gone was any stipulation for US withdrawal. Point 6 made clear that, whether because of the growing

AQI threat or their own interests, the Anbar awakening movement intended to fight AQI alongside the US military rather than on its own. The provincial security council would have found such a level of cooperation wholly unacceptable. The awakening movement's political ambitions were unmistakable. The first point called for the dissolution of the provincial council.[73] The provincial council elected the governor. Electing a new provincial council would automatically open up competition for a new governor. Power would never be far from the movement's view.

THE TOUGHEST TIMES

November 2005 to August 2006 was perhaps the most disappointing period of the war for the United States, especially in Anbar. The largest Sunni attempt yet to reject violence had come to naught; the clear, hold, and build effort in Ramadi had stalled; and AQI had emerged stronger than ever in the city. The formation of the Anbar awakening movement did not spell the end of AQI. It was only an opportunity to field much-needed police forces and, as every US officer realized, was sure to face hard fighting.

On August 16, Colonel Devlin (Zilmer's intelligence officer) published a report, later leaked to the *Washington Post*, that stated al-Qa'eda in Iraq could not be militarily defeated in Anbar. He pointed out that US forces were too few and that the central government was failing to address Sunni grievances. The absence of political reconciliation meant that a critical mass of Sunnis remained committed to violence. Other Marine officers concurred with his assessment—though they wanted it kept secret. Casey disagreed with Devlin, even though his own headquarters assessed that defeating AQI would take longer than initially planned and would not be achieved by the end of 2006. Devlin's report brought to light the dire situation in Anbar which had previously been shielded from Washington. Other intelligence reports tended toward far more optimism. Devlin's analysis came as a complete surprise. The report was discussed throughout the Pentagon and White House. It added to a growing perception in Washington that the war was going poorly. Washington's concern had already been raised by statements by General John Abizaid (commander of Central Command, which oversaw US military operations in the Middle East) to the Senate Armed Services Committee that Iraq could be moving into civil war and journalist Thomas Ricks's book *Fiasco* on the military's tactical errors.[74] The Bush administration would soon reconsider the entire Iraq strategy.

Given the situation, Devlin can be forgiven for believing the situation in Anbar was worse than perhaps it actually was. As he himself noted, the police and the budding tribal movement had real potential. Yet better to acknowledge the difficulties than groundlessly declare victory, as had so many before him. The evidence pointed to a difficult situation that would take months of hard fighting to overcome. Violence wracked the city of Ramadi, and the tribal movement was too small and too unproven for anyone to responsibly argue they could go toe to toe with AQI. The question at the middle of September 2006 was: Would the new tribal movement survive?

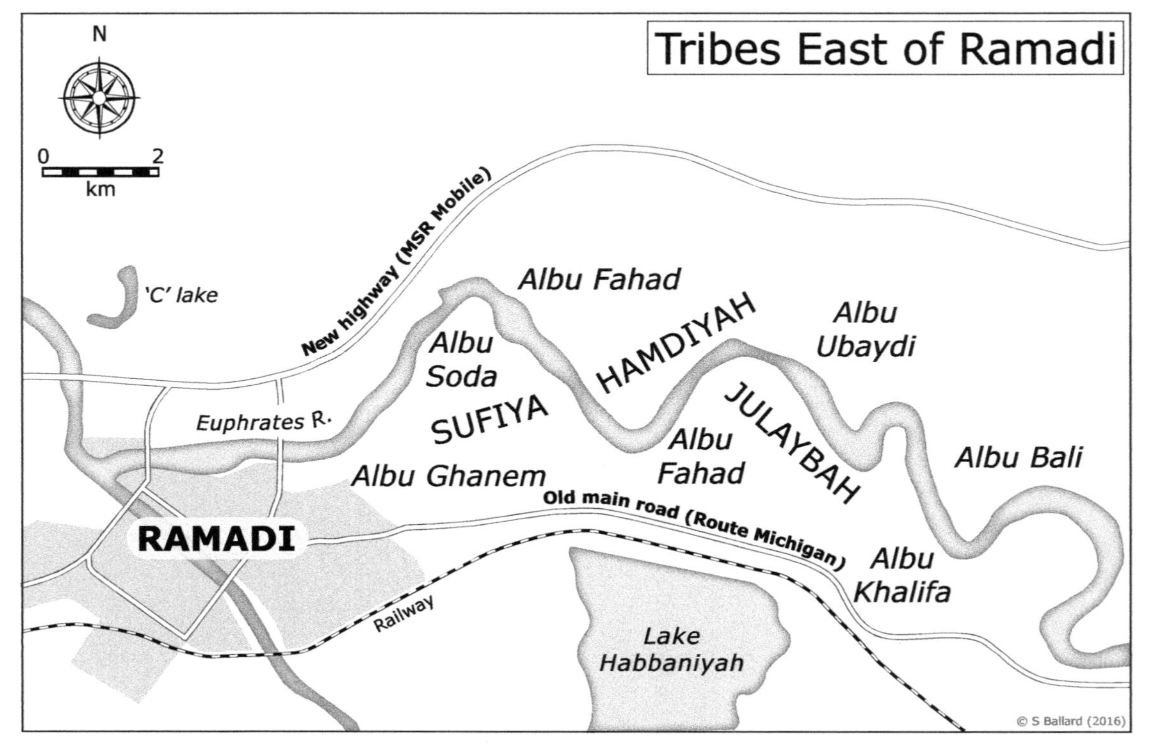

Map 8. Tribes East of Ramadi

CHAPTER 5

The Anbar Awakening

The declaration of the formation of Sahawa al-Anbar, or the al-Anbar awakening, set the stage for the climactic phase of the Anbar campaign. AQI could not afford to lose. In spite of their success in Ramadi, they had already been pushed out of Fallujah and al-Qa'im. Losing Ramadi would throw them into the backwaters of the province. Seven more months of fighting followed. This was no quick decision. This was hard-fought attrition.

The balance of forces hardly favored the new awakening movement. In spite of his public claims, Shaykh Abdul Sittar represented neither twenty-five tribes nor the people of Ramadi. Only three tribes really stood up to fight AQI—the Albu Risha, Albu Ali Jassim, and Albu Thiyab.[1] The Albu Assaf openly participated in the awakening and had a few men in the police but lived too far west to get into heavy fighting. Sittar also received moral support from Jassim Muhammad Salih, a former chief warrant officer of the Albu Soda of the eastern outskirts of Ramadi (a neighborhood known as the Sufiya).[2] The governor's tribe, the Albu Alwan, was outside the awakening movement, though the clique around the governor and the tribe's leadership had no love for AQI. A small number of Albu Alwan were in the police. Further weakening the movement was the fact that none of these tribes stood up as a whole. AQI had infiltrated them. Many tribesmen fought against their own tribal leaders. To give an example, in December 2006, a journalist, Thibauld Malterre would speak to a captured member of the Albu Thiyab tribe in a prison cell in the Jazirah police station who said: "I want to kill Americans because they occupy my country, and jihad is the will of God."[3] Between the three tribes, really just the cadre of leaders, 650 police, and 100–300 tribal militia openly opposed AQI. They were fighting a two-front war—one against AQI and the tribes aligned with them and another against AQI cells within their own tribes.

AQI, despite months of heavy combat, was in good shape. The western and southern outskirts of the city lay in their hands. Unopposed to AQI were the Albu Aetha, Albu Mar'ai, Albu Khalifa, Albu Ubaydi, Albu Bali, Albu Chulayb, Albu Ghanem, and Albu Fahad.[4] Even in the northwest, as noted above, AQI still had substantial influence. In downtown Ramadi, AQI could move freely throughout all but the western enclave that Captain Barela and his Marines had blocked off. The city's population served as a ready recruiting base. The religious leaders accepted AQI more than they did the government. The mishmash of different tribes made it difficult for any tribal leader to control any territory. In this environment, AQI's armed and organized cadres ran the streets. AQI's finances were healthy. Since May, revenue streams had increased markedly. In late September, AQI leadership allocated increased funds to Ramadi in order to defeat the awakening.[5]

The awakening movement did enjoy one advantage: cohesion. Infighting and incoherence historically curse tribal movements. The divided nature of tribes—with their numerous clans and sub-tribes—and competition over material gain tend to undermine tribal unity (asabiyya). In turn, military effectiveness falls.[6] As discussed, the fall of the Anbar provincial security council could largely be attributed to divisions within the Albu Fahad.

If infiltrated by AQI, the Albu Thiyab, Albu Risha, and Albu Ali Jassim were each still more cohesive than the other tribes around Ramadi. Close-knit sub-tribes and clans improved the unit cohesion and esprit de corps of the police and militias. The police had preexisting loyalties and a source of identity. I personally remember three Albu Thiyab and Albu Ali Jassim policemen enthusiastically telling me that they would crush the takfiri (a term for those who had corrupted Islam) under the heel of their boots. Two were in bright blue police shirts. The third was in a T-shirt with a kaffiyeh headscarf. At the same time they told me that they were proud to be police, they boasted about the strength of their tribes. Their pride and morale was tied to tribe.[7] Kinship, tribal culture, and geography meant that close-knit sub-tribes and clans surrounded the leaders of the Albu Risha, Albu Thiyab, and Albu Ali Jassim. AQI had infiltrated into their tribes, but these clans were in good position to fight back.

The Albu Thiyab militia, for example, was affiliated with the families of Hais, Colonel Tariq, Lieutenant Colonel Adnan (the commander of the Jazirah police station), and one other tribal leader named Shaykh Husayn. Their sons, nephews, and cousins had joined the police and ran the militia. These young men conducted the actual patrols around their homes and villages. Tariq's crew in Albu Thiyab territory could endure the hard summer of 2006 partly because they had all soldiered together in the border police. They knew and trusted each other intimately.[8] In one gun battle, a patrol under Husayn's cousin ran into an AQI checkpoint in their territory. Husayn's cousin killed two insurgents before he himself was killed in the exchange of AK-47 fire. AQI then came and shot up his funeral, killing two more tribesmen. This kind of tit-for-tat had silenced other tribes. With the Albu Thiyab, probably because of the close family bonds, it escalated the feud.[9]

It helped that Sittar and his allies lived in rural areas of homogeneous tribal identity. In contrast to the mishmash of downtown Ramadi, most people in Albu Thiyab territory were Thiyabi. The same was true of the other two tribes. Villages made up of the same family or clan could easily call their men to arms. Tribal leaders had real power in this environment. The countryside lacked the officials, businessmen, and high concentration of religious leaders, who vied with the tribal leaders for power inside downtown Ramadi. Furthermore, the territory of the three tribes bordered each other and the US military bases at Camp Ramadi and Camp Blue Diamond. They formed a solid defensive block—unlike the tribes interspersed in downtown Ramadi or those farther east, which were often at odds with their neighbors. The rural terrain itself also helped. Walled compounds surrounded by open fields with clear lines of fire made for solid defensive positions. Finally, Sittar's profits from smuggling along the highway to Jordan—the Albu Risha were well placed at the intersection of routes leading to Syria, Jordan, and Baghdad—allowed him to buy the loyalty of the tribesmen.

US commanders backed the awakening movement with reservations. In mid-September, Colonel MacFarland spoke to Brigadier General Reist about the awakening and Sittar's request to have Governor Ma'amoun and the provincial council removed (the first of the eleven points of the awakening's September 14 declaration). Reist agreed that the movement should receive US support but disagreed that the governor should be removed. In his assessment, doing so would violate the Iraqi constitution and paint the United States as a colonial power dismissive of democracy and Iraq's sovereignty.[10]

Nevertheless, MacFarland was allowed to support the new movement. Certain writers later accused the Marines of opposing the movement. This is untrue, in spite of their reservations. The unfortunate finger-pointing can be attributed to the normal friction between staffs and units on the ground that is a hallmark of military operations. Major General Zilmer and Brigadier General Reist knew that the awakening movement could be an invaluable ally against AQI and wanted the movement's fighters on the battlefield. They simply sought to avoid a feud with Governor Ma'amoun that would question US commitment to Iraqi sovereignty, as well as split the budding opposition to AQI.[11] From their perspective, Sittar and Ma'amoun needed to work together. The strategic value of a broad anti-AQI alliance and cooperation with the government outweighed the tactical expedient of empowering Sittar as much as possible. The blowback to an American move against the governor from Baghdad and the Western press could have upended the awakening altogether. Zilmer was careful in another regard as well. He knew that militias could easily turn into death squads. He kept an eye on this possibility. US support of death squads was not something he would tolerate. At this point, in his view, the police and neighborhood watch organizations did not appear to be death squads. Therefore, Zilmer endorsed the awakening movement. But the governor would stay in place. Resolving the dispute between him and Sittar became a priority.[12]

US support for the awakening movement took the form of money, military protection, training, and advising.[13] The money came partly through *solatia*, payments to the families of policemen who had been killed in the line of duty. Payments could exceed $10,000. Money also came through CERP (commander's emergency response program) projects. The passing of the US budget in June allowed US forces to contract projects again, ending the half-year pause. The United States spent $10 million on CERP projects in Ramadi from August 2006 to March 2007, compared to $5 million between August 2005 and July 2006. MacFarland allotted projects to friendly tribal areas and contracted the labor to the tribes. The idea was to funnel the projects through the tribal leaders so that they could win back the loyalty of their tribesmen. CERP projects gave tribal leaders access to jobs and money, which they could use to induce their tribesmen to join the police and stand against AQI. Sittar had explained that financial enticements would bring around hostile tribes and counter what AQI was offering. In other words, projects could make the tribal leaders the patrons of their people once more. A tacit agreement existed that tribal leaders would receive projects in return for police.[14] Captain Travis Patriquin, MacFarland's tribal engagement officer, illustrated the idea in an ingenious PowerPoint brief. Patriquin, who spoke Arabic, had formed a close friendship with Sittar. He was one of the first to recognize the opportunity represented in the awakening.

In August and October, MacFarland's commanders flooded the Albu Risha, Albu Ali Jassim, and Albu Thiyab territories with nearly $1 million in CERP projects—the largest sum spent in any single area of Ramadi over that period (see Table 5.1). Much less had been spent before then. Only two projects had been ongoing between the Albu Ali Jassim and Albu Thiyab territory earlier in 2006. The three tribal areas—which represented a small minority of the total Ramadi population—would receive a disproportionate amount of spending long into 2007 (see Table 5.2).

Table 5.1 Commander's Emergency Response Program (CERP) Disbursements in Ramadi

Month	Funds Disbursed
August 2005	$43,000
September 2005	$0
October 2005	$505,000
November 2005	$796,000
December 2005	$262,000
January 2006	$603,000
February 2006	$112,000
March 2006	$255,000
April 2006	$65,000
May 2006	$254,000
June 2006	$1,436,000
July 2006	$1,079,000
August 2006	$1,170,000
September 2006	$19,000
October 2006	$1,126,000
November 2006	$2,174,000
December 2006	$1,814,000
January 2007	$1,549,000
February 2007	$1,493,000
March 2007	$1,099,000

Source: Multi-National Forces-West CERP database, 2005–2007, unclassified, accessed in 2008.

The United States was clearly building up the power of the awakening movement's leaders.[15]

A few US battalion commanders demanded that shaykhs cough up police recruits before they would grant any projects.[16] Contractors connected to the tribal leaders—sometimes the tribal leaders themselves—usually ran the projects.[17] For example, in September, US forces demolished the buildings surrounding the government center in order to clear fields of fire. Two months later, US commanders went

Table 5.2 Distribution of CERP Funds in Ramadi (excluding condolences and city-wide distribution of medical assistance and generators)

Month	Awakening territory*	Western Ramadi	Tam'eem	Central Ramadi	Eastern Ramadi	Sufiya and Julaybah
June 2006	$81,000	$62,000			$40,000	$22,000
July 2006	$2,000	$28,000		$585,000	$65,000	$42,000
Aug. 2006	$471,000	$100,000				
Sept. 2006	$9,000					
Oct. 2006	$421,000	$423,000	$28,000			$2,000
Nov. 2006	$106,000	$1,519,000**	$2,000	$50,000	$137,000	
Dec. 2006	$773,000	$364,000	$114,000	$60,000	$397,000	$4,000
Jan. 2007	$931,000	$448,000		$106,000		$51,000
Feb. 2007	$405,000	$400,000	$96,000	$56,000	$45,000	$171,000
March 2007	$360,000	$143,000	$108,000		$182,000	$40,000

* Tribal territory of the Albu Risha, Albu Ali Jassim, and Albu Thiyab.

** $1.1 million went to rubble clearing near the government center. Ahmed al-Rishawi, Abdul Sittar's brother, took this contract.

Source: Multi-National Forces-West CERP database, 2005–2007, unclassified, accessed in 2008.

to Sittar's brother, Ahmed, to find contractors for a $1.1 million project to remove the rubble and guard the site.[18]

In certain cases, US commanders waived a bidding process. North of the Euphrates, they allowed the tribal leaders to use a sole source process, by which they could put forward a contractor of their choice. Even when US commanders did enforce a bidding process, a tribal leader usually had the power to ensure that his contractors, rather than outsiders, got the projects within his territory.[19] MacFarland and his superiors accepted that in order to build a viable opposition to AQI. There were other ways of economically empowering the awakening tribes too. MacFarland and Zilmer effectively granted Sittar economic power by turning a blind eye to his criminal activity along the highways near Ramadi. Regaining control of the main highway all the way past Rutbah to Syria and Jordan appears to have been one of Sittar's priorities, under the pretext of making it safe for travelers.[20]

Money helped the tribal leaders rebuild a position of authority within their tribes. US soldiers, Marines, tanks, and firepower helped them survive day to day. The leaders of the awakening movement were far more conscious of their own security, especially after the assassination of Khalid, than previous leaders who had opposed AQI. Their protective details (Sittar had fifty men guarding him) and standing neighborhood watches that defended the homes and families of policemen made this clear. US commanders reinforced these measures with fortifications and quick reaction forces.[21] Battalion civil affairs teams gave tribal leaders materials for fortifying their homes and setting up checkpoints. Sittar's compound had a wall three meters high, observation towers, and a US M1A1 tank standing guard. MacFarland pre-targeted the regions around tribal checkpoints for counter-battery fire and dedicated drones to surveillance duty over the homes of key tribal leaders.[22] Unlike Shaykh Nasr and the leaders of the Anbar security council, Sittar and his allies welcomed the US protection.

Finally, US forces arranged training for police recruits. All official police went through three forms of training. First, the police recruits attended six weeks of basic training in Jordan or Baghdad. The Ministry of Interior required this training before they would authorize pay. When they returned to Ramadi, MacFarland's artillery battalion ran a one-week advanced training course at Camp Ramadi. An innovation was to have sergeants from the Iraqi army do the actual instructing.[23] Once the police went into the field, US police advisory teams provided on-the-job training.

AQI AND THE ANBAR AWAKENING EXCHANGE BLOWS

During September and October, the awakening tribes and AQI struck at each other. The number of attacks in the Albu Risha, Albu Ali Jassim, and Albu Thiyab territory rose from forty-four in July to nearly one hundred in August and then again in September as the tribes and AQI exchanged blows. Zarqawi's successor, Abu Ayyub al-Masri, appears to have organized AQI's response. Despite a few conciliatory public statements (such as an internet posting reaffirming that AQI needed to work with the tribes to succeed), he resorted to more violence.[24] In the Arab press, he promised to kill Sittar personally. Sunnis working with the police were threatened rather than bought off. Abu Farouk, an AQI leader in Ramadi, called for an Islamic caliphate in Anbar and claimed that AQI had a "right to kill all infidels, like the police and army and all those who support them."[25] He made clear the incongruity between AQI's vision of Islam and the tribal system: "This tribal system is un-Islamic. We are proud to kill tribal leaders who are helping the Americans."[26]

Just four days after Sittar announced the formation of the awakening, a suicide car bomb exploded at a police station in western Ramadi, causing thirty-one US and Iraqi casualties. The assassination campaign persisted as well. Two attempts were made on Sittar's life before the end of October with suicide car bombs. One was laden with chlorine gas canisters. It caused no injuries. Unfortunately, this tactic would be seen again.

The police and their tribes weathered the onslaught and gave AQI a bloody nose. Because they were Sunni and fellow tribesmen, the local communities provided intelligence to the police, enabling them to kill or detain insurgents.[27] Each policeman killed or captured roughly twice as many insurgents as his counterpart in the Iraqi army. At this stage, many of the awakening movement's targets were members of their own tribes rather than foreign fighters. They also passed intelligence on to US forces, who then conducted their own raids. US commanders carefully coordinated their raids with Sittar and his allies.[28] The awakening movement formed "Thawra al-Anbar" (the al-Anbar Revolution), a raid force that took care of business rather quickly and efficiently.[29] Not only thugs and fighters but also leaders on US high-value target lists were killed or captured, including at least two AQI "emirs" (senior leaders within Ramadi): the infamous Abu Khattab and Khalid Ibrahim Mahal. The total number of publicized killings surpassed thirty by the end of October.[30] Rumors spread of executions and secret prisons. These activities were the most morally gray aspect of the awakening and justified Zilmer's earlier concern. He had the difficult job of balancing the military effectiveness of the awakening against the need to protect the innocent.

Around this time, Sittar, Hamid Hais, and Tahir Bedawi completed asserting control over their tribes. In October, violence declined within the Albu Risha, Albu Ali Jassim, and Albu Thiyab areas (though certainly not in Ramadi as a whole). Less than fifteen incidents occurred that month in those tribal areas. The number of incidents dropped further the following months. Lieutenant Colonel Adnan from the Albu Thiyab, commander of Jazirah police station, explained that the new police stations and police forces made the tribal leaders appear powerful to their tribesmen. They created a feeling of security. The longer the police survived, the more tribesmen joined them.[31] AQI leaders and cells fled from the awakening's tribal fighters to safer areas surrounding Ramadi. Inside their tribal areas, the awakening leaders used the police to enforce tribal law.

Sittar's skilled use of propaganda magnified the movement's tactical successes. He understood how to use rumor and the press to spread his propaganda far better than American officers ever had. No longer did the Iraqi people only hear the insurgent voice. Sittar put out word that the movement would hunt down and kill any outsiders in Ramadi. Statement after statement on the internet, al-Iraqiyya television, and publicly in Ramadi broadcast the killing of AQI leaders and their defeats in battle. The killings may have given the movement some credibility in the eyes of the population and helped build grassroots support. They certainly gave it notoriety. It was clear Sittar followed through on his threats. Sunnis may have respected Sittar for his willingness to fight—possibly even for his ruthlessness.[32]

All that said, these successes were just tactical. Other tribes still sided with AQI, the city itself remained in their hands, and the police were sustaining more casualties than they were inflicting. AQI had been bloodied, but so had the new movement.

At any point, AQI could have tried to negotiate with the awakening movement and accommodate their concerns. Yet they refrained. AQI remained dedicated to violence over compromise. Its leadership's one major political move, in coordination with affiliated groups, was the establishment of the Islamic State of Iraq. The move was ostensibly in reaction to the Iraqi parliament's passage of a law on October 11 in favor of federalism, which Sunnis deeply opposed. On October 18, dozens of AQI fighters marched in the streets of Ramadi in broad daylight to announce the city would be the capital of a new Islamic state under Abu Omar al-Baghdadi and built upon Iraq's Sunni provinces. In later years, AQI leadership would sometimes claim that this was their first declaration of the formation of a caliphate, before the well-known announcement in 2014 after the fall of Mosul.[33] Al-Jazeera broadcast the march. A similar march followed in Haditha.

AQI and its allies would now refer to themselves as the "Islamic State of Iraq." There is some debate in academic circles if AQI's decision to form its own state eventually led to a break with the central al-Qa'eda leadership, including Osama bin Laden and Ayman al-Zawahiri.[34] If true, it is misleading to refer to the Islamic State of Iraq as al-Qa'eda in Iraq. Nevertheless, for the sake of consistency, I will continue to refer to the organization as "AQI" until I discuss the events of 2013.

In terms of leadership, Baghdadi became the titular head of AQI. Masri continued to run day-to-day activities as deputy and war minister.[35] A longtime Iraqi member of AQI, Baghdadi may have been one of the early supporters of the idea of turning AQI and its affiliated groups into an Islamic state of their own. A few Western scholars see Masri as the shadow leader of AQI during this period, and Baghdadi as a mere symbol. Others see Baghdadi as a guiding thinker and unifying figure.[36] In any event, Baghdadi and Masri appear to have been able to work together without any undue rifts or rivalry.

The march and the announcement of the Islamic State of Iraq clearly demonstrated that neither the United States nor the tribes yet controlled the streets. Historically, the announcement marks the broadening of AQI's aims. For Ramadi, however, it was a supporting act in AQI's program of violence. Baghdadi, Masri, and Ramadi's AQI leaders (emirs) offered no compromise.[37] Baghdadi and Masri may have overseen instructions for AQI emirs to target the tribal leaders and police in priority over the US forces, since the former were the greater threat to AQI's existence.[38] According to the AQI spokesman, "They have to either join us in forming the Islamic State . . . or hand over their weapons to us before we are forced to act against them forcefully. It will not save them that they fought the Americans and resisted them in the last few years."[39]

Why AQI's leaders refused to compromise remains conjecture. A distorted interpretation of Islam is one possibility. To a greater extent than bin Laden or Zawahiri, AQI leaders tended to believe that Islam justified killing other Muslims. But this is probably not all that accounts for their stance. Resounding tactical success up to mid-2006 seems to have convinced at least some AQI senior leaders, probably including Masri, that they were on the right track and that popular backlash was unlikely. From their perspective, different tactics may have been unneeded because there had been no downside to brutality. One might say that tactical success crowded out moderation and compromise.

LOBBYING THE GOVERNMENT OF IRAQ

For the awakening tribes to succeed, Zilmer, along with other officers, believed they would need the approval of the

Iraqi government. Otherwise, their forces would be illegitimate, nothing more than an extralegal militia. Since large numbers of the tribal militias had become police, under the Ministry of Interior, the movement had already tied itself to the state. That theoretical tie needed to become real. The Ministry of Interior still had to officially accept what were tribal militiamen in blue shirts, pay them regularly, and promise that they would keep their jobs over the long term.

Sittar met with Prime Minister Nuri al-Maliki on September 27, 2006.[40] Maliki's exact views on the awakening movement at this time are unknown. There is evidence that he was initially reluctant to work with Sittar, recognizing that empowering a Sunni movement might eventually threaten his own regime. One of Maliki's close aides later said that the prime minister had problems with US overtures to Sunni groups.[41] Whatever the case, Maliki relented. He apparently considered AQI a greater immediate threat than a Sunni tribal movement. The fact the movement was based in Ramadi, distant from Baghdad, supposedly helped. According to one story, he begrudgingly accepted the awakening because they were out of the way in Anbar and not worth arguing over with American officials and officers calling for reconciliation.[42] Later in 2007, when asked about the possibility of future clashes between the movement and the Shi'a, one of Maliki's advisors responded, "Obviously some people see this as a threat, but when compared to other threats, this is a rather benign one."[43]

Maliki's endorsement became clear in October when the government took a series of steps to empower the awakening movement. First, Maliki awarded Sittar and his subordinates cash gifts and salaries.[44] Shortly thereafter, the Ministry of Interior appointed Hamid Hamad al-Showqat al-Thiyabi, a member of the movement, to be the new provincial chief of police. Hamid closely followed the interests of the awakening tribes and even funneled funds from the Ministry of Interior into their coffers. At the same time, the Ministry of the Interior gave Sittar the new title of "senior advisor for counterterrorism operations in Anbar." His responsibilities were undefined, which allowed him to keep doing what he was doing with the sanction of Baghdad. The government had effectively given the awakening leaders control over the police forces in Ramadi.[45] Meanwhile, like the United States, the Iraqi government turned a blind eye when Sittar regained control of criminal activity along the highways near Ramadi. It was an unwritten way of both rewarding him and approving of his growing status.[46]

Of greatest significance, in mid-October, the Ministry of Interior permitted the movement to create three "emergency" battalions, totaling 2,250 men.[47] This was a huge concession. For all intents and purposes, the government was permitting Sittar and his movement to field their own militia. Maliki was sanctioning the political and military power of the awakening movement, at the expense of government monopoly over the use of force.

The emergency battalions put Zilmer on the horns of a dilemma. Zilmer realized that they would be an invaluable asset. Nevertheless, he also feared that US commanders could be overly enthusiastic in the hunt for AQI and might flood the emergency battalions with weapons and lethal training, which would be illegal and would increase the chance that these forces could become death squads. Heightening his concern, around the same time that the emergency battalion issue arose, a separate tribal militia started working with the Iraqi army in Khalidiyah, a town between Fallujah and Ramadi. Masked in black hoods and brandishing AK-47s, they patrolled alongside the soldiers and dragged in unarmed insurgents for detention—the spitting image of a death squad.

In order to lay down the rules of the game, Zilmer drafted a letter that forbade US forces in Anbar from working with armed militias. The militiamen had to sign up to be police (he allowed the emergency battalions to count as police). Prior to training, they could start operating, but the process of becoming policemen had to be underway. Furthermore, US commanders could provide tribal leaders with projects, train their forces, and advise them in the field, but were forbidden from providing either weapons or pay. The only pay could come from the Ministry of Interior. This was Zilmer's check on death squads.[48]

In short order, the awakening tribes mobilized recruits for the emergency battalions. The first five hundred showed up for training with weapons, uniforms, discipline, and in many cases military experience. US forces in Ramadi put them through a basic training course. By January, all three emergency battalions had taken the field, armed and fairly well led, if still very much tribal militia organized along tribal lines.[49]

Getting the Ministry of Interior to pay all these new forces—both police and emergency battalions—was less simple. For all of 2006, the Ministry of Interior delivered pay intermittently and lagged in authorizing hiring orders for new police. Consequently, more police were on the job than the Ministry of Interior was ready to pay. Brigadier General Neller traveled to Baghdad weekly to negotiate with the Ministry of Interior. It was a laborious process, but by January the Ministry of Interior was paying all the police and emergency battalion militiamen, plus providing them with vehicles, weapons, and ammunition. Even then, the US forces were still providing fuel and trying to resolve radio communications issues.[50]

Maliki himself cautiously allowed support for the awakening to move forward. He would resist actually visiting

Ramadi until March, when General David Petraeus, then commander of all US forces, would convince him to go. He would defer Sittar's demand for provincial elections for years.[51]

INFIGHTING

Infighting is the bane of tribal movements. Although Sittar and his allies had (so far) cooperated with each other, the same could not be said for their relations with Governor Ma'amoun. On September 26, they sent a letter to the government requesting his removal. On television, they made their demands public. Their spokesman proclaimed,

> The governor and the provincial council did not have any role in the province ... I want to convey a fact that all Anbar tribal leaders do not want Ma'amoun as a governor and do not recognize the former provincial council because this council has spent three years ... without any role. On the contrary, the province became more chaotic during this period.[52]

At the root of the objections to Ma'amoun was his connection to the Iraqi Islamic Party, the leading political party in Anbar and an obstacle to Sittar's political ambitions.

Brigadier General Reist and Dr. Rafi al-Issawi, the minister of state for foreign affairs (Maliki's liaison with the leaders of Anbar), mediated the feud. Reist regularly encouraged Ma'amoun to cooperate with Sittar. On October 10, Reist and MacFarland brought Ma'amoun and Sittar together at Camp Blue Diamond (Saddam's old palace on the northern edge of the Euphrates) for a dinner. The meeting rapidly devolved into a shouting match. A week later, Zilmer and Reist tried again. They hosted a meeting at Camp Fallujah.

By the end of the meeting, following more shouting, Sittar praised Ma'amoun for his long-standing opposition to AQI and Ma'amoun called Sittar his brother. After that, though Sittar still despised the Iraqi Islamic Party, the two started meeting on their own in Ramadi and the feud became manageable.[53] They worked out an agreement that granted the awakening representation on the provincial council, which seemed to satisfy Sittar and the other awakening leaders for the time being. On November 14, at a meeting in Baghdad, the provincial council added eight new unelected awakening councilmen. The movement's political power was growing.

The resolution of the dispute between Ma'amoun and Sittar yielded tangible results on the battlefield. After agreement was reached, a substantial number of the governor's tribe, the Albu Alwan, aligned with the awakening movement. On November 12, 120 Albu Alwan tribesmen loyal to Shaykh Raad Sabah Mukhlif al-Alwani (a lesser tribal leader living in Ramadi) volunteered to be police. They were deputized and allowed to man a new police station in western Ramadi—the al-Warar police station. Under the tactical command of Lieutenant Colonel Salam Muhammed Abbas al-Alwani, a former member of Saddam's special forces, the al-Warar police would be at the sharp end of the campaign against AQI.[54] Unlike the other awakening tribes that were from the countryside, the Albu Alwan actually lived in downtown Ramadi and consequently had a better ability to gather intelligence. Once the al-Warar police took to the streets, Albu Faraj tribal leaders contributed more men to the movement as well (the success of the Albu Thiyab to their immediate west may have encouraged them). As had been the case elsewhere, infighting had wracked the tribe. Two tribal leaders had been competing for leadership. AQI had exploited the absence of authority to exert influence over the rank and file. Nevertheless, the Albu Faraj leaders would soon contribute larger numbers of men to the police (thirty to forty had joined previously) and would help form one of the three emergency battalions.[55] Overall, 700 new police and emergency battalion militia stood up to fight AQI during November; more than 1,300 operated in Ramadi in total.

DOWNTOWN RAMADI

Violence in *downtown* Ramadi had not let up. In the summer, scarcity of police had stopped US forces from oil-spotting the city. Now, expansion of the police allowed them to resume. Lieutenant Colonel William Jurney arrived in Ramadi in September 2006 with his battalion, 1st Battalion, 6th Marine Regiment (1/6), and took over 3rd Battalion, 8th Marine Regiment's area of operations in western and central Ramadi. Commanding the battalion in Fallujah in 2005 had given Jurney counterinsurgency experience. Careful study of the techniques his friend Dale Alford had used in al-Qa'im prepared him further. Jurney set up new outposts throughout his part of the city. He had a set-piece process. First, Iraqi army, Iraqi police, and his Marines searched the buildings within a targeted neighborhood. Next, they emplaced concrete barriers to obstruct insurgent vehicle movement. Finally, they built an outpost. Neighborhood by neighborhood, they repeated the process and put up outpost after outpost. Both police and Marines manned them.

Like Alford, Jurney emphasized developing the Iraqi army and police. He partnered every one of his platoons with an Iraqi army unit and augmented the police training teams with eight Marines, who lived and worked with the police in their stations. The police and Marines depended on one another to succeed: the police needed the Marines for the firepower and tactical skill to keep back AQI's cadres, who still outnumbered them; the Marines needed the police to man the increasing number of outposts and to figure out the identity and location of insurgents. According to Jurney, the police were critical to the spread of outposts.[56] Without the growth of the police, manpower and local knowledge to feed the growth of outposts would have been absent.

From their new posts, the police went after the insurgents. Lieutenant Colonel Salam's police showed particular aggressiveness—attacking concentrations of insurgents and mounting raids to capture insurgent leaders. How did the police and emergency battalions identify insurgents? Provincial Police Chief Abdul Salam, who briefly became provincial police chief after the Ministry of Interior removed Hamid for corruption, later explained: "The main thing is the cooperation of the tribes and the people and with the police. They give the police intelligence on the location of the insurgents. They take the police to the insurgents and point them out. They are sick and tired of insecurity."[57] In his view, the fact that the police were locals and possibly fellow tribesmen made the people trust them—far more than they trusted the Iraqi army or US soldiers and Marines.[58]

Abdul Salam's explanation simplifies the complexity of intelligence collection in Ramadi in late 2006. To some extent, locals actually did approach the police on their own. For instance, when the police and Marines set up an outpost in the heart of the dangerous Qatana district, in the middle of the city, local citizens came out in tears. Such happy moments were far from the case everywhere. People rarely rushed to embrace the police. The days of locals openly pointing out insurgents were months away. Shaykh Raad (the Albu Alwan tribal leader) and the other awakening leaders had to encourage locals to cooperate and provide intelligence, behind which lay an implicit threat that the police might treat the obstinate unkindly.[59]

In this environment where many people sympathized with the insurgents, the police had to find informants and go out on their own surveillance operations in search of insurgent activity.[60] Sergeant Paul Lindberg from Jurney's battalion described how the police worked: "They would get out there . . . go into the places where a lot of us could not go . . . they could get down in there and they probably knew half of the guys down there . . . because most of them are locals . . . they would really get out there and get information out of the people."[61] The fact that many police units and emergency battalions contained retired intelligence officers helped. The Saddam regime, after all, knew something of counterintelligence. A system eventually developed whereby the police received information directly from locals coming to a police post or via informants. The police post could take action on their own or relay the information to the joint coordination center, which would pass it on to the Iraqi army, US forces, or another police post for action. The system proved particularly useful in going after insurgents who lived outside the precinct of the post where the information had been received.[62]

Despite these successes, the battle was far from over. Tactically, AQI was faring well. Suicide car bombs crashed into police stations and fighters got the better of police and tribal militias in hit-and-run attacks. The al-Warar police in particular faced attacks by insurgents—sometimes from their own tribe—determined to defeat them. Galib Awda, a health care worker in Ramadi, told Martin Fletcher of the *London Times*: "These are the worst days in Ramadi . . . the main groups are all fighting for control of the city."[63]

On November 25, sixty to one hundred insurgents attacked the Albu Soda, a growing ally of the awakening tribes, in the Sufiya neighborhood east of Ramadi. It was one of AQI's largest attempts to quash the tribal movement.

Earlier in November, Jassim Muhammad Saleh al-Suwadawi, a former warrant officer in Saddam's military, had set up checkpoints in the Sufiya district. Insurgents, especially the Albu Fahad living further east, had previously used the area as a staging ground and as an eastern line of communication into downtown. The checkpoints inhibited insurgents from continuing to do either. AQI leaders approached Jassim and threatened that they would attack if he did not realign with AQI. Jassim refused. AQI attacked. Masri himself was reported to have helped plan the operation.[64]

The insurgents—largely from the Albu Fahad—came at the Albu Soda from two directions under the cover of a mortar barrage. Obstacles and IEDs cut off reinforcement routes. This well-resourced and well-organized attack put Jassim and his men (who numbered fewer than thirty) in a tough spot. From rooftops and windows, the tribesmen picked off the attackers, falling back when pressed too hard. Eventually, they ran low on ammunition. MacFarland's headquarters only learned of the attack when civilians in the area fled across the Euphrates and alerted the nearest Iraqi army post. Captain Patriquin then phoned Jassim and asked him to have his men wave their shirts over their heads so that US aircraft could identify the enemy. US aircraft could still not discern friend from foe and dropped no bombs during the AQI assault. Jassim and his outnumbered tribesmen were driven back. One of his homes was torched. US reinforcements took hours to get through the IEDs and obstacles to reach the beleaguered shaykh, by which time the attackers had withdrawn to fight another day. US air strikes and tanks managed to destroy a few vehicles leaving the battlefield, but that was it. Seven of Jassim's men and ten other tribespeople, including women, were killed. AQI dragged a few of the bodies behind their cars and pickups. AQI losses are unknown.[65]

Tactically, Sufiya was a clear-cut victory for AQI. Strategically, such victories mattered little when tribes kept getting up for another round. Only holding tribal territory could quash these tribes for certain. But that would require going toe to toe with the US military and winning, something out of the cards for AQI. The defeat had failed to compel Jassim to give up. He simply allowed a US company to set up an outpost meters away from his home. Jassim went on to formalize his participation in the awakening movement. Within days, he committed 176 men to the police. Jassim's tribesmen found IEDs that had been planted by other tribesmen, identified kidnappers for Americans to detain, and guided US forces on raids.[66] Meanwhile, facing strident and widespread complaints from the police and the tribal leaders that they were being left to face down insurgent assaults on their own, MacFarland and his battalion commanders took steps to communicate better with the police and to expedite reinforcements.

Other battles also showcased the fighting spirit of the early tribes of the awakening movement. On December 10, insurgents ambushed a patrol of forty police led by Lieutenant Colonel Salam in Ta'meem. At a range of roughly one hundred meters to the north, twenty insurgents opened fire on the patrol from one of forty multistory apartment buildings, known as the "white apartments" for their light tan color. Another twenty-five tried to block off reinforcements from a nearby combat outpost. The police took cover and, despite casualties, returned a hefty volume of fire. After thirty minutes, a contingent of Iraqi soldiers arrived under Colonel Mustafa, the Sunni battalion commander from Ramadi who paid special attention to the police. US reinforcements arrived next. Then, under cover of US and Iraqi army machine guns, the police assaulted the insurgent positions and cleared them out, on their own, without any US advisors. AQI stood and fought, their tactics sound. Without the heavy weapons of the US and Iraqi army, the police would have been mowed down. Especially fortuitous was a Bradley fighting vehicle that roared by, en route to the combat outpost, and blasted the apartment building with its 25-mm gun. Yet it was not the US and Iraqi soldiers that made the police go forward and then fight for thirty minutes inside the apartments. Their own motivation did that. No Sunni police had ever before shown such élan.[67]

The day had an amusing ending. Thirty tribesmen from an emergency battalion had rushed to reinforce the police, eager to get into the fight. They arrived after the battle had ended and mistakenly fired a broadside into a nearby police station undergoing construction. They must have been jealous of the accomplishments of Salam's police.[68]

With the support of the US military and Iraqi army, the awakening tribes persevered. Since September, they had just been a minority opposition to AQI, based on a handful of tribal elite. In spite of numerous tactical victories, AQI had not defeated them. Sittar's propaganda made the most of the movement's successes. The longer the movement survived, the more tribal leaders and fighters rallied to its colors. Provincial police chief Abdul Salaam said, "Abdul Sittar has much influence. Other shaykhs came around because someone of Abdul Sittar's weight leads the Anbar awakening. He has more influence and power than the government. This encouraged the shaykhs to help."[69] Many tribal leaders were fighting internal wars within their tribes against AQI influence. In October and November, only the Albu Risha, Albu Ali Jassim, and Albu Thiyab could really be described as united, having rooted out AQI from their ranks. Now the balance was shifting. By the end of 2006, over two thousand police and emergency battalion militia were completing training, about to take to the streets. The opportunity to stamp out the rebellion was slipping through AQI's fingers.

There is little evidence AQI realized what was happening. On the contrary, tactical success emboldened them. Few attempts at compromise seem to have been made. For instance, rather than use their tactical victory in the Sufiya to compromise with the Albu Soda from a position of strength, AQI distributed posters and flyers threatening to attack other tribes in a similar fashion unless they returned to the fold. Masri himself seems to have been detached from the reality of Ramadi. He apparently hid himself to evade targeting. He rarely went to Ramadi, or other battlefronts, and thus did not see the degree of tribal resistance. His chief judge described him as "totally isolated" and "almost absent from the details of what goes on in the battlefield."[70]

Others were more attentive. In Ramadi's eastern outskirts, sub-tribes of the fractious Albu Fahad were carefully watching the battle. The Albu Fahad had been beset by infighting since the death of Shaykh Nasr, its sub-tribes divided between the resistance and AQI. One Albu Fahad tribal leader later said that 20 percent of the tribe had fought with AQI and 20 percent had fought with the resistance.[71] A small number of obstinate resistance cells had carried on a secret war against AQI since early 2006. Shaykh Abdul Jabbar al-Fahadawi led one of the Albu Fahad sub-tribes north of the Euphrates. In late November, Colonel Tariq, the Albu Thiyab police commander, brought Shaykh Jabbar to meet Lieutenant Colonel John Tien, commander of 2nd Battalion, 37th Armored Regiment—the battalion operating north of the Euphrates (1st Battalion, 6th Infantry Regiment had gone home at the end of October). Jabbar was thinking about turning: his brother had been killed by AQI, he wanted projects, and he saw that other tribal leaders who had worked with the awakening movement had regained control over their territory. He refused to stand, though, unless US soldiers were posted alongside his police. It was not until December—after Lieutenant Colonel Tien mounted a clearing operation—that a small neighborhood watch (thirty to forty men) started fighting AQI out of a new police station near the village of Hamdiyah (Jabbar was lightly wounded during this fighting). Over the next month the neighborhood watch grew to 170 men. The Ministry of Defense recognized the neighborhood watch as police and allotted them pay.[72] Shaykh Muhammad of the Albu Ubaydi tribe, farther east, turned in January, after Jabbar, though fighting continued in their area for some time.

As the awakening expanded, Sittar convened regular meetings with the tribal leaders, clad in white and black robes, trimmed with gold, and wearing white or red-checkered head scarves. The tribal leaders would discuss security matters and reconstruction. The meetings were often at Sittar's compound by Camp Ramadi. Sittar was a prominent speaker, but that was more form than substance. It was the consensus between the leaders that mattered.

THE AWAKENING SPREADS

Between Fallujah and Ramadi, the Euphrates meanders through farmland, irrigation ditches, and palm groves interspersed with stand-alone homes and small villages. Approaching Fallujah lie the towns of Khalidiyah and Habbaniyah. For the better part of a year, Habbaniyah, Khalidiyah, and the surrounding countryside had been the scene of well-organized attacks against 3rd Brigade, 1st Iraqi Division. The brigade was the most battle tested and independent in Anbar. During the summer, two hundred locals joined the police in the area. They gave a mixed performance. They were nowhere near as aggressive as the police in Ramadi. In November, a tribal militia backed by a local tribal leader approached the US forces and the Iraqi army, willing to help fight AQI. Shortly thereafter, black-clad militia accompanied the Iraqi army and Iraqi police on a joint patrol in Habbaniyah and pointed out insurgents, whom the army then picked up—thirty-seven in all, two of whom were on a high-value target list. This was the patrol that upset Zilmer.[73] After the Zilmer letter, the militia continued to operate but unarmed—gathering intelligence and identifying insurgents for US and Iraqi patrols and checkpoints. There were of course plenty of suspicions that they were more aggressive outside the supervision of Marines.

To the southeast of Fallujah lies the town of Ameriyah. It had never been protected by Marines for more than a few weeks. In the spring of 2006, the Fallujah district police stood up detachments in Ameriyah. AQI hit them hard. Colonel Larry Nicholson, the Marine commander in Fallujah, had too few forces to permanently outpost the town or secure the supply lines leading to it. He pushed down relief columns every few weeks, but the police were still left fighting alone and unafraid. The aged Shaykh Khamis of the Albu Issa, known for his influence, supported the beleaguered police. His worn face—of a chain-smoker—and fragile frame obscured his power. Khamis had fled to Jordan following intimidation in 2005. With over ten different sub-tribes, he could not unite the entire Albu Issa tribe behind him, particularly from Jordan. Some of his sub-tribes aligned with AQI and the notorious Zoba'i tribe to the northeast.

In mid-2006, Shaykh Khamis returned from Jordan. He set loyal tribesmen to work collecting intelligence and reached out to other tribal leaders. They became the forward eyes of the police in Ameriyah. Major Daniel Whisnant, the nearby Marine company commander, worked with him closely. Whisnant had already served a very successful tour in North Babil, south of Baghdad, in 2004; he understood how to wage counterinsurgency. Whisnant eventually placed an outpost south of Khamis's house. Insurgent leaders actually tried to negotiate with Khamis—a sure sign of his success. They promised to relent on enforcement of Islamic law (shari'a) in return for his endorsement of the Islamic State of Iraq. Khamis told Whisnant that he could not trust AQI. Consequently, they fought on.[74]

The police fought on in the city of Fallujah as well. AQI had silenced religious leaders and crippled the city council. Yet stamping out the police proved difficult, though they intimidated many into deserting. How the police held together is unclear. The size of the police force—one thousand men—probably helped. They could suffer casualties and desertions and still function. So long as the police stood, Fallujah might suffer IEDs and assassinations, but the streets remained outside insurgent control. Reconstruction proceeded and the city remained a refuge for Sunnis fleeing Baghdad.[75]

PETRAEUS AND THE SURGE

On January 10, 2007, President Bush announced that a new strategy would be implemented in Iraq, known as "the surge." It ultimately reinforced the 140,000 US personnel with another 30,000.[76] The focus of the surge was stabilizing Baghdad. As a secondary effort, roughly 4,000 went to Anbar. To execute the new strategy, President Bush replaced General Casey with General David Petraeus. Since 2003, Petraeus had been the foremost advocate of improving US counterinsurgency techniques and had supervised the writing of a new counterinsurgency field manual, which was published in December 2006.

The surge came early to Anbar. The 15th Marine Expeditionary Unit (two thousand men) had arrived at the end of November, actually separate from the official surge decision. Two companies, roughly four hundred men, of its single battalion (2nd Battalion, 4th Marine Regiment) went to Ramadi. The battalion had just over nine hundred men total. The other two companies and the battalion headquarters went to Haditha. The headquarters of the Marine Expeditionary Unit went to Rutbah to try to exert better control over the highway between Ramadi and Jordan.

The official surge sent no new units to Anbar. What it did was extend the deployments of the 15th Marine Expeditionary Unit for forty-five days and two other Marine battalions for ninety days. This provided additional manpower and compensated for the loss of manpower rotating out of Anbar. One of those battalions was Jurney's. It would now overlap with its replacement, 2nd Battalion, 5th Marine Regiment, set to arrive in February. The extension was a relief because 1st Battalion, 37th Armored Regiment, covering southern Ramadi, would depart in February and would not be replaced. Second Battalion, Fifth Marine Regiment could take over their area of operations. The net gain in numbers was only three hundred men, but it was a gain nonetheless (as the armored battalion had few infantry to patrol the streets). The net gain for Ramadi overall was 700 Marines, out of a total of roughly 4,600 Americans in the city (minus the brigade headquarters).

Surge reinforcements were only part of the equation. As impressive as the seven hundred Marines were the over two thousand new policemen and emergency battalion members who took to the streets between January 1 and March 31, 2007. By the end of March, over four thousand police would be working in Ramadi (see Table 5.3). More and more police

Table 5.3 Police and Emergency Battalion Personnel in Ramadi

Date	Number of Recruits	Number of Active Police/ Emergency Battalion
January 2006	1,000	0
February 2006	0	0
March 2006	0	0
April 2006	0	0
May 2006	50	400
June 2006	35	200
July 2006	330	400
August 2006	150	400
September 2006	25–50	650
October 2006	400	650
November 2006	400 (500 ERU)	1,350
December 2006	800 (1,000 ERU)	2,230
January 2007	1,000	3,150
February 2007	NA	3,900
March 2007	NA	4,470

Source: Visit to police recruitment, Camp Blue Diamond, Ramadi, July and August 2006. Rick Jervis, "Police in Iraq See Jump in Recruits," *USA Today*, January 15, 2007. Carter Malkasian, Working papers on impact of police, Center for Naval Analyses, December 2006 to July 2007.

meant more and more outposts and less and less freedom of maneuver for AQI.

Zilmer, Neller, Reist, and the rest of I Marine Expeditionary Force only witnessed the opening act of the surge. They redeployed back to the United States in February, before the fruits of their labor became evident. They had guided US forces through the grim spring and summer of 2006 and then tightened pressure on AQI through the autumn. The awakening movement had been cultivated under their eyes. They had acted responsibly by trying to limit the chances that tribal militias would commit atrocities and trying to tie them to the government. Their efforts to ensure that tribal militia became official police were tireless. By arranging for regular funding, they ensured the new tribally based police would survive for years. When US forces would ultimately leave Anbar, the tribally based police would have salaries and a reason to stay together. The US-funded Sons of Iraq militias that would be formed in Baghdad and elsewhere in 2007 and 2008 would be less fortunate. Maliki refused to bring them into the official government structure. This allowed him to dissolve the Sons of Iraq once he had no more use for them, opening the door for AQI's revival.

MacFarland and his brigade headquarters redeployed at roughly the same time. They had been in Iraq fifteen months, having been extended in September. MacFarland's willingness to seize opportunity and then back Sittar to the hilt had fueled the awakening. His method would be a model for turning tribes throughout Iraq, and later influence similar efforts in Afghanistan. More than anyone else, he made tribal engagement and building local forces part of the American way of war. Among many other painful casualties, MacFarland returned home without one far-seeing member of his staff—Captain Travis Patriquin, the Arabic speaker who had bonded with Sittar and other tribal leaders. An IED had killed him on December 6. He had given everything to make the awakening succeed.

On February 9, II Marine Expeditionary Force (II MEF), commanded by Major General Walt Gaskin, succeeded I Marine Expeditionary Force (I MEF). Brigadier General John Allen was responsible for tribal engagement and economic development activities. He soon developed a deep understanding of tribal dynamics and close relationships with the tribal leaders. Brigadier General Charles Gurganus took over Neller's duties overseeing army and police advising and training.

The nine hundred Marines of 2nd Battalion, 5th Marine Regiment arrived in southern Ramadi in February 2007. Lieutenant Colonel Kasniewski, the battalion commander, immediately pushed his Marines out on patrol. They set up small posts and tried to control every corner. Every two hours, Marines patrolled from these posts. The insurgents fought back hard. As the Marines stretched out, they stood up new neighborhood watch organizations. The Marines identified the mukhtars (community leaders) and had them bring all the local men together. The men were largely unemployed and willing to join the neighborhood watch in return for fifty or one hundred dollars per month. As elsewhere, the neighborhood watch provided the Marines with vital boots, eyes, and ears to combat the insurgents. The members readily pointed out AQI insurgents and the locations they frequented.[77] Captain Rod McHaty, Kasniewski's intelligence officer, highlighted the importance of the police: "I believe that we actually own the streets when we conduct foot patrols and engage the locals. But the main reason for the turnaround in the security here is the willingness of the people to join the Iraqi police force and protect their neighborhoods."[78]

In addition to the activities of the new Marines, the new US brigade commander in Ramadi, Colonel John Charlton, who had succeeded Colonel MacFarland, launched a series of clearing operations that established new outposts in Ramadi. Operation Mufreesboro in late February cleared the Milaab district and set up a new police station. Operation Okinawa, in mid-March, placed two new outposts in the center of Ramadi. Five hundred police and emergency battalion militia took part, clearing buildings and shops on their own.

The additional men on the streets made a difference. So did the outposts. By March 2007, the number of outposts and bases in Ramadi, including new police stations and joint security stations, had grown from thirteen in late 2005 to over fifty. In Ramadi, attacks involving eight or more insurgents had been roughly twenty to thirty per month for over a year. Massing for such attacks required freedom of movement for the insurgents. They had to be able to gather unseen by police or US forces. In March, the number of attacks by eight or more insurgents dropped to five. This implies that only then did enough Marines, soldiers, and police patrol and outpost the city to curtail insurgent freedom of movement.

While the military and police forces impaired AQI's freedom of movement, the Iraqi government hit their pocketbook. First, in January 2007, Maliki decreed that only government gas stations could receive gas. Private gas stations, which were the majority of the gas stations in Anbar and often fell under AQI, were embargoed. Then, in the middle of February 2007, the 4th Iraqi Division occupied the Bayji oil refinery. The government enforced a new rule that all Anbar tankers receiving oil must have the approval of Governor Ma'amoun. The governor would approve no one working with AQI—although he probably approved plenty of tankers connected to the awakening tribal leaders. Next, in March, the Marines started escorting tankers to and from Bayji, making it difficult for AQI to hijack fuel trucks. These three measures squeezed one of AQI's sources of funding and allowed the awakening tribal leaders to expand their own control over oil smuggling. The tribal leaders had been given an edge in gaining control over their own tribes.[79]

As his power increased and US Marines and soldiers secured more ground, Sittar was able to reduce AQI's other black-market funding sources as well. He spread his forces along the main highway through Rutbah to the Jordan and Syria border crossings at Walid and Trebil. He gained greater influence over extortion and taxation along the route. He also asserted a degree of oversight of the crossing of goods at the customs posts themselves. This was all lucrative for his finances, and damaging to those of AQI.[80]

On top of the loss of freedom of movement and funding, detainee releases from US detention facilities had stopped. Since 2005, detainees had been regularly released, partly for lack of evidence, partly to reduce prison crowding. In December, Lieutenant General Raymond Odierno, Chiarelli's replacement as the new commander of Multi-National Command-Iraq (MNC-I), the operational headquarters for the country, had met with Zilmer and his staff. After receiving a brief on the detainee release problem, Odierno asked what he could do. Neller asked him to stop releasing detainees who had come from Anbar. Too many were going straight back into AQI's ranks. Odierno did just that. For the next six months, no more detainees were released into Anbar province. Another of AQI's pools of fighters had been shut down.[81]

As fighting dragged on, brutality escalated. AQI stopped trying to avoid civilian casualties. Suicide car bombs now killed or wounded civilians, something unheard of in the past. This paled in comparison to the final development in suicide car bomb tactics—the use of chlorine gas canisters. These horrible innovations struck Ramadi, Habbaniyah, Fallujah, and Ameriyah between October 2006 and April 2007. Their explosion released a cloud of chlorine gas. They were indiscriminate; anyone near the explosion inhaled the gas and suffered its effects. A chlorine attack on an emergency battalion in January killed ten and wounded sixty-one. In all, chlorine-laden suicide car bombs killed or wounded 381 Iraqis, mostly civilians.

As if the chlorine gas was not enough, AQI started executing women and children. In January, AQI killed a whole family (including four women and two children) in Hamdiyah in order to deter Shaykh Jabbar's Albu Fahad subtribe from working with the awakening movement.[82] That same month AQI decapitated two twelve-year-olds from the Albu Ghanem tribe, which had formed a small neighborhood watch, and left their heads on the parents' doorstep.

Brutality backfired. In the case of the Albu Ghanem, their shaykh called for vengeance and joined the awakening movement. Similarly, the Islamic Army, part of the resistance, protested the chlorine gas attacks on their website. One of the Islamic Army's commanders said: "Al-Qa'eda has killed more Iraqi Sunnis in Anbar province during the past month than the soldiers of the American occupation have killed within three months. People are tired of the torture . . . we cannot keep silent anymore."[83]

Amid the new brutality, suicide bombings continued to inflict losses on the awakening tribes. On February 14, a suicide car bomb killed Lieutenant Colonel Salam, the Albu Alwan police commander who had made such a mark since his tribe had stood up in November and whose men had shown such élan at the "white apartments" back in December. His men would keep fighting without him.

By March 2007, the tribes unaligned with the awakening tribes had winnowed down to the Albu Mar'ai (south of Ramadi), the Albu Bali (between Ramadi and Fallujah), the Albu Khalifa (between Ramadi and Fallujah), and the Albu Fahad faction that lived south of the Euphrates and east of Ramadi in the area known as Julaybah.

Fox Company of 2nd Battalion, 4th Marine Regiment and new police in Ramadi went into the Albu Fahad territory south of the Euphrates. On January 26, Marines and police established Combat Outpost Julaybah but, throughout February, faced heavy violence. A former general within the Saddam fedayeen, Major General Kadhim Muhammad Faris headed into Julaybah. Faris was a member of the Albu Fahad from Julaybah and had worked with the resistance since at least 2004. The Marines nicknamed him "the Bear," for his size. The Iraqis knew him as "the Slapper," for his giant hands and what he did with them to prisoners.[84] Faris mobilized a militia and ruthlessly hunted AQI, including any Albu Fahad in their ranks.

In early March, forty-three tribal leaders from the Khalidiyah area met with one of Sittar's representatives (his "nephew") at Camp Habbaniyah. The tribal leaders agreed to align with Sittar. Faris had organized the tribal leaders and the 150-man militia that showed up at Camp Habbaniyah a few days later. Brigadier General Gurganus (Brigadier General Neller's successor) forbade the militia from being armed. Undeterred, Faris continued with his work.[85] Large numbers of former Ba'athists and military officers resided in Khalidiyah. Faris assumedly used old networks and Ba'athist methods to find and remove insurgents. In the course of the fighting, two police were kidnapped. Open protests broke out. Women took to the streets. With the support of the people, the militia captured the kidnappers and freed one of the kidnapped police. Locals cheered from their rooftops. When an emergency battalion reinforced the militia, the mosques called for jihad on AQI and, on March 13, the Albu Fahad shaykhs in Julaybah announced their intention to build a local police force. The Albu Mar'ai south of Ramadi did the same shortly thereafter.

COLLAPSE OF AQI IN RAMADI

At this point, the awakening movement had turned most of the tribal leaders of Ramadi. The elite of the tribes were with Sittar and his original allies. The awakening now fielded substantial groups of tribal fighters from nearly every tribe: the aristocratic Albu Assaf, the urban Albu Alwan, the warrior Albu Fahad, and the obstinate Albu Ghanem and Albu Mar'ai. It would be a mistake to think all the tribesmen of each tribe had turned. Large numbers were unaligned or even with AQI. But the tribal leaders could now mass thousands in police and militias. Resistance groups had also turned, attacking AQI either on their own or alongside the awakening. Meanwhile, the two army brigades in the city had continued to improve under US advising, and they helped backstop the tribes.

Nearly seven months had passed since Sittar had announced the formation of the Anbar awakening, ten since Zilmer had launched the operation to clear Ramadi, and sixteen since Shaykh Nasr and his colleagues had created the Anbar provincial security council. Over those last seven months, AQI's losses had accelerated. The jump was due to the Iraqi police and the emergency battalions. From January to August 2006, in operations without the police, US and Iraqi security forces had killed, wounded, or captured between 1,000 and 1,400 insurgents per month (an average of 1,200) throughout Anbar. Operations involving the police (or the police on their own) had accounted for less than 10 percent of the total, between 90 and 130 per month over the summer. From October 2006 to March 2007, the number killed, wounded, or captured rose to 1,400–1,700 per month. Losses inflicted by the US forces and Iraqi army on their own held relatively steady at 1,100–1,200 per month. Losses inflicted in operations involving the police and emergency battalions now accounted for over three hundred every month, roughly 25 percent of the total. From December to February, the number exceeded four hundred per month; in March, over five hundred. The vast majority were insurgents the police had captured, usually through intelligence provided by tribal or local sources. Missing in these figures are the untold numbers killed, captured, or executed in tribal hits and raids.[86]

In spite of losses, month after month, AQI had been able to hold. Total numbers of attacks in Anbar remained high: an average of seventy per day, the same as the previous seven months.[87] Insurgents managed to kill or wound over four hundred American and Iraqi military and police per month in January, February, and March 2007, a number exceeding all but six of the thirty-four months between March 2004 and December 2006. These facts suggest that up through the middle of March 2007, AQI could replace a good number of its losses. Otherwise, numbers of attacks and American and Iraqi casualties should have dropped further. No decisive battle or strike against their leadership had knocked AQI out. Nor had the tribal movement torn out AQI's support base in one fell swoop. Ramadi had been a slow, grinding battle of attrition.

Nevertheless, by the middle of March 2007, AQI had reached the end of its rope. Losses had sapped their strength and their pool of replacements had diminished as tribal allies defected, tribal leaders reasserted control over their tribes, and the police and Marines clamped down on downtown Ramadi. An AQI emir who was in Anbar for a year over 2006 and 2007 penned an in-depth analysis of the causes of defeat, captured in 2007. "The Islamic State of Iraq is faced with an extraordinary crisis, especially in al-Anbar," he wrote.[88] Determined to keep fighting and signal strength, the emirs—seemingly backed by Baghdadi and Masri—had pressed military operations without proper preparation. At the same time, foreign fighters had insisted on "carrying out operations and going into battles" after the tide had already turned against them, exhausting the local fighters.[89] Through such means, AQI was apparently able to sustain a high tempo, but at the cost of pushing its fighters to the breaking point. As defeats mounted, fighters came under more and more stress. Foreign fighters and suicide bombers had great trouble operating in Anbar, constraining the supply of outside reinforcements. The emir explained that Iraqi civilians were reluctant to help foreign fighters, out of fear of the tribal movement: "Civilian supporters in some Governorates are afraid because of coercion and the renegade movement among the tribes and their oppression against the Mujahidin and their supporters."[90] "We found ourselves in a circle not being able to move, organize, or conduct our operations," he summarized. "Too often [leaders] lack leadership and military experience, they suffer from lack of support from local residents and are forced to have to confront more than one enemy at a time."[91]

Sometime between March 29 and March 31, 2007, AQI pulled back from Ramadi. Attacks fell sharply from roughly one hundred per week in Ramadi (a figure that had held for months) to under forty. They would drop to under twenty in April and then ten in June. In Anbar as a whole, the average number of attacks fell from seventy to fifty per day. By July, the number would be twenty per day. AQI cadres retreated to the desert or villages along the western Euphrates. Several cells took refuge in the desolate Thar Thar region between Ramadi and Lake Thar Thar to the north. The security situation compelled Baghdadi and Masri to stop letting foreign fighters into the province. AQI's emirs and facilitators kept many of the remaining foreign fighters and suicide bombers out in the desert, on the outskirts of villages, and in safe houses where they would be hard to target.[92] In late June, roughly seventy insurgents made an abortive attempt to reinfiltrate into Ramadi through marshy ground, known as "Donkey Island," south of Ramadi. Soldiers and Marines quickly detected and defeated them in the Battle of Donkey Island (June 30–July 1, 2007).[93]

Exactly why AQI retreated from Ramadi at the tail end of March 2007 remains unknown. One possibility is that the AQI leadership made a careful and deliberate decision to stop fighting. American observers have hypothesized that the AQI leadership ordered its remaining cadres out of the city. A few reports of insurgents falling back and then probing the outskirts of Ramadi, looking for an opportunity to return, support such a hypothesis.

Another possibility is that morale broke down: leaders gave up and fled; fighters laid down their arms. Rather than a deliberate withdrawal, it was a spontaneous collapse. Certain evidence supports this hypothesis as well, such as reports that insurgent leaders had been fleeing Ramadi one by one since February. The AQI emir who authored the 2007 letter lamented that the rise of the tribes "created panic, fear, and the unwillingness to fight. The morale of the fighters went down."[94] His writings verge on admitting to outright collapse:

> The Mujahidin's family faced troubles ... especially in al-Anbar and particularly in (al-Ramadi and al-Gharbiyyah) as the Ansaris [Iraqi members of AQI] are facing huge administrative problems as there is a lack of assistance and an increased number of martyrs within their families. There are, captured and fleeing Mujahidin, who have no one but a merciful God. This hardship ... caused depression and sadness and the feeling of hopelessness in improving their condition. Their desire to fight has been weakened ... in addition to the burdened Emirs who have responsibilities beyond their capabilities, with lack of supporters and increasing apostasy.[95]

He even went so far as to describe AQI's fighters as mutinous.[96] Nevertheless, information is too sketchy to know why AQI resistance broke exactly when it did.

Whether retreat was deliberate or spontaneous, the actions that brought AQI to its perilous condition can be more easily discerned. We know that AQI had trouble moving about Ramadi, especially after new US surge forces and unprecedented numbers of police arrived in early 2007. In this sense, the surge helped but should be put in context. It is hard to argue that the new surge forces—amounting to something less than a battalion—suddenly turned the course of the battle in roughly a month, when five US battalions had been fighting in and around Ramadi for over half a year. This is not to mention the new Iraqi forces. The new police and emergency battalion militia—plus the tribesmen fighting as part of neighborhood watches—far outnumbered the new surge forces. We also know that the police and US special operations forces had captured or killed cell leader after cell leader. By February, AQI's command-and-control structure was fraying. Continuing to fight in that environment probably was becoming untenable. On top of this, AQI had lost its power to cow the tribes. After the remainder of the Albu Fahad flipped in the middle of March, few major tribes stood with AQI and tribal leaders had greater influence over individual tribesmen than had been the case since at least the fall of Saddam. Even if AQI could still draw from some disaffected tribesmen, their reservoir of manpower was much shallower and their resources—because of the measures against their oil smuggling and tribal recapture of sectors of the black market—much smaller.

AQI had gotten itself into this hole partly through failing to compromise with the tribal elite. The organization had asked for too many spoils, imposed its reading of Islam too enthusiastically, and let violence supplant negotiation. Violence could only go so far. It could not overrun a Marine outpost or repulse a Marine assault. It is impossible to know whether any awakening leader would have accepted a compromise—certainly not Sittar, Hais, or Tariq. They were risk takers in pursuit of political supremacy in Anbar. If they had been willing to fight at the ebb of their power (spring 2006) and risk the Carthaginian peace that defeat surely would have brought, why would they have compromised later, when their tribal movement was far stronger? Moreover, none of these leaders trusted AQI, who they believed were dedicated to the destruction of the tribal system. Nevertheless, AQI *might* have been able to reach a compromise with other tribal leaders who had accepted AQI for much of the preceding year. Through compromise, AQI *might* have been able to contain the movement. It was only in late 2007 that AQI's leadership acknowledged that their strict and unbending treatment of Sunni competitors had contributed to their downfall.

In any event, something more than US forces and AQI's violence was needed to throw the tribal movement over the top. Nor were new tactics enough. From June 2006 onward, Marine and Army units refined their tactics. They set up more outposts. They advised and partnered closer with the Iraqi police and army. They used more project funds and in a more targeted manner. They implemented counter-intimidation measures to protect tribal leaders. Their predecessors had explored most of these tactics. What had dissuaded them from implementing them was less lack of imagination than scarcity of US and Iraqi forces and Iraqi disinterest. Of note, the foremost reason that US commanders did not protect the earlier Anbar security council movement was that its leaders demanded distance. To be implemented, new tactics depended upon other factors—adequate US forces, adequate Iraqi forces, and most of all an Iraqi willingness to fight. This brings us to the nature of the Iraqis themselves.

What repeatedly staved off defeat was the nature of the awakening tribesmen—their leadership, cohesion, and their morale. Again and again they withstood heavy blows, such as assassinations, suicide car bombs, and battlefield defeats. Earlier tribal movements, including those that had also enjoyed US support, had cracked under the weight of far lesser reverses. The original awakening tribes kept on fighting. While other tribes backed off after an assassination, they sought revenge. The cohesion of the Albu Risha, Albu Ali Jassim, and Albu Thiyab; Sittar's grasp of propaganda; aggressive hits on enemy leadership; robust measures to protect themselves; and the élan of the individual tribal fighter brought success where others had failed.

CHAPTER 6

The Land of the Islamic State

After March 2007, the awakening movement expanded throughout Anbar. Tribes rose up in Haditha and around Fallujah. As in Ramadi, they cooperated with the United States, secured their territory, and fought AQI. In Fallujah, the Ministry of Interior appointed a new police chief in early 2007, filling a void that had existed since summer 2006. He ruled with a heavy hand. Assisted by a new set of Marine operations and outposts, he suppressed the stubborn insurgent activity in the city of mosques. Shaykh Khamis and the Albu Issa gained the upper hand south of Fallujah. The tribe rose to preeminence in the Fallujah region.

Brigadier General John Allen, responsible for working with the government and tribes, facilitated the progress. He negotiated with many of the tribal leaders who had yet to join the awakening movement. The heads of several tribes were taking refuge in Amman—Shaykh Mishen of the Albu Jumayli from Fallujah, Shaykh Majid and Shaykh Amer of the Albu Assaf from west of Ramadi, Shaykh Khamis of the Albu Fahad from Ramadi (Nasr's brother). Allen convinced them to return to Anbar and support the awakening. In certain cases, the leader brought his tribe into the awakening. In other cases, much of the tribe was already fighting but the leader's presence brought added support and resources.

As AQI was defeated, the tribal leaders across Anbar met and coordinated their activities. It was less that the awakening movement spread to new areas and organized resistance to AQI than that tribes rose up and then aligned with the other tribes of the awakening movement, never viewing themselves as subservient. The awakening movement tied together the tribes of Anbar, stretching from al-Qa'im to Fallujah. The big-name tribes were anchors: the Albu Mahal in al-Qa'im, the Albu Nimr in Hit, the Albu Fahad in Ramadi, and the Albu Issa and Albu Jumayli near Fallujah. Abdul Sittar claimed leadership, but he was really just the most powerful Ramadi figure. By the end of the summer, province-wide, violence on the part of AQI or any other insurgent group had dropped to record lows.

Meanwhile, the idea of an awakening spread beyond Anbar to Baghdad and other provinces. Sunni tribal leaders from across the country learned what was happening in Anbar. Sittar and his brother, Ahmed al-Rishawi, even hosted a few of them at their home. Battles were still raging in Baghdad between Shi'a militias, AQI and the resistance, and US forces. Various Sunni tribal leaders and resistance commanders were interested in re-aligning to secure their interests. Under General Petraeus's direction, US forces directly paid Sunni tribes, resistance cells, and neighborhoods to form militias and fight AQI. In the process, the new Sunni militias could keep out the Shi'a militias that had been attacking them. The Sunni militias were dubbed the "Sons of Iraq." Unlike the Marines, Petraeus was unable to get Maliki to place these militias into the police and allocate a salary. The Sons of Iraq were too close to the center of national power. So Petraeus paid them directly with US military funds. Roughly 100,000 stood up. They helped turn the tide against AQI throughout Iraq.[1]

On September 4, 2007, President George W. Bush visited al-Anbar. He went to al-Asad airbase in the western desert and met with the leaders of the awakening movement and Prime Minister Maliki. The meeting was televised, Sittar seated right next to President Bush. Sittar had become great, perhaps the most famous Sunni in Iraq. He overshadowed other Sunni tribal leaders, including those with far more tribesmen and more distinguished lineages.

One of the tribal leaders with the highest status by birth was Shaykh Ali Hatim Abdul Razzaq Ali al-Sulayman al-Assafi. Ali Hatim was a young, up-and-coming Baghdad politician, born into the direct line of the head tribal leader of the entire Dulaymi confederation, the "shaykh of shaykhs." Abdul Razzaq, who had led the Dulaymi until his death, was his father. Ali al-Sulayman, who had led the confederation during the founding of Iraq, was his grandfather. Amer, the current shaykh of shaykhs, was his uncle. Ali Hatim had been absent from the front during the battle for Ramadi, but supported the awakening politically. His family had fallen out of favor and commanded the Dulaymi tribes in name only. Ali Hatim was ambitious and wanted to regain ascendancy. He looked down on the smaller Albu Risha tribe and dismissed Sittar, who he said "was given much more prominence than he deserved."[2]

Brigadier General Allen found himself mediating between the various parties ostensibly united against AQI. Sittar and Governor Ma'amoun were still balancing against each other. Allen tried to tie the tribal leaders to the government and government programs and funds.[3] Of equal concern, as the awakening grew, different tribal leaders competed with each other more and more, demanding Allen's careful attention. The return of traditional heads of the tribes from Jordan added to the intrigue. The old leaders competed with the new order that had risen through the war against AQI.

From July 2006 onward, AQI tried to kill Sittar in eleven separate bombings. On September 14, 2007, the twelfth attempt got him, exactly a year to the day of the announcement of the awakening and ten days after the meeting with Bush.[4] The attackers had infiltrated into his security detail and laid an IED on his own property, in a spot he frequented near his horse stables. He drove over it. Rumors have persisted ever since that it was members of the awakening movement, jealous of his rising power, who killed him, not AQI.

Sittar's death yielded no advantage for AQI. The tribal leaders now had too much power. US soldiers and Marines were still present en mass. AQI had suffered too many losses. Sittar's brother, Ahmed, succeeded him as head of the Albu Risha and leading figure in the awakening. Ahmed was a capable politician and diplomat. He lacked Sittar's fire, but with fighting subsiding, a calmer temperament seemed appropriate. The different tribal leaders continued to cooperate, though with a constant undercurrent of competition. They quietly questioned Ahmed's dominance. A few complained about the small size of his tribe and his status in the tribal hierarchy.

The province enjoyed a degree of calm surreal to Marines who had served there a year or two earlier. Shops and restaurants opened up in former Fallujah and Ramadi war zones. Marines could walk the streets without body armor. In September 2007, US forces even held a five-kilometer race through downtown Ramadi. Reconstruction work accelerated. Allen organized the expenditure of tens of millions in commander's emergency response program (CERP) projects, which both improved the lives of the people and kept the tribal leaders empowered. IEDs and suicide bombers never disappeared entirely. On June 26, 2008, a suicide bomber in Karma, near Fallujah, tragically killed a Marine battalion commander, a tribal leader, and several other Iraqis. Throughout Anbar, twenty-two Marines were killed between February 2008 and February 2009 (in contrast to ninety between February 2007 and February 2008).[5] Nevertheless, the Marines found themselves worrying about local politics more than security.

After 2007, the tribal forces and police grew to twenty-nine thousand in Anbar, with an additional four thousand Sons of Iraq militia on the eastern edge of the province next to Baghdad. The two Iraqi army divisions in the province developed as well. They numbered over twenty-one thousand and continued to receive US training and mentorship.[6] The 1st Iraqi Division won acclaim when Maliki deployed its headquarters and one of its brigades to Basra to put down Moqtada al-Sadr's March 2008 uprising. With ample US air support, they attacked and defeated al-Sadr's militias. They were soon dispatched throughout the country as a fire brigade, much to the pride of their Marine advisors.[7]

In 2008, the United States started to draw down its forces in Iraq. The numbers of the surge were no longer necessary. Relatively low levels of violence in Anbar allowed the Marines to secure permission from Washington to leave. The Marines did not see themselves as the force for a long-term occupation. In Washington, plans were then forming to send them to more war in Afghanistan. Their generals refocused upon that older war.

Over 2008 and 2009, the Marines gradually withdrew from Anbar. At the same time, they reduced their funding of reconstruction projects and the tribal leaders. In the assessment of the Marine commanders, tribal leaders seemed to have sufficient businesses and inroads into the government to operate on their own. US commanders generally expected the tribal leaders would be able to keep order. In

January 2010, Major General Richard Tryon, the final Marine Expeditionary Force commander, departed Anbar, almost six years after the first Marines had arrived in February 2004. US Army units covered Anbar until the final US military withdrawal in 2011. Violence in Anbar remained low-scale, erratic, and manageable.

During this time, the tribal leaders retained their dominance. So did tribalism. With the urgency of war now lifted, tribal politicking intensified. Ahmed, Sittar's brother and successor as the leading shaykh of the awakening, was growing in political power. Certain awakening tribal leaders distanced themselves from him. These included Wissam al-Hardan, one of the early members of the movement. Competition worsened when Ahmed tried to turn the awakening into a political party in order to compete in the January 2009 provincial elections. A new provincial council would be elected, which would select the new provincial governor. Various awakening tribal leaders broke off from Ahmed's new party. Hamid al-Hais of the Albu Thiyab ran against Ahmed. Hais had been at the forefront of the 2006 fighting, alongside Sittar. The Iraqi Islamic Party of Governor Ma'amoun also ran against Ahmed's party.

The elections were a success in Anbar: the Iraqis ran it themselves; there was no violence; three hundred thousand people voted. Ahmed's coalition won, ensuring the political dominance of his faction and accomplishing his and Sittar's long-standing goal of replacing Ma'amoun.[8] Qassim al-Fahadawi, a well-respected, non-Iraqi Islamic Party politician, became the new governor, working closely with Ahmed. Electorally, Ahmed had come out on top. Politically, the awakening movement was no longer a bloc in pursuit of common political goals. It was a natural turn of events.

The tribes had another problem. The side effects of working so closely with the government and the Americans were emerging. The awakening leaders had always been an elite. Loyal sections of their tribes supported them. The general population—the masses in the cities and disfavored tribal sections—obeyed, but with varying degrees of sympathy. An August 2007 ABC news poll had found that a mere 23 percent of respondents in Anbar had confidence in their local leaders.[9] For some part of society, sympathy for AQI and, to a greater extent, antipathy toward American occupation lived on. The awakening tribal leaders were easy targets for criticism. Their actions had gone against the grain of Iraqi and Islamic identity. A number of locals accused them of having been American stooges and spies. Neighbors of Shaykh Raad Sabah Mukhlif, the determined Albu Alwan leader of 2006, dubbed his street "the Street of the Lackeys."[10] The tribal leaders had a credibility problem.

Even with the politicking and the credibility problem, the different tribes individually remained determined to suppress the old enemy. The Ramadi tribal leaders continued to hold in check what remained of AQI. They still spoke with each other about security matters. Their tribesmen still joined the police. Outside Ramadi, discussions were more tenuous, but ties between the Albu Nimr, Albu Mahal, and Albu Issa endured. Until 2013, common opposition to AQI lived on in this loose inchoate form. The tribal leaders were still dominant.

SECTARIAN DIVISIONS

The last US military forces withdrew from Iraq on December 18, 2011, after negotiations for a status of forces agreement between the United States and Iraq fell through. A small military contingent was embedded in the US embassy to oversee funding of the Iraqi military and maintain contact with its leadership. Together with two consulates, the embassy was all that was left of US presence in Iraq.

Sectarianism had begun to reassert itself ahead of the withdrawal. As Adeed Dawisha has argued in his book *Iraq: A Political History from Independence to Occupation*, the Shi'a political leadership feared a Sunni resurgence, because of Saddam's and AQI's histories of violence.[11] This fear was a powerful force against Sunni-Shi'a reconciliation. Maliki depended on the support of a coalition of Shi'a groups, armed with militias, to maintain his premiership. He had to heed their sectarian defensiveness and demands. It compounded his own biases toward oppressing the Sunnis.

One possible Sunni threat were the Sons of Iraq. Maliki had resisted the program from the beginning. In late 2008, the Iraqi government received control of the Sons of Iraq from the US military. Over the next years, Maliki and the Shi'a-controlled Ministry of Interior arrested and killed Sons of Iraq militiamen in Baghdad and Diyala provinces, supposedly using US-provided information on names and identities.

Equally offensive to Sunnis were the March 2010 parliamentary elections. Ahead of the elections, in January, the Iraqi Accountability and Justice Commission threw out five hundred candidates for ties to the Ba'ath Party. Included were seventy candidates from Ahmed's awakening party. Ahmed threatened to boycott. Although he never carried out his threat and many of the candidates were later reinstated, the incident was another step in Sunni disenfranchisement.

The outcome of the elections further outraged Sunnis of Anbar. Extensive Sunni votes went to Ayad Allawi's bloc. It narrowly won the plurality. Ahmed and the awakening party tallied poorly. By law, winning the plurality should have guaranteed Allawi the right to form a government. Because they were heavily represented in Allawi's bloc, Sunnis should have gained positions in that government. Maliki foiled the Sunnis' chance. He formed his own new coalition and compelled Allawi to concede. Anbar Sunnis saw these events as an orchestrated government campaign against them. They would remember the elections as proof the government was untrustworthy and the constitution bankrupt.[12]

With the US withdrawal, things only got worse. One day after the last American soldier (outside the US embassy) left, Prime Minister Maliki took the alarming step of trying to arrest Vice President Tariq al-Hashemi, the highest-ranking Sunni in the government. Maliki accused Hashemi of running death squads. Hashemi fled the country. His Sunni bloc in parliament boycotted the national government. Maliki tried Hashemi in absentia and sentenced him to death.

The Hashemi incident magnified Sunni distrust of the government. During 2012, a Sunni federalist movement gained momentum. The idea was for Anbar and other Sunni provinces to have autonomy from the national government. Several Anbar leaders, including Ali Hatim, spoke out against the government. Most Anbar tribal leaders supported the idea of federalism in theory. Maliki negotiated with them and tried to address a few of their grievances. He was somewhat successful, at least temporarily, in breaking Anbar leaders off from the rest of the Sunnis. In the end, unlike the leaders of other Sunni provinces, the Anbar leaders never insisted upon federalism. Consequently, while he sent military forces into other Sunni provinces, Maliki left Anbar alone.[13] Elsewhere in Iraq, Maliki arrested thousands of supposed Ba'athists. He also disarmed the Sons of Iraq. Anbar had few Sons of Iraq, so few Anbaris lost their jobs. Well aware of events in Baghdad, the people of Anbar still heard and saw what was happening.

It was Maliki's next move that brought the people of Anbar to the streets. On December 19, 2012, government forces raided the home of the finance minister, Dr. Rafi al-Issawi. Issawi was out, but ten of his bodyguards were arrested on allegations of terrorism. Issawi fled to Anbar. He was from the powerful Albu Issa tribe of Fallujah. A Sunni hero, he had treated wounded Iraqis at the Fallujah hospital during the worst days of 2004. In Fallujah, Issawi met with the Fallujah tribes. Their leaders decided to protest and block the highway from Baghdad to Jordan and Syria. In the ensuing days, protests occurred around Fallujah and throughout Anbar against Maliki. The demands of the protests broadened to include fairer Sunni inclusion in the government, the release of Sunni prisoners, and an end to government violence and security operations against Sunnis. The Arab Spring protests that had spread across the Middle East in 2011 inspired Iraqi Sunni leaders and protesters. Thousands took to the streets in Fallujah and Ramadi, as well as Samarra, Mosul, and Kirkuk. Issawi and other Anbar leaders denounced Maliki and condemned his policies.[14]

Most of the Anbar tribes and the awakening tribal leaders backed the protests. From Ramadi, Ali Hatem declared his support. He was looking to promote himself as the leader of Anbar tribes and a major Sunni leader in Iraq. His rival, Ahmed, ultimately did the same. As Sittar's successor and still the most influential awakening tribal leader, Ahmed had long managed a cooperative relationship with Maliki. After Issawi's bodyguards were arrested, Ahmed at first concurred with the government's move. The outbreak of the protests, however, forced him to break with Maliki or risk losing his popular support base.[15]

The protests put the tribal leaders in an untenable position. The tribal leaders depended on the government for the money, salaries, and privileges to dominate Anbar. The protests pressured them to relinquish their ties to the government in order to avoid immediate discredit and loss of their tribesmen's support, which would in turn imperil their long-term authority over the province. In one instance, a delegation of high-standing tribal leaders won a set of concessions from Maliki on Sunni demands only to have Issawi and other protest organizers reject them. The delegation went along. By supporting the protests, however, tribal leaders had to accept mass popular activity, with thousands of people out on the streets. They had to allow other leaders to speak to the people, thus opening their own authority to challenge. Religious leaders and AQI supporters who had formerly been under the tribal thumb could come out, rally the people, and implicitly challenge the tribal leaders, who were now without government support.

When Ahmed stopped working with the government in early 2013, Maliki turned to Hamid al-Hais and Wissam al-Hardan. They were two of the founding members of the awakening and had opposed Ahmed in the 2009 provincial council elections. They went with Maliki. On February 27, 2013, Hardan was "elected" to be the new head of the awakening by a faction of other awakening leaders, supposedly under government duress. The title carried little weight. In contrast to the earlier tribal politicking, this fracturing of the awakening movement had significant military implications. The government threw out tribesmen affiliated with Ahmed and his allies from the police force and left those of Hais and Hardan.[16] Baghdad installed a new police chief who was very close to Maliki. Six thousand police were dismissed, reducing the size of the Anbar police force from twenty-nine thousand to twenty-three thousand at best.[17] The decrease would ease AQI's return. Meanwhile, Hais and Hardan criticized those awakening tribal leaders who were supporting the protests, saying they were endangering the unity of the country. By openly criticizing the protests, Hais and Hardan unwisely hacked away at their own popular legitimacy and at the old idea of an awakening.

While the police in Anbar divided, the Iraqi army weakened. The edge the Americans had trained into the army dulled. New recruits received poor training. Officers became involved in corruption. Maliki gutted the army of the experienced commanders who had been trained by the Marines, especially the Sunnis, and put in less-skilled loyalists.[18] Even the 1st Iraqi Division, once the pride of the army, degenerated.

Protests persisted for months, if with fewer day-to-day participants than at first. Tents popped up at sit-in sites on the outskirts of Fallujah and Ramadi. A tent camp pitched right outside Ramadi on the highway to Jordan became the heart of the protest movement, dubbed the "Square of Pride and Dignity." Tribal leaders convened meetings in the camp and donated supplies and food.[19] Every week, protests heated up at Friday prayers, when Muslims tend to leave their homes to go to the mosque for their afternoon prayers. Many protesters were upset at all politicians, including Sunni ones, rather than just the Shi'a and Maliki.[20]

The religious leaders of Anbar were at the forefront of the protests. Abdul Malik al-Saadi, a highly respected and highly educated Iraqi religious leader living in Amman, visited and encouraged the protests. He criticized Maliki, elections, and the government as sectarian and called on soldiers to desert. One Ramadi tribal leader said: "We follow Abdul Malik al-Saadi; we heed his advice on how to formulate our demands to the government and how to negotiate with it. He is our spiritual leader." Another protester echoed him: "When it comes to tribal matters, we follow Ahmed Abu Risha, and when it comes to religious matters, we follow Abdul Malik al-Saadi."[21] The protests had no single leader, but imams and scholars called people to the streets and helped organize.[22] They lent the protests legitimacy. Their presence communicated that the arrests were a crime that affected the entire Sunni community.

Through the protests, religious leaders regained prominence lost after the success of the awakening movement. After 2006, influential religious leaders had generally been those who supported the awakening, such as representatives of the government-funded Sunni Endowment. The larger mass of religious leaders had suffered a loss in power. The awakening tribal leaders saw it as within their writ to control what religious leaders preached. They had tried to suppress religious leaders who did not share their views and bring in a high-standing few who endorsed them. Additionally, religious leaders themselves had wanted to stay away from the awakening. Mass popular protests opened the door for every religious leader to play a role and rise in stature. Many religious leaders called for armed struggle against the government. The few who advocated a peaceful approach found themselves challenged and often outbid by those who decried the oppression of the Sunni people. Now bereft of government or American largesse, the tribal elite could not impede religious leaders empowered by mass popular activity. They could not buy them or the people off. Nor could they argue with them without appearing disrespectful of Islam. Religious leaders who supported AQI were thus able to reassert their influence.[23]

In April 2013, the Iraqi army opened fire on protesters in Hawija, in northern Iraq. At least 120 civilians were killed or wounded. Outraged, Sunnis in the north started ambushing and attacking government forces. The Iraqi army then launched a series of operations to quash them, resulting in more violence and deaths. Protests in Sunni provinces intensified. Ahmed and Ali Hatim mobilized tribal militias to defend Anbar against the army.[24] The Ramadi police, still manned by locals, refused to execute arrest warrants against Ahmed and other protest leaders.[25] Maliki tried to send in security forces to do the job, but the tribal police and militias fought them off. By May, sectarian violence throughout Iraq was returning to the levels of the 2006–2007 civil war.[26]

For its part, the United States largely stayed out of the fray. It continued to work through the government and refrained from reestablishing assistance for the Sunnis or siding with them diplomatically in a manner sufficient to get Maliki to back down. For most of 2013, even diplomatic contact was limited. The Sunnis were left to their own devices to contend with Maliki.[27]

THE ISLAMIC STATE

After 2006, Abu Omar al-Baghdadi remained head of AQI. Abu Ayyub al-Masri, the Egyptian who had first succeeded Zarqawi in June 2006, continued to play a large role as deputy and war minister. In 2007 and 2008, as tribes and resistance groups beyond Anbar turned, Baghdadi had tried to moderate AQI's aggressiveness and reunite with the resistance. It was to no avail.[28]

Between 2008 and 2010, US leaders and intelligence analysts assessing the situation concluded that AQI had been severely defeated.[29] They overestimated the scale of the defeat. AQI had never disappeared from Iraq, or from Anbar. Cells, fighters, and commanders repaired to the deserts, the villages on the edges of farmland, and clandestine life in the cities. The resurgent tribes and the US military could push AQI into hiding, but they could not extinguish popular sympathy for them. Every month, suicide car bombs went off in Baghdad. AQI demonstrated its resilience days after the US withdrawal when seventeen bombs shook the capital. In Anbar, the tribes kept AQI more suppressed than elsewhere, but here too hidden sympathy survived. The release of nine thousand prisoners from US detention facilities between 2008 and the end of 2009 re-seeded Anbar with AQI supporters—though the tribal leaders did their best to remove their most dangerous enemies in the lot. Every week a handful of attacks in Fallujah marred the peace.[30] Even Ramadi was vulnerable. In December 2009, a suicide bomber injured Governor Qassim in Ramadi and killed several others.

The effectiveness of Baghdadi and Masri as leaders is a matter of some conjecture. On the one hand, they were in charge as AQI was crippled in 2006 and 2007. On the other hand, they managed to keep the organization alive during the ensuing years of hardship.[31] They succeeded in sustaining the steady barrage of suicide bombings in Baghdad from 2008 onward. They also ran an effective assassination campaign against Sons of Iraq militia commanders in and around Baghdad.[32] Their luck ran out in April 2010. US and Iraqi special operations forces killed both men in a house in the Thar Thar area of Salahudin province.

In May 2010, *Abu Bakr* al-Baghdadi became the new leader of AQI. Abu Bakr al-Baghdadi was a member of the Albu Badr tribe, which claims descent from the Quraysh, the tribe of the Prophet Mohammed. Baghdadi held a doctorate in Islam, religious credentials that few Iraqis could match. Under his leadership, AQI gained a deeper legitimacy. The organization matured and became a dire threat to Anbar and the state of Iraq.[33]

AQI leaders appear to have spent years plotting their resurgence in Anbar. From at least 2010, Baghdadi's subordinates had recognized the Anbar awakening as the United States' decisive move in their loss of power. They aimed to reverse-engineer it. Presumably Baghdadi himself agreed. Baghdadi's subordinates planned to attack the police and army where vulnerable in order to expand their influence in Anbar. At the same time, they proposed to copy the US model and turn tribes away from the government and toward AQI.

Money and weapons would be given to the tribes to bring them over. It was thought that AQI's legitimacy as Muslims and respect for Islam would naturally appeal to the tribes.[34] Baghdadi seems to have moved forward with this plan.

Baghdadi took advantage of the civil war in Syria that had started in 2011 and escalated in 2012. The regime lost much of the country, including the territory next to Anbar. Those regions became safe havens for AQI. Baghdadi relocated portions of AQI to the Euphrates river valley in eastern Syria. AQI had long had cells and operatives in Syria. The enhanced presence amid the civil war allowed AQI to attract more Syrians and larger numbers of foreign fighters.[35] Fighters located in Syria traveled back and forth into Iraq, launching raids and suicide bombing missions.

As had been the case in 2006 and 2007, many AQI commanders and fighters were locals. A few of AQI's top leaders even used names (nom de guerre) that hinted they were from Anbar, such as Abu Ahmad *al-Alwani* and Dr Wa'el *ar-Rawi*.[36] Their most prominent field commander in Anbar was Shaker Waheb al-Fahadawi, a twenty-seven year old with Zarqawi's taste in fashion: black garb, long hair, beard. Waheb was a member of the Albu Fahad tribe. US forces had detained him in 2006, when he was studying computer science in Ramadi, and sent him to prison. He escaped in 2012, after six years of heavy exposure to AQI from the other prisoners. He became an AQI field commander in Anbar, a good example of the persistent draw of AQI on young men out of the Albu Fahad and other awakening tribes. Waheb gained notoriety in August 2013 for executing a group of Syrian truck drivers in Anbar. He would play a leading role in future offensives.[37]

In April 2013, Baghdadi gave his organization a new name: the Islamic State of Iraq and al-Sham (Syria). As their ambitions grew regionally and internationally, members soon referred to themselves as simply the "Islamic State."[38] The Islamic State had an edge over other Sunni groups fighting the regime in Syria or opposing the government in Iraq, including Sunni political parties and tribal leaders. By claiming to form a new state across existing borders—tied together by the universal Islamic faith—the Islamic State appeared to be succeeding where others had failed.[39] Syria and Iraq had been the sites of the first two caliphates after the death of the Prophet Mohammed. The Islamic State's presence in both countries lent the new "state" great credibility. Competitors in Syria and Iraq could match neither the Islamic State's ideas nor its morale and military organization. Other groups, including "Islamist" political parties, often had tribal, nationalist, or secular origins and lacked the Islamic State's closeness to Islam. For their book *ISIS: Inside the Army of Terror*, Michael Weiss and Hassan Hassan interviewed several Islamic State members and found that the Islamic State's dedication to Islam and fighting injustice had inspired many Sunnis to join. "ISIS," they wrote, "more or less had a monopoly on the global Salafist-Jihadist narrative."[40] Writing in 2015, Khalil al-Anani of Johns Hopkins University would echo them: "The Islamic State . . . aims to represent itself as the most authentic and realistic alternative for Islamists. By declaring a caliphate . . . and creating a state, they claim to have achieved what other Islamists failed to do."[41] In Syria, the other Islamic opposition groups refused to attack the Islamic State.[42] In Iraq, neither the tribes nor Sunni politicians—secular competitors—would be able to win over the masses or organize to the extent of the Islamic State.

At this point, tens of thousands of tribal militia, police, and army still operated in Anbar. The Islamic State had to whittle down the leadership and wait for fractures between the tribes and the government before Anbar could be conquered. The Islamic State went after tribal leaders in

Anbar, trying to kill off their most determined opponents. In January 2013, a suicide bomber killed Shaykh Aifan Sadoun al-Issawi, a member of parliament. He had been an effective adversary of AQI in the Fallujah area in 2007. After the death of Shaykh Khamis from natural causes, he had been the leading shaykh of the Albu Issa tribe. The Albu Issa were now without a strong leader. Later in the year, the Islamic State killed Shaykh Khalid al-Jumayli, a leader of the populous Albu Jumayli tribe, also around Fallujah. As 2013 wore on, coordinated assaults and suicide bombers periodically struck security posts in the province. Throughout Iraq, the Islamic State was carrying out thirty suicide bombings per month, compared to five to ten per month in 2011 and 2012.[43]

Over 2013, Baghdadi's forces consolidated their position in the western desert. Refuge in Syria helped them mass against the army. In June, the Islamic State launched attacks in al-Qa'im, Rawah, and Hit. Their fighters moved freely about Rutbah (near the Jordanian border) and Rawah (between Haditha and al-Qa'im), and were active in Haditha. The 7th Iraqi Division responded with a series of methodical operations that accomplished little. The army moved too slowly.[44]

Sectarian tension fed the growth of the Islamic State. Maliki's measures inflamed fears of Shi'a and Iranian expansionism. Many Sunnis turned to the Islamic State as a protector or check on the government. A year later, US advisors in Anbar would hear that local Sunnis joined the Islamic State because of disenfranchisement.[45] Without this sectarian rift, the Islamic State would surely have had less support.

While carrying out small terrorist attacks in the cities and larger operations in the western desert, the Islamic State exploited the deepening rift between the government and the Anbar tribes. They sought to break it open. Inflaming the protests against the Iraqi government would serve this purpose. The Islamic State participated in the protests that took off in

Anbar in 2013. Their fighters appeared in the streets, especially during the latter half of the year. Their flags could be seen in the crowds, even in Ramadi. Islamic State leaders started calling for protesters to take up arms against the government.[46]

The renewed stature of religious leaders in rallying and organizing the protests served as an avenue for the Islamic State to expand its own influence. Religious leaders tended to view the Shi'a government as destroying the faith. They tended to believe that Anbar had to be defended against this dire threat. In this view, it was better to work with the Islamic State and accept their version of change than oppose it and thereby help the government. Moreover, few wanted to object to a movement so vigorously claiming Islamic credentials. Even religious leaders uncomfortable with the Islamic State often said nothing.[47]

According to later American observers, plenty of Anbar Sunnis tacitly supported the Islamic State. They seemed to consider its strictness a minor irritant. The government that had arrested their leaders seemed far worse.[48] Various resistance groups and former regime military accepted the Islamic State, including many that had worked with the awakening in 2006 and 2007. Tribesmen entirely unaffiliated with the Islamic State declared themselves part of the movement, regardless of the direction of their tribal leaders. The Albu Fahad tribal leader admitted: "Tribesmen just started calling themselves Islamic State and al-Qa'eda."[49]

Amid the protests and their enmity toward the Iraqi government, the tribal leaders ended up abiding the Islamic State. Undoubtedly, they had trouble controlling the situation. The protests had given the Islamic State a forum to compete for the hearts of the people. Rafi al-Issawi explained the dynamic in a later interview: "There was no direct relationship at all between the demonstrations and tribes ... and Al Qaeda ... People got very upset, very angry about the government's behavior and the Iraqi army's behavior . . . The people started to look at the army as an enemy rather than as a national army."[50] That led to an environment that fostered the Islamic State:

> When [the Islamic State] came as defenders of Sunnis, we knew that they were criminals, that they were not Sunni defenders. When they presented themselves, people said, "Well, it may be possible to save us from the government, from the army which is not a professional national army, but one that killed and arrested Sunnis."[51]

An influential Albu Nimr tribal leader put it another way: "The question of 2013 and 2014 that every shaykh faced was: 'Is fighting the Islamic State a possibility if doing so is in support of a Shi'a government and against Islam?'"

In Ramadi, Ahmed al-Rishawi advocated that protesters distance themselves from the Islamic State and negotiate with the government. He even advised letting the police and army attack the Islamic State. Set on his rivalry with Ahmed, Ali Hatim demurred and refused to oppose the Islamic State. As a member of the traditional ruling family of the Dulaymi tribal confederation, Ali Hatim had always wanted to regain undisputed leadership of the Anbar tribes. At this point, his politicking was deepening the divisions between the tribes and improving the chances of the Islamic State. Overestimating his own tribal power, he argued that he could sweep away the Islamic State once the government re-formed. Certain other tribal leaders followed the same logic, thinking they could exterminate the Islamic State once the government had conceded. Years later the influential Albu Nimr tribal leader said the main reason for the growth of the Islamic State in Anbar was that "Disparate tribes allowed the Islamic State to grow after Maliki created opportunity."[52] Ahmed found his own calls to oppose the Islamic State without robust support. The fact he did not attack the Islamic State directly on his own is a sign of the power of both the divisions between the tribal leaders and the openness toward the Islamic State among the general population.

The Islamic State gained a foothold in a few neighborhoods of downtown Ramadi where tribal influence was low. One video on the web showed Islamic State fighters in central Ramadi parading by cheering civilians.[53] During 2013, the Islamic State doubled the number of attacks they were conducting in the city from eight or ten to twenty per month, often bombings or hits on tribal leaders and police officers. There were occasional suicide car bombs as well.[54]

THE RISE OF THE ISLAMIC STATE

In December, clashes between the tribes and the Iraqi army escalated out of control. On December 28, Maliki arrested Ahmed al-Alwani, a member of parliament from Anbar who had spoken at protests over the past year. Government forces raided his home in Ramadi, killing several guards, his brother, and his sister, and injuring his wife and child. Once more, Sunnis were outraged, especially Anbaris. Forty-four members of parliament resigned. The tribal leaders again deployed their militias and their police, this time on a wider scale. Old resistance groups mobilized in opposition to the government. Religious leaders called Sunnis to arms. Two days later, Maliki sent in the army to clear out the protesters in Ramadi. Tribal militias repulsed them. At least seventeen people died in the clashes between the army and tribal militias. The army and tribal militias also fought around Fallujah and in the western desert. Skirmishes went on for three days. The army performed poorly. The militias captured two tanks and several Humvees, foreshadowing events to come.

Stunted, the army temporarily withdrew from both Fallujah and Ramadi before trying again on January 2.[55]

On January 1, the Islamic State launched its own attack. Cells within the cities moved to seize control while convoys of pickups, loaded with hundreds of fighters, drove in from the desert and outlying villages.[56] Large numbers of Islamic State fighters flowed in from the Euphrates west of Ramadi, where they had taken refuge over the previous years.[57] Reinforcements from Syria were among them. The Islamic State filmed one convoy of pickups crossing the border. Fighters attacked police stations and occupied mosques.

Over the next two days, the military situation was hugely confused as the army confronted the tribes and the Islamic State at once.[58] The two divisions of the army in Anbar were largely out of the cities and at 60 percent strength after Maliki's mismanagement. They were in no position to combat the Islamic State. Where attacked, the soldiers again performed poorly. Their leadership was weak. It did not help that on December 21, the Islamic State had ambushed and killed the commander of the 7th Iraqi Division, along with twenty-four of his men. Under Islamic State attack, soldiers often fled and abandoned their weapons, equipment, and vehicles, sometimes shedding their uniforms and donning civilian clothes to avoid being targeted.[59] Large numbers of Humvees and tanks fell into the Islamic State's hands. So many soldiers deserted that the two divisions in Anbar dwindled to under 30 percent strength.

At this critical moment, the tribes went their separate ways. The confusion of the situation afflicted the tribes as it had the army. The tribes were still confronting the army when the Islamic State attacked. Under untoward pressure, they succumbed to the fractures that curse tribalism.

Some tribal militias and affiliated police aligned, or realigned, with the government in order to fight the Islamic

State. Those of the Albu Risha, the Albu Thiyab, the Albu Aetha, parts of the Albu Fahad, the Albu Nimr near Hit, and the Albu Mahal around al-Qa'im were in this camp. Ahmed, Hais, and Hardan came back together. Although their political rivalry prevented cooperation to the degree of 2006 and 2007, each directed their tribesmen to resist the Islamic State. Present in Ramadi, Ahmed declared himself and his Albu Risha tribesmen against the Islamic State and behind the government.[60] He negotiated an agreement with Maliki for his tribal fighters to attack the Islamic State alongside the Iraqi army. Additionally, he tried to organize a government and tribal counteroffensive against the Islamic State fighters in Fallujah.[61] Maliki was willing to fund new emergency reaction units for the mission. "All the tribes of Anbar are fighting against al-Qaeda . . . We are happy this fight is taking place. We will confront them face to face, and we will win this battle," Ahmed announced to the press, notwithstanding the fact that a united tribal movement no longer existed.[62]

Other tribes aligned with the Islamic State against the common government enemy. A set of tribal leaders, including those from former awakening tribes such as the Albu Faraj, issued a public announcement of hostility against any tribe or group fighting the Islamic State or standing with the government. Certain tribal leaders swore loyalty to Baghdadi. Often, these were the tribes and tribal leaders that had lost out in the spoils of the awakening. Leading awakening tribes such as the Albu Risha, Albu Nimr, and Albu Alwan had dominated since 2007 and sometimes mistreated other tribes (and even groups within their own tribes). The mistreated tribal leaders now exploited the opportunity to reorder the hierarchy.[63] They let their tribesmen join the Islamic State in battle or provide logistics support. A few tribes that had prospered in the awakening also lent support. Ali Hatim, at odds with Ahmed, continued to oppose the government. He and his allies publicly endorsed fighting against the government and alongside the Islamic State. A number of their tribesmen broke from the original awakening tribes.[64] Sections of the Albu Fahad, especially average tribesmen, did the same, splitting the tribe once more. Around Fallujah, reportedly few if any tribesmen opposed the Islamic State in the beginning of 2014.[65] Key Albu Jumayli tribal leaders aligned with the Islamic State.

Still other tribes stood back and tried to stay out of it, often unwilling to work with the sectarian government.[66] Shaykh Raad and half the Albu Alwan, seething over the arrest of Ahmed al-Alwani, did this, though they later realigned with the old awakening tribes when the Islamic State threatened their survival.[67]

The Islamic State overran police checkpoints and stations throughout the province. In coordination with other hardline groups, they took Fallujah rapidly.[68] The religious leaders rose up and sided with the Islamic State. The police put up scant resistance. Islamic State fighters burned down the police headquarters and hoisted their flags across the city. The police chief and a handful of tribal fighters tried to mount a counterattack, to no avail.[69] The army, already exiled to the desert outside the city, lobbed in artillery and mortar rounds, missing any Islamic State fighters but killing seventeen civilians.[70] Abdullah Janabi, the resistance leader of the first battle of Fallujah, returned and resumed organizing against the government from within the city. On Friday, January 3, thousands of Islamic State fighters, carrying their black flags, and the people of Fallujah filled the streets for prayers. Photos of the event spread across the internet—a sorrowful image for any American who had fought in Fallujah.

In Ramadi, the Islamic State quickly seized whole neighborhoods and moved against the government center and the old awakening strongpoints in the western part of the city and its environs. It was a combined effort. Islamic State cadres residing in downtown neighborhoods attacked from within. Meanwhile, outside forces converged from multiple directions, overrunning the northeastern (Albu Faraj region), eastern (Sufiya), and southern outskirts of the city.[71] Shaker Waheb led a force that captured police posts in the heart of the city. Suicide bombers targeted tribal and army patrols and posts.[72] The government center was defended by police under Major General Faris al-Fahadawi, aka "the Slapper," who had mobilized militias and rooted AQI out of Albu Fahad territory in 2006 and 2007. He was now working for the Ministry of Interior. In spite of the confusion in the city, he and his men resisted the Islamic State attacks.[73]

Islamic State fighters captured the eastern and southern portions of Ramadi. Faris's police, the Iraqi army and special operations forces (dispatched by Maliki) managed to hold on to the main Iraqi army bases and the government center. The old Jazirah tribal redoubt, where the Albu Thiyab, Albu Ali Jassim, Albu Aetha, and Albu Risha fought hard, also held out, as did some Albu Fahad east of the city. Rafi Abdul Karim Mukhlif al-Fahadawi commanded these Albu Fahad and vigorously defended his family's territory. Rafi was the brother of Shaykh Nasr, assassinated by AQI back in 2006 for his leadership in the Anbar security council, the first group to oppose AQI in Ramadi. In 2006, the family had gone to Jordan. This time they stood.[74] Nevertheless, after a week of fighting, the Islamic State had seized much of Anbar and Ramadi.

In June 2014, the Islamic State launched an even larger offensive and conquered Mosul and cities farther south along the Tigris. The Islamic State now controlled almost all Sunni Arab Iraq. In form and name, Baghdadi had established a state. Shortly thereafter, the Islamic State's spokesman, Abu Mohammed al-Adnani, announced the establishment of a new caliphate and proclaimed Baghdadi caliph. On July 4, Baghdadi spoke before his followers at Mosul's Great al-Nuri Mosque. Members of the Islamic State pledged allegiance to him as caliph. The pledge had Islamic meaning that helped suppress divisiveness within the state.

In the years between 2008 to 2015, a cascading set of actions can be seen to have unwound stability. In 2006 and 2007, the awakening had empowered a small tribal elite. Military power and a degree of common purpose, rather than overwhelming support from the people, enabled them to rule. The system started to fall apart very early. First, tribal politicking resumed, weakening the unity of the awakening movement. Second, Maliki began stripping the Iraqi army of competent leaders and proper support, crippling the tribe's backstop in any future battle. Third, Maliki executed his series of ill-advised arrests, leading to the mass popular protests that curtailed the tribal leaders' monopoly on power. The Islamic State demonstrated marked advantages over the tribal leaders in mobilizing support once people could mass in the streets. Fourth, violence between the tribes and the army broke out, shattering the tribal-army unity needed to defeat a determined adversary. Taking advantage of all these factors, the Islamic State finally attacked at the end of 2013 and overwhelmed the weakened army and tribes. Tribal and sectarian dynamics had unraveled the successes of America's time in Anbar.

AMERICA'S SECOND WAR IN ANBAR

For over two years, the Islamic State would control most of Anbar. Violence harkened to the worst of 2004–2007. US military operations resumed after the Islamic State swept into Mosul in June 2014. During that summer, President Barack Obama successfully pressured the Iraqi parliament to relieve Maliki. Obama withheld substantial military assistance until he was gone. The parliament selected Haider al-Abadi, a Shi'a from the Da'wa party, as the new prime minister. Abadi (who had lived in Britain) was far more progressive than Maliki. But Abadi had a weak base and depended on Ayatollah Ali al-Sistani and Moqtada al-Sadr for political support against powerful Iranian-sponsored Shi'a rivals. These rivals stymied Abadi's attempts to reach out to Sunnis or re-form the broken army.

Marines came back to al-Asad airbase in late 2014 and set up a training and advising command. They were forbidden to go into combat. Their job was to train and advise Iraqi army units and coordinate operations. Most important, they arranged US air strikes, which improved the Iraqi soldiers' chances against the Islamic State cadres.

The weaknesses seen in early 2014 in the government, Iraqi army, and tribes continued through 2015. The Iraqi army displayed markedly lower morale and resilience than the Islamic State. Soldiers deploying to Ramadi reported that as many as 80 percent of their colleagues deserted before arriving in the city.[75] Iraqi army offensives were methodical and rarely successful. US advisors often assessed that soldiers had very poor morale. They commented that the Iraqi army would attack only with overwhelming superiority, and the smallest setback could cause soldiers to flee, leaving their weapons and uniforms behind. Iraqi generals were known to despair that their army was nothing, a shadow of Saddam's army of the 1980s. In contrast, Islamic State fighters launched attacks against superior numbers and showed a willingness to close on objectives.[76]

The roots of the Islamic State's morale probably had something to do with Shi'a oppression of the Sunni and the Islamic State's own string of victories. Additionally, the Shi'a soldiers of the Iraqi army were surrounded by an angry Sunni population at the same time they were fighting a deadly foe. Commanders and soldiers were inclined to fortify themselves in bases and protect themselves rather than take risk. The Islamic State's appeal to Islam also very well played a role. US commanders assessed army soldiers to be far less ideologically inclined than their more aggressive Shi'a militia counterparts. The Iraqi army stood for a vague attempt at nationalism while the Islamic State stood for both Sunnism and Islam. "There is no sense of nation," said one general, an astute observer of the Iraqi army, "The republic goes no farther than Baghdad."[77]

The remnants of the tribal movement fought on after the battles of January 2014, diminishing over the course of the year. In al-Qa'im, on the border with Syria, the Albu Mahal and their thousands of fighters resisted the Islamic State for months. In the end, exhausted, Shaykh Sabah and the Albu Mahal tribal leaders stood aside. Between June 21 and 23, 2014, they surrendered al-Qa'im to the Islamic State.[78] Next, in October, the Islamic State captured Hit and the nearby home villages of the Albu Nimr.[79] The Islamic State massacred approximately 350 Albu Nimr tribesmen, many in public executions, often burying them in mass graves.[80] The tribe's lead shaykhs escaped to Jordan. Pockets of tribal resistance in the western desert—including smaller groups of Albu Nimr—survived near al-Asad airbase. A core of the 7th Iraqi Division defended the airbase and surrounding villages.

Around Ramadi, Ahmed's attempt to form a new movement against the Islamic State collapsed. By siding so openly with the government, he lost credibility in the eyes of Sunnis. Many viewed him as a sellout. He, Hais, and Hardan were dubbed "Baghdad Sunnis." Abdul Malik al-Saadi, the highly respected Sunni religious leader, said the attempt at a new awakening was illegitimate because of its ties to the government. Even among the Ramadi tribes still fighting, Ahmed had trouble inspiring. Unlike his brother Sittar, Ahmed was a politician, not a warrior. He was unskilled at building a cohesive military force. Had he been alive, Sittar might have masked collaboration with Maliki and uttered only invective in public. Nor did Ahmed lead from the front and go into battle with his tribesmen and the police. That had never been his place. Much of his time was spent in meetings in Baghdad, Amman, or Dubai, periodically seeing old American friends who hoped he could rekindle the awakening. In January 2015, Islamic State cadres overran Ahmed's compound on the western outskirts of Ramadi and burned it to the ground. Ahmed was forced to take refuge in Irbil and Dubai.[81] The time of the house of Sittar had ended.

Ali Hatim fared no better. The Islamic State took over his lands and subsumed his followers. He decamped to Irbil in disgrace. What remained of the old awakening leadership lost influence over other former awakening tribes and within their own tribes. Tribesmen could turn away from the movement because it had worked with the government bent on destroying the Sunnis. Tribesmen were less obliged to listen to the instructions of a tribal leader who had collaborated or worked with Ahmed. In Rafi al-Issawi's words, "You see, when [Sunnis] fight [the Islamic State], people . . . blame them for fighting Sunnis who are protecting you, while no one is fighting Shi'a militias that are killing our brothers."[82]

The few tribal leaders and tribesmen still fighting had such enmity with the Islamic State that their only choice was to carry on. Faris, Tariq (the former border policeman and determined Albu Thiyab commander from the awakening), and Rafi al-Fahadawi are good examples. With his Albu Fahad militia, Rafi al-Fahadawi continued to defend his tribal territory just east of Ramadi. The family's long opposition to AQI meant that their people within the tribe could only expect retribution at the hands of the Islamic State and tribal rivals. Rafi 's elder and very tribal brother remembered: "With our own capability and limited money, we fought."[83]

The United States tried to work again with the tribes, but the government was lethargic and obstructive. Certain tribes produced lists of thousands of tribesmen ready to fight. The government approved a fraction of the total number and favored weaker tribes and more pliable tribal leaders over the more powerful. The government was even ambivalent toward the tribes *already* fighting the Islamic State. When Rafi al-Fahadawi and his family asked for weapons and ammunition, the government provided nothing. Anti-Islamic State tribal leaders such as Rafi al-Fahadawi could carry on because they had their own sources of wealth and stockpiles of weapons. Shi'a politicians distrusted the Sunnis and did not want to rearm them. Their fears were not without merit. Certain tribesmen told Marine advisors that they opposed the Islamic State but would switch sides and help them if Shi'a militia came near.[84] The US forces in Anbar ended up working with a core of two thousand fighters around al-Asad and another few hundred around Ramadi.

Ramadi hung on into 2015. After January 2014, roughly two hundred thousand civilians fled to Jordan and Kurdish territory in Iraq.[85] The army and a handful of tribal militia and police defended the city's western sections. The frontline swayed back and forth. The army concentrated upon their bases—the bases on the edges of the Euphrates that had been occupied by US Marines and soldiers and before that had been the palaces of Saddam. A combination of police and army garrisoned the government center. The Islamic State controlled the highway and main road leading to Baghdad, partly surrounding the army and tribes. Resupply for the army had to come via long circuitous desert roads. Many Sunni tribes in and around Ramadi assisted the Islamic State against the government. They gave the Islamic State cash to pay its fighters and smuggled small arms and weapons into the city.[86]

The Islamic State prepared a bold assault on the Ramadi government center. Baghdadi called for recruits from Syria for the assault.[87] Twelve cars and captured Iraqi army armored vehicles were loaded with explosives to be used as suicide car bombs or—in the latter cases—suicide tank bombs. This was one of the Islamic State's trademark tactics. They took their captured Humvees, MRAPs, and main battle tanks, packed them with explosives, and plowed them into Iraqi army and police posts. Unlike a car, their heavy armor was impervious to army and police AK-47 and machine-gun fire. Because more explosives could be used and the armor created a tighter shell, the blast was far more destructive than that of a normal suicide car bomb. It could obliterate well-constructed fortifications.

On May 15, 2016, the twelve suicide car and tank bombs filed behind a bulldozer into Ramadi and headed toward the government center, defended by the army and police. Faris again commanded the police, having been fired and rehired a few times since January 2014. The soldiers hunkered down and got out of the way of the bombing column. The twelve suicide bombs exploded against the government center's concrete barriers. The shock wave collapsed buildings throughout the surrounding neighborhood. What happened next is only rumor. Some say the defenders panicked and ran. Others say a few soldiers, police, and Faris fought until they were overwhelmed and forced to retreat. In either case, the government center fell.[88] After that, the army's morale cracked. Whole units got ready to evacuate. A few did not wait. Lines of army vehicles could be seen leaving the city.

The next day, the Islamic State hit the bases, deploying another twenty suicide car and tank bombs. The suicide tank bombs ran right against the Iraqi army bases, blew up, and breached the fortifications. Other suicide car and tank bombs followed in their wake, driving directly onto the bases, tearing apart the defenders. US air strikes came too late to break up the Islamic State attacks. By the end of May

17, the Iraqi army in Ramadi was in full retreat, surrendering its bases and equipment to the Islamic State. Without the army, the tribal militia in downtown Ramadi held on a little longer but eventually also gave up.

Collapse spread to the remaining tribal areas resisting the Islamic State. Rafi al-Fahadawi and his tribal fighters were still successfully defending their territory when the Islamic State assaulted the army bases. Panicked army soldiers filtered through around 3 am on 17 May. They commandeered civilian cars and trucks and fled farther eastward to the army base at Habbaniyah. The sight of the rout shook the morale of the tribal fighters. Rafi and his men were convinced that they too must fall back. They thought that if the army is retreating then the Islamic State force must be large and powerful. Without the army, Rafi doubted his fighters could survive. They retreated and later took position on a new army line that formed closer to the army base at Habbaniyah. Perhaps another 150 tribal fighters in parts of the old tribal redoubt in the Jazirah kept up a sporadic resistance.[89]

A HARD LANDING

By the summer of 2015, the United States had witnessed eighteen months of nearly unbroken defeat in Iraq and Anbar. In September 2015, Sean MacFarland, now a lieutenant general, became the commander of US forces in Iraq and Syria. He knew Ramadi, Anbar, and the tribal leaders better than anyone. He was as thoughtful and anxious to exploit opportunity as he had been in 2006. He immediately increased the air strikes available to Iraqi forces. At the same time, through careful diplomacy, he nudged the government and a few of the military commanders into greater action. Tellingly, even he withheld from rekindling the awakening. He realized that the movement was too broken and discredited to be resurrected.

In a protracted and slogging battle between June 2015 and February 2016, the Iraqi government laid siege to Ramadi. The Iraqi army gradually surrounded and isolated the city. Several hundred soldiers were killed in the process.[90] MacFarland and his generals patched together maybe a thousand tribal fighters. Tariq led a unit of Albu Thiyab. Rafi al-Fahadawi, helped by former governor Qassim al-Fahadawi, led his group of Albu Fahad. MacFarland advised the Iraqi generals and ensured they had sufficient air and logistic support. Throughout the autumn, US air strikes pounded the city.

At the end of December, Prime Minister Abadi (who had succeeded Maliki over a year earlier) sent in two thousand Iraqi special operations forces, known as the counter-terrorism service (CTS). They penetrated into the city under the cover of heavy US air strikes. At the height of the battle, the United States was conducting roughly forty air strikes per day.[91] Six months earlier, that had been more than the number of strikes across *all* Iraq and Syria. Now Ramadi rated it alone. US bombs broke up Islamic State counterattacks. City blocks were flattened, adding to the devastation wrought by the Islamic State's suicide tank bombs seven months before. Buildings that evaded air strikes were pockmarked with artillery and mortar impacts. The grand mosque somehow survived with just a few holes.[92] The Iraqi commanders levied special destruction upon neighborhoods in the northeast of the city where the Islamic State had received popular support. There, US bombs left little standing. Step by step, the Iraqi special operations forces cleared neighborhood by neighborhood. Scattered tribal cadres filled in behind them. By mid-February, the battered shell of Ramadi had been retaken.[93]

In the course of the offensive, Rafi al-Fahadawi upheld his family honor. He and his men recaptured their territory east of the city and then followed the Iraqi special operations forces into the city itself. It is a bittersweet intermission to a tale that had begun exactly a decade earlier with the leadership of his brother, Shaykh Nasr, within the Anbar security council. This had been the first real resistance to AQI in Ramadi. In that struggle, Nasr had been assassinated, the tribe had suffered multiple fractures, and the family had retreated to Jordan. After suffering months of tribal infighting, the family ultimately joined the awakening only to face defeat again with the Islamic State and the loss of their tribal land. In the end, Nasr's family endured to rule their ground, now under his younger brother. Such is what it means to fulfill the role of shaykh: guiding a family and their immediate tribesmen through the tides of state power, foreign invasion, popular uprising, and religious movements, retreating and aligning however necessary—so that family and tribe survive.

In the aftermath of the battle, police and army garrisoned the city. The Iraqi army and special operations forces worked with the tribal militias that had been fighting the Islamic State. They recruited another few thousand militia. The city was a wreck. The development work of 2006–2009 had been demolished. Reconstruction would have to start all over again. The United Nations Development Program instituted projects to reestablish power and sanitation. Nevertheless, for years, the hospital was inoperable, the bridges were demolished, the barriers that control Euphrates water flow were busted, and employment was depressed. Half of Ramadi's population were displaced or refugees. The governor and other officials and provincial council members lived in Baghdad. Prime Minister Abadi let the city fall under a myriad of military and police commanders—a mess of competing chains of command—with some delegation to tribal leaders for social matters. These were the pro-government tribal leaders who depended on the Shi'a government to survive and were not a threat. Most ominously, Shi'a militia tied to Iran and deepy anti-Sunni, sat on parts of the highways outside the city. They had kept out of the battle for Ramadi. Now they remained as a check on Sunni power.

The confidence of Abadi's government and its military forces rose in the wake of Ramadi. Over the next six months, the government recaptured Hit and Fallujah. Although the Islamic State ceased to control Fallujah and Ramadi outright, violence continued. The Islamic State still managed mass attacks on government positions surrounding Ramadi, Fallujah, and Hit on a regular basis. The Islamic State's future in Anbar was unclear. The Sunni people were ambivalent. There was no widespread anti-Islamic State uprising. Marine advisors reported that most local people would not oppose the Islamic State.[94] The advance of Shi'a dominance over Anbar raised the specter of grievance and oppression. Peace did not break out. Counterinsurgency against the Islamic State commenced once more. At the time of writing (spring 2017), it had yet to end.

The remains of the awakening were a ruined city, a weak army, and a residual grouping of tribal leaders and their supporters. The Iraqi army was a wisp of its former self, ineffective on the offensive, reliant on Iraqi special operations forces and a generous serving of American bombs. The impression of years of careful US training and advising had been temporary. The tribal leaders and militias that had somehow stuck out it out were tarred by their closeness to Baghdad and too few to reclaim their former dominance.

With the expansion of Shi'a power over Anbar, Sunni political authority was more circumscribed than ever before. The Shi'a army and militias controlled the roads and cities, what Sunni leaders had traditionally seen as the heart of their power. The Shi'a commanders, soldiers, and militiamen set up their own taxation of commerce, obstructed Sunni refugees from returning home, and detained innocent civilians on charges of "collaboration" with the Islamic State.

The awakening had not only failed to contain the Islamic State; it had failed to protect Anbar against the Shi'a, one of the motivations behind the formation of the movement in the first place.

In light of the cascading set of events from 2008 to 2015, the unraveling of the successes of 2006 and 2007 seems almost inevitable. Sectarian friction and fears inexorably drove Sunni and Shi'a apart. It was more than the biases of Maliki. Sunnis also received scant assistance under his successor Abadi. While the United States withdrew and the government grew hostile, tribal authority fragmented. It was too fragile to hold down AQI on its own. It depended on outside resources that were temporary and a unity that ran against the grain of the tribal structure itself. At the same time, AQI and then the Islamic State were persistent. The group was ingrained in Sunni society, able to survive during times of adversity and prevail when its adversaries were fractious.

The government's arduous recapture of Ramadi cannot mask the larger lesson. The accomplishments of 2006 and 2007 had crumbled. From the beginning of January 2014 to the end of June 2016, the situation had been worse than during the dark summer of 2004. The Islamic State had controlled much of Anbar for over two years. A credible threat to the United States homeland had re-emerged. The United States had been forced to re-enter a full-blown war, the very thing the awakening was supposed to prevent. Years of effort and sacrifice had come close to naught. Nothing symbolizes that better than the destruction of the city of Ramadi itself.

CHAPTER 7

Lessons from the Past

> The tribes, having lost their traditional rulers, were soon torn by bitter internal feuds. The tribes were splintered to fragments and reduced to innumerable chaotic little sections, but the central government was not strong enough itself to assume direct control. The petty chiefs, released from the authority of their patriarchal princes, fought, murdered and robbed one another with impunity.
>
> —John Bagot Glubb, former British political officer in Ramadi, describing the Iraq of 1920[1]

I left Anbar at the end of August 2006. I missed the September 14 announcement of the awakening by two weeks and change. For years, one of my biggest regrets was not extending another two months to see the awakening take off. We had been studying the tribes and could see a few tribal leaders turning against AQI. It was too early to know where things would go. Until recently, just hanging around a few weeks longer seemed like something I should have done. I would have been lucky enough to catch Sittar's announcement. Today, I am more ambivalent. I fear I might have drawn too many of the wrong lessons.

The rise of the Islamic State erased the major accomplishments of 2006 and 2007. The awakening was broken. As the war against the Islamic State plodded into its fourth year, no groundswell of Sunnis rushed back to the government. Ramadi itself was retaken by elite Iraqi special operations forces and hundreds of US air strikes. The latter betrays the ultimate failing of the awakening. Without the United States, it was unsustainable. The United States was dragged back into a long war. US Marines were again on the ground. US aircraft were again bombing Iraqi cities. The awakening had been nowhere near decisive enough to free the United States from war in Anbar.

A realistic appraisal of the US effort in Ramadi and the awakening would be that, over the short term, it yielded a temporary and uneasy stability. Over the long term, it yielded a residual tactical opposition to the Islamic State. After stability collapsed, the remnants of the awakening movement delayed Islamic State success with a spirited if inadequate defense of their territory. Without the US effort and the awakening, Anbar could have lost five or so years of uneasy stability and the Islamic State may have had an easier time emerging. This is a much more modest assessment of the impact of the awakening and US effort in Anbar than the traditional one of a lasting tipping point.

That is not to say that the history of the awakening is devoid of value. On the contrary, much should be remembered in what Americans and Iraqis accomplished. The willingness of US commanders to adapt and experiment should be copied. Colonel Sean MacFarland's work with the awakening movement is a model of initiative. Lieutenant Colonel Bill Jurney's outposts, patrolling, and living with Iraqi police and soldiers demonstrate how counterinsurgency-style tactics can make a difference on the street. Brigadier General Bob Neller's tireless negotiations to get the government to officially endorse, arm, and pay the tribal police show the level of attention that can be required to tie militias to a government. For any tactician, officer, or civilian working in a conflict zone, these examples merit study. Although unlikely to win a war outright, they may lead to better results than other methods—at least under certain circumstances.

The awakening also offers a wealth of insights into working with tribes. It joins a long list of cases where outside powers have found tribes to be allies against common enemies. Having devoted a bit of my own time to this subject, I hesitate to draw lessons, knowing dynamics change from place to place. I would note how MacFarland strove to build trust with the awakening leaders. Trust is a worthy first principle of building relationships with tribal leaders. Another valuable insight is how money was essential to giving tribes the resilience to compete with AQI. Woe to the general who sends men and women to fight terrorists without generous funds. Above all, the awakening should draw attention to the morality of empowering tribes. In the environment of an insurgency or civil war, tribes can be especially prone to seek power and exact vengeance against rivals. These tendencies can compel tribesmen to kill, execute, or torture innocent people. When working with tribes, the United States can inadvertently abet this behavior. During 2006 and 2007, US commanders tried to prevent such abuses, but rumors abounded. Today, what really happened is unknown. We can only guess if they were killing AQI fighters in the heat of battle or innocent civilians in cold blood. The possibility of atrocity is the issue that anyone working with tribes must have in the forefront of their mind. That is why, whether successful or not, Major General Zilmer's steps to prevent human rights abuses deserve praise.

Moving up from the tactics and the actions of American commanders, we should reconsider why the awakening succeeded in 2006 and 2007. A necessary condition was the presence of US Marines and soldiers. They accounted for the bulk of the fighting and AQI losses. They freed up key neighborhoods and prevented AQI from outright overwhelming the awakening. It is worth remembering that the causal weight of

US soldiers and Marines transcends the question of whether the 2007 surge created the awakening. Ramadi received its most substantial reinforcements *prior* to the surge and the awakening started before the surge was even announced. So, for Anbar, the 2007 surge matters little. The basic *idea* of the surge, however—that US soldiers and Marines were necessary for short-term success—is substantiated. Minus those Marines and soldiers, AQI surely would have crushed any tribal movement.

Contrary to what has sometimes been claimed, sudden tactical innovation by US forces may have played a lesser role. It is debatable how much innovative tactics—versus continued US presence and operations—enabled the awakening to succeed. The improved funding and counter-intimidation measures of autumn 2006 did not spare the awakening from severe AQI attacks. AQI inflicted at least as much damage to the early awakening as it had to the Anbar security council in late 2005 and early 2006. Sittar and his early allies simply had the guts to persevere.

A second necessary condition for the success of the awakening is the struggle for power between the tribes and AQI. The presence of US forces alone was insufficient to cause the awakening. Internal dynamics also played a key role. The rise of AQI pushed aside the tribal leaders and edged in on their territory and smuggling. The tribal leaders were losing their position in society. Partly for this reason, a few in Ramadi decided to resist, first in 2005 and then again in 2006. The same thing had happened in al-Qa'im in mid-2005 with the Albu Mahal tribe. This is not an argument about AQI's brutality. That factor matters less than claimed at the time, demonstrated by the fact the awakening leadership had been fighting AQI *before* the worst acts of brutality occurred. The tribal leaders had reason to fight regardless of AQI's brutality. In certain cases, AQI's uncompromising position and brutality inflamed the reaction and offended potential allies, forgoing a chance to limit the damage. This nuanced understanding of the role of brutality nonetheless contrasts with the idea it *caused* the awakening.

The reason to be careful about overemphasizing brutality is that doing so obscures the real sympathy for AQI in Anbar. Overemphasis can imply that Sunnis spontaneously rejected AQI: brutality has no sympathizers, so AQI must have been hated. Overemphasis also can idealize the awakening tribes. It frames their motives as good—selflessly defending the people against a cruel scourge—and whitewashes their sins (while burying our own sense of responsibility). The awakening tribes were hardly that good. They committed their fair share of killing and oppression. In sum, a pure brutality argument understates sympathy for AQI within Anbar society and overstates sympathy for the tribal leaders. In the aftermath of 2007, such misunderstanding may have blinded us to AQI's longevity and the possibility of a future Islamic State.

These two necessary conditions—US troops and the struggle for power—only partially explain why the awakening succeeded. Throughout Anbar, of those tribal leaders who rose up against AQI in 2005 and 2006, many failed—even if they had US support. Notably, both conditions had existed during the awakening's immediate and unsuccessful predecessor—the Anbar security council—in late 2005. At least one other condition matters for explaining the awakening's 2006–2007 success. That condition is the esprit de corps and cohesion of the clans that started the movement. It is something more than the mere presence of Sittar, who was one of several determined figures. The success of the awakening depended on the nature of the Albu Risha, Albu Thiyab, and Albu Ali Jassim tribesmen that surrounded the initial awakening leaders. This was a small core of tribesmen. They were willing to bear casualties. Divisions within the tribes were shallow enough to be overcome. The awakening movement's predecessors in 2005 lacked these traits. Their tribes were severely riven by internal infighting. Their tribesmen, perhaps because the spirit of cohesion was so diffuse, broke after a few casualties. If the Albu Risha, Albu Thiyab, and Albu Ali Jassim tribesmen had done the same, the awakening would have failed.[2]

The historiography of the success in Anbar has been too focused on how various actions such as a US surge or better tactics or cruel brutality changed the course of the Iraq war. It has neglected deeper dynamics. It has neglected the esprit de corps and cohesion of the early awakening tribesmen. These were themselves a function of kinship, geography, and tribal culture. Close-knit familial relations and rural life in homogenous villages tied tribesmen together. Trust and family bonds hindered AQI from dividing them or convincing them to give up. Tribal culture reinforced fighting spirit. The clans and families at the forefront of the awakening had a tradition of fighting together in the military or as smugglers. These tribes were also low ranking in tribal status. Desire to rise in rank may have motivated risk taking and accustomed these clans and families to adversity. And tribal culture demanded revenge against wrongs, a value that was probably stronger in the more communal and rural environment in which these families and clans lived. To explain the outcome of the awakening, all these dynamics have to be explored.

The dynamics should not be assumed to be static. Group cohesion does not appear to change rapidly—given that many of the tribes that fought hard against AQI also fought hard against the Islamic State—but it can shift over time as family relations, rivalries, and common experiences shift. As a tribe's power grows or shrinks, the ties that bind can thin or thicken. Cohesion can waver if traditions of fighting or smuggling together are diluted when a tribe rises in status and wealth. The willingness to take risks can likewise fall. Under long periods of adversity, trends may go in the other direction. Tribes can learn from past defeats. The need to stick together can reinforce ties and group cohesion. Such shifts that can be seen in fractures that emerged between and within the tribes as the awakening expanded and how certain families went to ground against AQI but later fought against the Islamic State.

Over the wars in Iraq and Afghanistan, American soldiers, Marines, and civilians learned to appreciate how culture and history deeply affected their day-to-day work. Thus it is with utmost irony that explanations for the outcome of awakening, an event used to justify new ways of waging war, have turned to numbers and tactics—standard military explanations—more than how kinship, geography, and culture bind men together to endure hardship. Take away that endurance and an armed force can break, regardless of its foreign support or numerical superiority. As ibn Khaldun, the famous fourteenth-century Arab scholar, wrote: "Group feeling produces the ability to defend oneself, and to press one's claims."[3] The value of the study of the people who are fighting and what binds them together should be remembered.

WHY THE AWAKENING BROKE DOWN

Today, study of why the awakening succeeded is overshadowed by the rise of the Islamic State. Indeed, rather than understanding the causes of success, the greatest value of studying Ramadi and the awakening is understanding what happened eight years later. Study illuminates why the great victory collapsed. Three reasons stand out. Each can be detected in 2005, 2006, and 2007.

The first and most obvious is that Maliki's government turned against the Sunnis. The defensiveness of Shi'a politicians and parties in the wake of decades of Sunni oppression—a manifestation of the sectarian divide—propelled Maliki to ill-advised lengths. By striking at key Sunni politicians and political interests, he endangered Anbar's political representation and created a fatal rift between the tribal movement and the government. Maliki tried to mitigate the rift by appeasing Anbar leaders in 2012 and then trying to help Ahmed al-Rishawi in 2014.

He failed. His actions induced a popular reaction that peeled away tribes and gave the Islamic State space to grow powerful. Consequently, the government found itself fighting the tribes at the moment of the Islamic State assault. Without the tribes, the army lacked numbers and popular support. Without the army, the tribes lacked heavy firepower. Divided, they fell.

Sectarian division had deep roots that preceded the rise of the Islamic State. They are evident in 2005 and 2006 in the prolonged constitutional debate, election campaigning, government formation, and ultimately civil war in Baghdad. During late 2006 and 2007, as the awakening got started, the modus vivendi between Maliki and the tribal leaders against AQI shielded Anbar from the full force of sectarianism that would later engulf it. At this time it was convenient for Maliki to empower the awakening. Hence his meetings with Sittar and eventual willingness to grant the tribes assistance. The bloodshed in Baghdad and difficulty US leaders encountered in ensuring that government assistance and salaries reached Anbar foreshadowed deeper divisions to come. So did the attitudes of the people of Anbar themselves. The distrust among the Anbar people and tribal leaders alike toward the government and Shi'a was palpable. After all, the awakening appealed to tribal leaders partly because it better enabled them to defend themselves politically and militarily against the state and Shi'a. Colonel Devlin's intelligence assessment of August 2006 highlighted what many Americans saw at the time:

> Al-Anbar Sunni have little hope for national reconciliation or re-integration into the national polity ... their greatest fears have been realized ... These fears ... are reinforced by actions of the Shi'a-dominated government, including the failure to pay ISF [Iraqi security forces] in al-Anbar, ... bureaucratic attacks on popular Sunni political and military leaders, and minimal support for local government institutions and initiatives from Ramadi to al-Qa'im.[4]

The second reason that the Islamic State could conquer Anbar is that the awakening movement could neither sustain nor hold itself together. The tribal leaders were a small elite that needed both money and guns to quiet most of the population. Their personal resources—based on the black market and business—were limited. Once US dollars and forces disappeared, their ability to keep Sunnis behind them and prevent the Islamic State from regaining ground diminished. The level of power that they could self-sustain was insufficient. On top of this, the tribal leaders feuded and competed with each other. These feuds were in the nature of the tribal system. When confronted with the Islamic State, the propensity was toward division rather than coming together for the sake of a common good. The tribes went their own way. Unity had been their last hope of holding out against the Islamic State.

Issues with the sustainability and unity of the tribes were evident from 2005 to 2007. Until the awakening, the tribes had been unable to succeed on their own. AQI had been edging out the tribal leaders. From 2006 onward, the tribes depended on the United States and the government to gain ascendancy. Money, weapons, quick reaction forces, advisors, and close air support came from these two sources. Before these lifelines were set, the tribes had been unable to compete with AQI. There were few reasons to believe they would do any better in 2014. Infighting compounded their trouble. Some tribes had aligned with the resistance, others with AQI. Even after the awakening movement gained momentum, its various leaders quarreled with each other. There were rifts within specific tribes as well. The Albu Fahad, for example, was deeply divided between pro-resistance and pro-AQI factions. This all serves to make the point that the tribal system was inherently unstable.

The instability of the tribal system fits too well within the wider history of tribes. The trend has been noted by

T. E. Lawrence, ibn Khaldun, and numerous other Arabists and scholars. The demise of the awakening echoes the British empowerment of many of the same Dulaymi tribes in the 1920s. When British support ceased, so did tribal dominance. In the Middle East and parts of South Asia, tribes are both a changing and a permanent social structure. They give people identity. Consequently, they are a means of instilling order. At the same time, their decentralization, unending inter- and intra-tribal competition, and bounded territorial authority push tribal order toward breakdown and conflict. In the best of worlds, a low level of violence waxes and wanes between tribes that is annoying yet manageable for a central government. In the worst of worlds, a more united and inspiring movement, such as the Taliban or AQI, exploits the breakdown and takes over. The latter transpired all too often in the early twenty-first century.

The third and last reason for the conquest of Anbar is that AQI and then the Islamic State enjoyed a critical mass of Sunni support. The Islamic State proved to have sufficient roots and appeal in Anbar to hold its own against the tribes and the government. The movement could endure, gradually re-energized by the sectarian strife and Syrian civil war, until its adversaries imploded.

The depth of support for AQI was grounded in 2005 and 2006. During those years, AQI rose up on its own and overwhelmed the tribes. The network managed to dominate Ramadi, gaining widespread support from locals. AQI gathered this momentum naturally, with limited outside help, thanks in part to ideology. Sunnis may have questioned the AQI version of Islam, but jihad against the infidel appears to have been inspiring. The appeal to Islam drew followers just as kinship drew people to the tribes. The difference was that Islam held universal legitimacy whereas kinship pertained solely to a tribesman's tribe. On this score, AQI, with its unrelenting commitment to jihad and young energetic imams, outbid the more secular resistance and the tribal leaders, who were rarely known for their piety. Tribal links and shaykhly authority had difficulty competing until US commanders started empowering the tribal leaders—a fact that Americans forgot in the exhilaration of the awakening when the tribes appeared victorious. In reality, AQI had a sustainability that surpassed that of the tribes.

The larger lesson is that internal cultural, historical, and social dynamics—sectarian divides, age-old tribalism, and the influence of groups claiming Islamic legitimacy—could not be redirected in the span of a few years. The very name "the awakening" imagines an event that sets history on a better course. I remember well the sense among American civilian officials and military officers in 2007 that the people of Anbar had awoken to the dangers of extremism and decided to stand up for themselves and against violence. Today, the awakening seems to have changed very little. It appears to have succumbed to the very sectarian, tribal, and religious forces that many thought it had overcome.

The awakening and its aftermath also serve as a reminder that intervention has a strong potential to cause instability and harm. In Iraq, the US invasion toppled over order and let sectarian, tribal, and religious dynamics run their course. The United States had neither the patience nor the endurance to wrestle with these dynamics over decades in order to enforce some kind of stability or insure its own glorious victories. The people of Anbar would have been better off had the United States stayed out of Iraq in the first place.

THE SHADOW OF ANBAR

The history of Anbar to 2016 redirects the initial interpretation of the awakening and the US military campaign in Anbar. The perspective of 2007–2012 was that Anbar was the foremost example of how counterinsurgency and US intervention can succeed. Whether due to US forces or a reaction to AQI brutality, the interpretation was the same: near total victory. It was the great tipping point. This interpretation has been disproven. The success of Anbar has been shorn by the 2014 defeats. The awakening and US military success in Anbar can no longer be seriously used to argue that military intervention in broken countries can lead to quick and long-lasting success, even if the interventions deploy the right numbers and methods.

Instead, Anbar is the foremost example of how the greatest successes of intervention can be evanescent. This reinterpretation endows Anbar with an even greater meaning. The most successful example of intervention and counterinsurgency was bound to deeper sectarian, cultural, and religious forces. In the end, these forces proved insensitive to the impact of a few years of US presence. If the most successful example of intervention and counterinsurgency was trapped by these forces, why should we expect anything different elsewhere? Anbar exemplifies how intervention itself is a costly, long-term project, and how success may only be sustained through a prolonged commitment of troops—perhaps not tens of thousands of troops but certainly thousands, along with funding of tribes or other partners. Anbar deserves to be remembered because it seems to have come so close to proving otherwise. It is a sober definition of the limits of success.

Such a long-term commitment, possibly indefinite, raises the expected cost of any intervention. Success should not be presumed to occur within a few years. The United States may have to pay for troop deployments for decades and accept the accompanying casualties. This should give any general, secretary of defense, senator, or commander-in-chief pause. The prospect of protracted costs should devalue intervention, and even deter the endeavor entirely. Living with instability somewhere in the world may be better than the financial and human expenses of addressing it. If the dangers of staying out are too high, then understanding that military commitment is likely to be severely prolonged should encourage thrifty strategies that are manageable over the long term. For the leader looking to withdraw from an intervention what should be remembered is that the host nation is unlikely to sustain our successes, or perhaps even survive itself. Rather, defeats should be assumed. Realism at the end of intervention is almost as important as realism at the beginning.

For the outsider, intervening in an insurgency or a civil war is a learning experience. The imperative to work with the people demands knowledge of society, culture, politics, and history—in all their complexity. Having spent some time in Iraq, Afghanistan, and Honduras, I am impressed by how much we can never learn. The longer I study a conflict, the less I believe that I know. We face an unavoidable dilemma of making decisions with incomplete knowledge or making no decisions at all. Every decision stands a reasonable chance of being a misstep. Friction is inevitable. So it is unsurprising that we overestimated the permanence of the 2007 success in Anbar. What we can do now is take heed and be wary of our ability to change foreign lands.

My personal experience in Iraq has been the dark days of 2004 to 2006, and more recently—in brief visits—the war against the Islamic State. This vista reveals the harsh realities of intervention. The lessons are grim. They are more cautious guides for future policy than history written from the viewpoint of victory. That said, it is better to see something than not. I think I still regret my decision to leave Anbar in August 2006 and miss the fleeting moment of America's greatest success in Iraq.

Notes

Chapter 1

1. Karen DeYoung, "Pakistan Will Give Arms to Tribal Militias," *Washington Post*, October 23, 2008. Linda Robinson, "What Petraeus Understands," www.foreignpolicy.com, September 2008, accessed December 6, 2008.
2. Malou Innocent, "A Model for Modern Counterinsurgency," *Armed Forces Journal*, August 2008.
3. Greg Jaffe, "Tribal Connections," *Wall Street Journal*, August 8, 2007. Niel Smith and Sean MacFarland, "Anbar Awakens: The Tipping Point," *Military Review* (March–April 2008): 41–53. Frederick Kagan, "The Gettysburg of This War," *National Review*, September 3, 2007.
4. Smith and MacFarland, "Anbar Awakens," 41.
5. For a detailed review of this line of thought, see Stephen Biddle, Jeffrey Friedman, and Jacob Shapiro, "Testing the Surge: Why Did Violence Decline in Iraq in 2007," *International Security* 37, no. 1 (Summer 2012): 20–23, 27.
6. Bob Woodward, "Why Did Violence Plummet? It Wasn't Just the Surge," *Washington Post*, September 8, 2008.
7. John Keegan, *The Face of Battle* (New York: Penguin, 1976), 50.
8. See Fuad Khuri, *Imams and Emirs: State, Religion, and Sects in Islam* (London: Saqi, 2006), 52–56. Philip Khoury and Joseph Kostiner, eds., *Tribes and State Formation in the Middle East* (Berkeley: University of California Press, 1990), 27–29. Thomas Barfield, *Afghanistan: A Cultural and Political History* (Princeton, NJ: Princeton University Press, 2010), 82.
9. "President Bush Addresses Nation on Iraq War," Transcript, *Washington Post*, January 10, 2007.

10. Robert Gates, speech at West Point, February 25, 2011.
11. For description, see Michael O'Hanlon and David Petraeus, "America's Awesome Military," *Foreign Affairs* 95, no. 5 (September/October 2016): 12–13.
12. Transcript of Iraq Hearing Statements, CNN.com, September 10, 2007.
13. For a reasoned argument, see John McCary, "The Anbar Awakening: An Alliance of Incentives," *The Washington Quarterly* 32, no. 1 (January 2009): 55–56.
14. Bing West, *The Strongest Tribe: War, Politics, and the Endgame in Iraq* (New York: Random House, 2008), 364–366.
15. David Kilcullen, *The Accidental Guerrilla: Fighting Small Wars in the Midst of a Big One* (New York: Oxford University Press, 2009), 151–176.
16. Austin Long, "The Anbar Awakening," *Survival* 50, no. 2 (April/May 2008): 67–94.
17. Biddle, Friedman, and Shapiro, "Testing the Surge," 7–11. The only academic book on the entire Anbar campaign is Richard Schultz, *The Marines Take Anbar: The Four Year Fight against Al Qaeda* (Annapolis: Naval Institute Press, 2013). Another book on Anbar is Jim Michaels, *A Chance in Hell: The Men Who Triumphed Over Iraq's Deadliest City and Turned the Tide of War* (New York: St. Martin's, 2010).
18. Anthony Shadid, *Night Draws Near: Iraq's People in the Shadow of America's War* (New York: Henry Holt, 2005). Mark Kukis, *Voices from Iraq: A People's History, 2003–2009* (New York: Columbia University Press, 2011). J. Kael Weston, *The Mirror Test: America at War in Iraq and Afghanistan* (New York: Knopf, 2016). Gary Montgomery and Timothy McWilliams, eds., *Al-Anbar Awakening, Volume II: Iraqi Perspectives* (Quantico, VA: Marine Corps University Press, 2009). See also Marc Lynch, "Explaining the Awakening: Engagement, Publicity, and the Transformation of Iraqi Sunni Political Attitudes," *Security Studies* 20, no. 1 (2011): 36–72.
19. Sterling Jensen, "Iraqi Narratives of the Anbar Awakening," doctoral dissertation, King's College London, 2014.

Chapter 2

1. Benjamin Bahney, Howard Shatz, Carroll Ganier, Renny McPherson, and Barbara Sude, "An Economic Analysis of the Financial Records of al-Qa'ida in Iraq," RAND Corporation research study (Santa Monica, CA: RAND Corporation, 2010), 25.

2. Phebe Marr, *The Modern History of Iraq*, 3rd ed. (Boulder, CO: Westview Press, 2011), 156–158, 163.
3. Gertrude Bell, *The Arab of Mesopotamia*, ed. Paul Rich (New York: Lexington Books, 2001), 140.
4. Adeed Dawisha, *Iraq: A Political History from Independence to Occupation* (Princeton, NJ: Princeton University Press, 2009), 73.
5. A few tribes fall under the Shammari, Ubaydi, or Anaiza tribal confederations, which are based in northern Iraq or Saudi Arabia. They still deal with the other Dulaymi tribes.
6. The Albu Fahad, Albu Halbusi, Albu Issa, and Zo'bai were originally part of the Shammari confederation. The first three are now treated as Dulaymi.
7. Toby Dodge, *Inventing Iraq: The Failure of Nation Building and a History Denied* (New York: Columbia University Press, 2003), 87.
8. Dawisha, *Iraq: A Political History from Independence to Occupation*, 73.
9. For more information on tribes in Iraq see Faleh Jubar, "Sheikhs and Ideologues: Deconstruction and Reconstruction of Tribes under Patrimonial Totalitarianism in Iraq, 1968–1998," in *Tribes and Power: Nationalism and Ethnicity in the Middle East*, ed. Faleh Abdul-Jabar and Hosham Dawod (London: Saqi, 2003), 69–109; and Patricio Asfura-Heim, "'No Security Without Us': Tribes and Tribalism in Al Anbar Province, Iraq," CNA Research Memorandum, June 2014.
10. Dawisha, *Iraq: A Political History from Independence to Occupation*, 296.
11. Marr, *The Modern History of Iraq*, 206, 235. Marr's book is widely respected as one of the best on the history of Iraq. Adeed Dawisha's *Iraq: A Political History from Independence to Occupation* is another strong history. It includes significant discussion on recent conflict. For a detailed discussion of tribes and the Iraqi state, see Fanar Haddad, *Sectarianism in Iraq: Antagonistic Visions of Unity* (New York: Columbia University Press, 2011), 95–99.
12. Dawisha, *Iraq: A Political History from Independence to Occupation*, 296.
13. Marr, *The Modern History of Iraq*, 158, 206, 235.
14. For more information, see Thair Karim, "Tribes and Nationalism: Tribal Political Culture and Behavior in Iraq, 1914–20," *Tribes and Power: Nationalism and Ethnicity in the Middle East*, ed. Faleh Abdul-Jabar and Hosham Dawod (London: Saqi, 2003), 300–304.
15. There is very little written in English on Islam in Iraq's Sunni regions, let alone Anbar. One of the best sources is an unpublished manuscript by Patrick Carroll, entitled "Getting to Know the

Imams and the Mullahs: Remembering the Non-Kinetic Lessons from Iraq and Afghanistan." An Arabic-speaking Marine officer, Carroll spent several years in Iraq and worked closely with the religious leaders of Fallujah.

16. Hanna Batatu, *The Old Social Classes and the Revolutionary Movements of Iraq: A Study of Iraq's Old Landed and Commercial Classes and of its Communists, Ba'thists and Free Officers* (London: Saqi, 2004), 954.
17. Patrick Carroll, "Getting to Know the Imams and the Mullahs: Remembering the Non-Kinetic Lessons from Iraq and Afghanistan," 105.
18. Richard Bulliet, *Islam: The View from the Edge* (New York: Columbia University Press, 1994), 182.
19. Patricio Asfura-Heim, "Tribal Customary Law and Legal Pluralism in al Anbar, Iraq," in *Customary Justice and the Rule of Law in War-Torn Societies*, ed. Deborah Isser (Washington, DC: US Institute for Peace, 2011), 271.
20. Batatu, *The Old Social Classes and the Revolutionary Movements of Iraq*, 165–167.
21. Basim al-'Azami, "The Muslim Brotherhood: Genesis and Development," in *Ayatollahs, Sufis, and Ideologues*, ed. Faleh Abdul-Jabar (London: Saqi, 2002), 165, 167. Abdul-Halim al-Ruhaimi, "The Da'wa Islamic Party: Origins, Actors and Ideology," in *Ayatollahs, Sufis, and Ideologues*, ed. Faleh Abdul-Jabar (London: Saqi, 2002), 149.
22. Thamer Ibrahim Tahir al-Assafi and Sheikh Abdullah Jallal Mukhlif al-Faraji, *Al-Anbar Awakening, Volume II: Iraqi Perspectives*, ed. Gary Montgomery and Timothy Williams (Quantico, VA: Marine Corps University Press, 2009), 32. For more information, see Karim, "Tribes and Nationalism: Tribal Political Culture and Behavior in Iraq, 1914–20," 300–304.
23. Asfura-Heim, "Tribal Customary Law and Legal Pluralism in al Anbar, Iraq," 272.
24. For information on the conventional war, see Bing West and Ray Smith, *The March Up: Taking Baghdad with the 1st Marine Division* (New York: Bantam Books, 2003).
25. National Surveys of Iraq, Oxford Research International, March 2004. By comparison, 64 percent of southern Iraq (Shi'a dominant) viewed the invasion as liberation.
26. Scott Johnson, "Inside an Enemy Cell," *Newsweek*, August 18, 2003.
27. Ibid.

28. Bradley Graham, "Top Iraq Rebels Elude Intensified U.S. Raids," *Washington Post*, February 15, 2005.
29. Daniel Byman, "Understanding the Islamic State—A Review Essay," *International Security* 40, no. 4 (Spring 2016): 127, 131.
30. Mohammed Hafez, *Suicide Bombers in Iraq: The Strategy and Ideology of Martyrdom* (Washington, DC: US Institute for Peace Press, 2007), 71. Discussions with 3rd Battalion, 7th Marine Regiment, Camp al-Qa'im, March 30, 2004.
31. Zarqawi letter, www.cpa-iraq.org/transcripts/20040212_zarqawi_full.html.
32. Ahmed Hashim, "The Insurgency in Iraq," *Small Wars and Insurgencies* 14, no. 3 (August 2003): 9.
33. Zarqawi letter, www.cpa-iraq.org/transcripts/20040212_zarqawi_full.html.
34. Mia Bloom, *Dying to Kill: The Allure of Suicide Terror* (New York: Columbia University Press, 2005), 170–171.
35. For more information, see Ben Connable, "Warrior-Maverick Culture: Evolution of Adaptability in the U.S. Marine Corps," doctoral dissertation, King's College London, 2016, 152–154.
36. Charles Clover, "Smiles and Shrugs Speak Volumes about Nature of Attacks on American Troops," *London Financial Times*, September 25, 2003.
37. Discussion with 505th Iraqi Civil Defense Corps (ICDC) Battalion, Camp Fallujah, March 23, 2004.
38. Meeting with 3rd Brigade, 82nd Airborne Division, 3rd Brigade headquarters, Camp Fallujah, March 8, 2004.
39. Address by Lieutenant General Ricardo Sanchez, Camp Fallujah, April 3, 2004. I MEF brief to General John Abizaid, Camp Fallujah, April 9, 2004.
40. Camp Fallujah, I MEF refugee planning meeting, April 20, 2004.
41. Paul Bremer, *My Year in Iraq* (New York: Simon and Schuster, 2006), 326–327, 333–334.
42. I MEF commanders' discussion, Camp Fallujah, April 13, 2004.
43. Discussions with 2nd Battalion, 4th Marine Regiment (2/4), 1st Marine Division Headquarters, Camp Pendleton, March 22, 2005.
44. Report to Congress, "Measuring Stability and Security in Iraq," Department of Defense, July 2005, 6.
45. Iraq Center for Research and Strategic Studies (ICRSS) poll, April 20–29, 2004.

46. George Casey, *Strategic Reflections: Operation Iraqi Freedom, July 2004–February 2007* (CreateSpace Independent Publishing, 2015), 41–42.
47. For further information see John Sattler and Daniel Wilson, "Operation Al Fajr: The Battle of Fallujah—Part II," *Marine Corps Gazette* (July 2005): 12–24; and Bing West, *No True Glory: A Frontline Account of the Battle for Fallujah* (New York: Bantam Books, 2005).
48. Meeting with General George Casey, I Marine Expeditionary Force forward headquarters, Camp Fallujah, March 18, 2006.
49. Of the ten divisions, those in Shi'a and Kurdish areas were locally based and could not be deployed to fight the insurgency in Sunni areas.
50. Discussion with Shaykh Sabah al-Sattam Effan Fahran al-Shuji al-Aziz, Jordan, May 31, 2006.
51. Shaykh Sabah al-Sattam Effan Fahran al-Shuji al-Aziz in *Al-Anbar Awakening, Volume II: Iraqi Perspectives*, ed. Gary Montgomery and Timothy Williams (Quantico, VA: Marine Corps University Press, 2009), 140–141.
52. Ibid., 141.
53. Hannah Allam and Mohammed al Dulaimy, "Iraqis Lament Call for Help," *Philadelphia Inquirer*, May 17, 2005.
54. Ellen Knickmeyer and Jonathan Finer, "Insurgents Assert Control over Town near Syrian Border," *Washington Post*, September 6, 2005.
55. Discussion with Shaykh Sabah, Jordan, May 31, 2006.
56. Ibid.
57. "Iraq's Desert Protection Force at War," *Front Page*, January 1, 2006.
58. Discussions with 3rd Battalion, 6th Marine Regiment (3/6), Camp al-Qa'im, February 21, 2006.
59. Ibid.
60. Discussions with Regimental Combat Team 7 (RCT-7), Camp al-Asad, February 23, 2006.
61. Discussions with 3rd Battalion, 6th Marine Regiment (3/6), Camp al-Qa'im, February 21, 2006; Discussion with 3rd Brigade, 7th Iraqi Brigade military transition team, Camp al-Asad, July 15, 2006.
62. Discussions with Regimental Combat Team 7 (RCT-7), Camp al-Asad, July 15, 2006.
63. Combating Terrorism Center, "Analysis of the State of ISI, 2006–2007," translated document, 2007, https://www.ctc.usma.edu/posts/analysis-of-the-state-of-isi-english-translation-2; Discussion with 5th Marine Regiment, Washington, DC, June 2007.
64. Ambassador Zalmay Khalilzad, press release, October 26, 2005, and speech on Iraq's Constitution, August 1, 2005.

65. World Public Opinion Poll; Iraq Poll, BBC ABC News, ARD German TV, *USA Today*, March 2007.

Chapter 3

1. Meeting with General George Casey, I Marine Expeditionary Force forward headquarters, Camp Fallujah, March 18, 2006.
2. Borzou Daraghi, "Death's at the Door in Iraq," *Los Angeles Times*, July 23, 2006.
3. Al Anbar Survey 5: December 2006. Al Anbar Survey 6: January 2006. Al Anbar Survey 7: May 2006, June 10, 2006, 43. Al Anbar Survey 8: August 2006, September 2006. The surveys benefited from the rigorous and professional supervision of an experienced political scientist.
4. Fallujah City Council Meeting, Mayor's Complex, Fallujah, February 28, 2006. Discussion with claimants, Civil-Military Operations Center, Fallujah, April 26, 2006.
5. Interviews of Sunnis, State Department visit to the Fallujah Liaison Center, Fallujah, July 14, 2006.
6. Discussion with Brigadier General David Reist, CNA, Alexandria, Virginia, April 22, 2009.
7. Fallujah City Council Meeting, Mayor's Complex, July 25, 2006.
8. Fallujah City Council Meeting, Mayor's Complex, August 1, 2006.
9. Discussion with junior imams, Government Center, Ramadi, April 23, 2006.
10. Discussion with Ubaydi tribe, Ramadi gas station, August 6, 2006.
11. Discussion with religious student, Government Center, Ramadi, July 10, 2006.
12. Ibid.
13. "State of the Insurgency in Al Anbar," I MEF G-2, August 17, 2006. Ahmed Hashim, *Iraq's Sunni Insurgency*, The International Institute for Strategic Studies Adelphi Paper 402 (February 2009): 16–17.
14. "Jazirah" is also the name of the desert between the Euphrates and the Tigris north of Baghdad. For this reason, the green region north of Ramadi is sometimes called "the Ramadi Jazirah."
15. Governor Ma'amoun, Anbar Mayor's Conference, Fallujah, August 3, 2006.
16. Lin Todd, "Iraqi Tribal Study—Al Anbar Governorate," Quantum Research International, June 18, 2006, 4–7, 4–8, 4–10, 4–14. John Bagot Glubb, *Arabian Adventures* (London: Cassell, 1978), 57.

17. Al Anbar Survey, September 2005; Discussion with 6th Civil Affairs Group, Ramadi, March 12, 2006.
18. Major Alfred Connable and Brigadier General James Williams in *Al-Anbar Awakening, Volume I: American Perspectives*, Eds. Gary Montgomery and Timothy McWilliams (Quantico: Marine Corps University Press, 2009), 114, 126.
19. This "leadership" was the Mujahedin Shura, a council established in January 2006 of AQI and affiliated insurgent and terrorist organizations. Ahmed Hashim, *Iraq's Sunni Insurgency*, The International Institute for Strategic Studies Adelphi Paper 402 (February 2009): 23.
20. Discussion with Iraqi police, Fallujah police headquarters, August 12, 2006. Bobby Ghosh, "In Iraq's Old Battlefields: Two Kinds of Americans," *Time*, October 8, 2010, www.content.time.com.
21. Combating Terrorism Center, "Analysis of the State of ISI, 2006–2007," translated document, 2007, https://www.ctc.usma.edu/posts/analysis-of-the-state-of-isi-english-translation.
22. Meeting with Governor Ma'amoun, Ramadi Government Center, March 12, 2006.
23. Correspondence with Dr. Ben Connable, August 17, 2016.
24. Ansar al-Sunna was another Salafist group operating in Ramadi. They too wanted to establish an Islamic state in Iraq. I do not mention them in the text because I have been unable to determine what operations they conducted. Discussion with 2-28 Brigade Combat Team, Camp Ramadi, March 15, 2006.
25. Miriam (head of a women's nongovernment organization in Anbar) in *Al-Anbar Awakening, Volume II: Iraqi Perspectives*, 20.
26. Major General Tariq Yusef Mohammad al-Thiyabi in *Al-Anbar Awakening, Volume II: Iraqi Perspectives*, 182.
27. Discussion with 3rd Battalion, 8th Marine Regiment and 2-28 Brigade Combat Team, Camp Ramadi, May 2, 2006. Discussion with I Marine Expeditionary Force foreign area officer, February 27, 2006.
28. Discussion with 1-506 IN, Camp Corregidor, April 4, 2006.
29. Discussion with 3rd Battalion, 8th Marine Regiment and 2-28 Brigade Combat Team, Camp Ramadi, May 2, 2006. Discussion with I Marine Expeditionary Force foreign area officer, February 27, 2006. Author brief to I Marine Expeditionary Force, August 23, 2006.
30. Discussion with interpreters, Ramadi Government Center, March 12, 2006.
31. Governor Ma'amoun, al-Anbar Mayor's Conference, Fallujah, August 3, 2006.

32. Description by Governor Ma'amoun, Government Center, Ramadi, April 23, 2006; "State of the Insurgency in Al Anbar," I MEF G-2, August 17, 2006.
33. Description by Governor Ma'amoun, Government Center, Ramadi, April 23, 2006.
34. Discussion with Colonel Fadil, director general of internal security, Ramadi, March 12, 2006; Combating Terrorism Center, "Analysis of the Islamic State of Iraq," 23.
35. There is a debate in academic circles over how much money AQI in Anbar received from oil smuggling and international financing. Captured AQI ledgers account for minor revenues from these sources, yet they feature prominently in interviews with Iraqis and analyses from the time. The most detailed study of AQI ledgers is Benjamin Bahney, Howard Shatz, Carroll Ganier, Renny McPherson, and Barbara Sude, "An Economic Analysis of the Financial Records of al-Qa'ida in Iraq," RAND Corporation research study (Santa Monica, CA: RAND Corporation, 2010).
36. Bahney, Shatz, et al., "An Economic Analysis of the Financial Records of al-Qa'ida in Iraq," 40–45.
37. Combating Terrorism Center, "Analysis of the State of ISI, 2006–2007."
38. Discussion with 1-506 IN, Camp Corregidor, Ramadi, August 11, 2006.
39. Hashim, *Iraq's Sunni Insurgency*, 34.
40. Finding evidence of AQI murder of civilians was a difficult task amid the intensity of day-to-day fighting and the unclear information in many of the stories that US forces heard.
41. Discussion with Brigadier General David Reist, CNA, Alexandria, Virginia, April 22, 2009.
42. Discussions with Task Force 1-172, Camp Ramadi, March 14, 2006. Meeting with 2-28 Brigade Combat Team, Camp Ramadi, March 8, 2006.
43. Discussion with 3rd Battalion, 7th Marine Regiment, Camp Hurricane Point, Ramadi, March 11, 2006; Discussion with Task Force 1-172, Camp Ramadi, March 14, 2006.
44. Discussion with 2-28 Brigade Combat Team, Camp Ramadi, March 15, 2006.
45. Discussions with Task Force 1-172, Camp Ramadi, March 14, 2006.
46. Meeting with Major General Huck and Ms. Lane Bahl (US State Department), Camp Fallujah, February 25, 2006; Discussion with 3rd Battalion, 7th Marine Regiment, Camp Hurricane Point, Ramadi, March 11, 2006.

47. Brigadier General James Williams in *Al-Anbar Awakening, Volume I: American Perspectives*, 114.
48. Bill Roggio, "Ramadi Revisited," *The Long War Journal* (blog), November 11, 2005, www.longwarjournal.org/archives/2005/11/ramadi_revisite.php, accessed June 18, 2009.
49. Jim Michaels, *A Chance in Hell: The Men Who Triumphed Over Iraq's Deadliest City and Turned the Tide of War* (New York: St. Martin's, 2010), 56.
50. Meeting with Major General Huck and Ms. Lane Bahl (US State Department), Camp Fallujah, February 25, 2006.
51. Discussion with 3rd Battalion, 7th Marine Regiment, Camp Hurricane Point, March 11, 2006.
52. Meeting with Anwar Kharbite, Government Center, Ramadi, February 26, 2006.
53. Meeting with Sunni business, tribal, and religious leaders, Amman, Jordan, May 22, 2006.
54. Comments by Shaykh Khamis Abdul Karim Mukhlif al-Fahadawi, Sunni conference, Jordan, May 29, 2006.
55. Meeting with Anwar Kharbite, Government Center, Ramadi, February 26, 2006.
56. Al-Anbar Security Council Petition to Iraqi Prime Minister, December 22, 2005.
57. Discussion with Task Force 1-172, Camp Ramadi, March 14, 2006.
58. Discussion with civil affairs officer with 1-506th IN, Government Center, Ramadi, March 13, 2006; Discussion with 3rd Battalion, 7th Marine Regiment, Camp Hurricane Point, March 11, 2006.
59. Discussion with Brigadier General Jim Williams, Camp Fallujah, March 3, 2009.
60. Discussion with 3rd Battalion, 7th Marine Regiment, Camp Hurricane Point, March 10, 2006; Michaels, *A Chance in Hell*, 71.
61. Discussion with Task Force 1-172, Camp Ramadi, March 14, 2006. Discussion with 3rd Battalion, 7th Marine Regiment, Camp Hurricane Point, March 11, 2006. Discussion with civil affairs detachment, 1-506 IN, Ramadi, March 13, 2006.
62. Letter to Mujahedin Shura Council, IZ-060316-01, Combating Terrorism Center at West Point, released April 2006. Bill Roggio, "The Sunni Awakening," *The Long War Journal* (blog), May 3, 2007, http://www.longwarjournal.org/archives/2007/05/the_sunni_awakening.php, accessed June 3, 2009; "State of the Insurgency in Al Anbar," I MEF G-2, August 17, 2006.

63. Sabrina Tavernise and Dexter Filkins, "Local Insurgents Tell of Clashes with Al Qaeda's Forces in Iraq," *New York Times*, January 12, 2006.
64. Correspondence with Dr. Ben Connable, August 18, 2016.
65. Discussion with 3rd Battalion, 7th Marine Regiment, Camp Hurricane Point, Ramadi, March 11, 2006.
66. Ellen Knickmeyer, "Ramadi Insurgents Flaunt Threat," *Washington Post*, December 2, 2005.
67. Letter to Mujahedin Shura Council, IZ-060316-01.
68. Ibid.
69. Ibid.
70. On December 1, just three days after the meeting at the government center, two hundred AQI fighters staged a show of force in the middle of Ramadi. The fighters left behind flyers promising to target each Sunni leader participating in the provincial security council. Knickmeyer, "Ramadi Insurgents Flaunt Threat."
71. Discussion with Shaykh Tariq al-Halabsa, Amman, May 22, 2006.
72. Letter to Mujahedin Shura Council, IZ-060316-01.
73. Ibid.
74. Discussion with Anwar Kharbite, Government Center, Ramadi, February 26, 2006.
75. Letter to Mujahedin Shura Council, IZ-060316-01.
76. Ibid.
77. Discussion with 1st Brigade, 1st Iraqi Division, Combat Outpost, July 10, 2006. Lydia Khalil. "Anbar Revenge Brigade Makes Progress in the Fight against al-Qaeda." *Terrorism Focus*, vol. 3, no. 12 (March, 28 2006).
78. Meeting with Colonel Fadhil, director general of internal security, Government Center, Ramadi, March 12, 2006. Discussion with Task Force 1-172, Camp Ramadi, March 14, 2006. Discussion with 2-28 Brigade Combat Team, Camp Ramadi, March 13, 2006. Discussion with Governor Ma'amoun's personal security detail, Ramadi, March 12, 2006. Discussion with provincial minister of tribal affairs, Government Center, Ramadi, March 14, 2006. Lydia Khalil, "Anbar Revenge Brigade Makes Progress in the Fight against al-Qaeda." *Terrorism Focus*, vol. 3, no. 12 (March, 28 2006).
79. "Al Qaeda in Iraq Situation Report," Combating Terrorism Center at West Point, released April 20, 2006.
80. Discussion with Shaykh Sabah, Jordan, May 31, 2006.
81. Discussion with Shaykh Hamid Rashid, Amman, May 22, 2006.

82. Conference with al-Anbar shaykhs, Jordan, May 29, 2006.
83. Discussion with Imam Abdur Qadr al-Ubaydi, Amman, May 22, 2006.
84. Bruce Pirnie and Edward O'Connell, *Counterinsurgency in Iraq (2003–2006)* (Santa Monica, CA: RAND Corporation, 2008), 59. Al Anbar Survey 5: December 2006; Al Anbar Survey 6: January 2006. Al Anbar Survey 7: May 2006, June 10, 2006, 43. Al Anbar Survey 8: August 2006, September 2006. Separate polling in May 2006 found that over 80 percent of the respondents in Ramadi believed violence could force a US withdrawal.
85. Al Anbar Survey 11: September/October 2006, October 2006.
86. Meeting with Brigadier General James Williams, Camp Fallujah, March 3, 2006.
87. Discussion with junior imams, Government Center, Ramadi, April 23, 2006.
88. Ibid.
89. Ibid.
90. Meetings with Khalef al-Aliyan, Baghdad, June 17, 2006.
91. Discussion with Jalal al-Gaoud, Albu Nimr tribal leader, Jordan, June 1, 2006.
92. Discussion with Albu Fahad tribesmen, Ramadi, July 8, 2006.

Chapter 4

1. Ramadi Planning Discussion, Camp Fallujah, March 27, 2006. I MEF Operational Planning Team, Camp Fallujah, March 30, 2006.
2. Brief to General John Abizaid, Camp Fallujah, March 26, 2006.
3. Discussion with Major General Robert Neller, Camp Courtney, Okinawa, June 15, 2009.
4. 3rd Brigade of the 7th Iraqi Division evidently was exempt from this concern because of the Albu Mahal rivalry with AQI.
5. Fallujah City Council Meeting, Mayor's Complex, May 2, 2006.
6. I Marine Expeditionary Force staff meeting, Camp Fallujah, May 2, 2006.
7. Meeting at I Marine Expeditionary Force, Camp Fallujah, July 13, 2006; Meeting with I Marine Expeditionary Force and Dr. Salam al-Zob'ai, Camp Fallujah, July 3, 2006.
8. Comments by Major General Richard Zilmer, Camp Fallujah, July 3, 2006.
9. Discussion with Kilo Company, 3rd Battalion, 8th Marine Regiment, Government Center, Ramadi, April 23, 2006.

10. Discussion with 3rd Battalion, 8th Marine Regiment, Camp Snake Pit, Ramadi, May 1, 2006.
11. Observation of claims processing at Iraq-US civil military operations center, ECP-8, Ramadi, July 11, 2006.
12. 1-506 IN patrol report, April 6, 2006. 1-506 IN patrol report, April 7, 2006.
13. Meeting with Colonel John Gronski, Camp Ramadi, May 6, 2006.
14. I Marine Expeditionary Force meeting with Multi-National Forces—Iraq (MNF-I), Multi-National Corps—Iraq (MNC-I), and Multi-National Security Transition Command—Iraq (MNSTC-I), May 17, 2006.
15. Discussion with Lima Company, 3rd Battalion, 8th Marine Regiment, Camp Snake Pit, Ramadi, June 11, 2006. Discussion with governor's personal security detachment, Government Center, Ramadi, June 25, 2006.
16. Discussion with Lima Company, 3rd Battalion, 8th Marine Regiment, Camp Snake Pit, Ramadi, June 11, 2006.
17. Ibid.
18. Discussion with Lima Company, 3rd Battalion, 8th Marine Regiment, Camp Snake Pit, Ramadi, June 11, 2006. Discussion with governor's personal security detachment, Government Center, Ramadi, June 25, 2006.
19. Niel Smith and Sean MacFarland, "Anbar Awakens: The Tipping Point," *Military Review* (March–April 2008): 43.
20. Discussion with 1st Brigade, 1st Iraqi Division (1-1 Iraqi Brigade) headquarters, Combat Outpost, July 10, 2006. Discussion with 3rd Battalion, 8th Marine Regiment, Government Center, July 9, 2006. Discussions with 3rd Battalion, 8th Marine Regiment, Snake Pit, June 5, 2006.
21. Brief to General George Casey, 2-28 Brigade headquarters, Camp Ramadi, May 6, 2006. Discussion with Anbar shaykhs, al-Anbar Economic Summit, Dead Sea, May 29, 2006.
22. I MEF Commanders' Conference, Camp Fallujah, June 13, 2006.
23. Discussion with 1-506 IN, OP Eagle's Nest, Ramadi, August 11, 2006.
24. Al Anbar Survey 7: May 2006, June 10, 2006, 43.
25. Discussions with 1-1 Iraqi Brigade military transition team, Combat Outpost, July 10, 2006. Discussions with 1st Brigade, 1st Iraqi Division, Combat Outpost, July 10–11, 2006. Discussions with 1-506 IN, Camp Corregidor, July 10–12, 2006.

26. Brief with 1st Brigade, 7th Iraqi Division, Camp Ramadi, March 15, 2006. Discussion with military transition team for a battalion in 1st Brigade, 7th Iraqi Division, Ramadi, July 6, 2006. Provincial Reconstruction Meeting, Government Center, Ramadi, March 13, 2006.
27. US units also occupied Sunni residences as observation posts.
28. Discussion with Brigadier General Razzaq, Combat Outpost, April 11, 2006. Discussion with 1-1 Iraqi Brigade, Combat Outpost, July 2006.
29. I Marine Expeditionary Force Commanders' Conference, Camp Fallujah, August 8, 2006.
30. This was particularly the case in downtown Ramadi.
31. "The Secret Letter from Iraq," *Time*, October 6, 2006.
32. Discussion with 1st Brigade, 1st Armored Division, Camp Ramadi, July 28, 2006.
33. Review of police registration lists, 1st Battalion, 6th Infantry Regiment, Camp Blue Diamond, Ramadi, July 9, 2006. Martin Fletcher, "Fighting Back," *London Times*, November 20, 2006.
34. The head of the Albu Thiyab, according to their tribesmen, was Hamid Turki. Discussion with 1st Battalion, 6th Infantry Regiment, Camp Blue Diamond, Ramadi, July 8, 2006. The head of the Albu Ali Jassim was Mohammed Ouda. Discussion with Colonel Adam Strickland, former foreign area officer in Anbar, August 22, 2016.
35. Khalid was a former general. He and his son were not technically tribal leaders (shaykhs).
36. Discussion with 1st Battalion, 6th Infantry Regiment, Camp Blue Diamond, Ramadi, July 8, 2006. Discussion with 1st Battalion, 6th Infantry Regiment civil affairs team leader, Pentagon, May 5, 2009.
37. Governor Ma'amoun was aware of the fighting. In March, he had wanted Sittar and Ahmed to receive slots for their tribesmen in police recruitment. Meeting with Governor Ma'amoun, Government Center, Ramadi, March 21, 2016.
38. Dr. Thamer Ibrahim Tahir al-Assafi and Sheikh Abdullah Jallal Mukhlif al-Faraji in *Al-Anbar Awakening, Volume II: Iraqi Perspectives*, Eds. Gary Montgomery and Timothy McWilliams (Quantico: Marine Corps University Press, 2009), 35.
39. Discussion with Brigadier General David Reist, CNA, Alexandria, Virginia, April 22, 2009.
40. Discussion with 1st Battalion, 6th Infantry Regiment, Camp Blue Diamond, Ramadi, July 8, 2006.

41. Mark Kukis, ed., *Voices from Iraq: A People's History, 2003–2009* (New York: Columbia University Press, 2014), 158.
42. Discussion with 1st Brigade, 1st Armored Division, Camp Ramadi, July 28, 2006.
43. Discussion with Colonel Adam Strickland, former Marine foreign area officer in Anbar, August 22, 2016. Discussion with Brigadier General David Reist, CNA, Alexandria, Virginia, 22 April 2009. Sheikh Wissam Abd-al-Ibrahim al-Hardan al-Aethawi in _ Al-Anbar Awakening Volume II, 59. "Maliki: Iraq Able to Keep Security After U.S. Exit," *Associated Press*, 14 July 2007.
44. *Voices from Iraq: A People's History, 2003–2009*, 159. Major General Tariq Yusef Mohammad al-Thiyabi in *Al-Anbar Awakening, Volume II: Iraqi Perspectives*, 184, 192.
45. Sheikh Ahmad Bezia Fteikhan al-Rishawi in *Al-Anbar Awakening, Volume II: Iraqi Perspectives*, 45.
46. Meeting with Task Force 1-172, Camp Ramadi, March 14, 2014.
47. Major General Tariq in *Al-Anbar Awakening, Volume II: Iraqi Perspectives*, 179, 183.
48. Khalid Al Ansary and Ali Adeeb, "Most Tribes in Anbar Agree to unite Against Insurgents," *New York Times*, September 18, 2006.
49. Statements on the part of future awakening tribal leaders that AQI was evil is widely documented and appears in the statements of several US military officers and civilian officials.
50. Ahmad al-Rishawi in *Al-Anbar Awakening, Volume II: Iraqi Perspectives*, 45.
51. Discussion with 1st Battalion, 6th Infantry Regiment civil affairs team leader, Pentagon, May 5, 2009.
52. Discussion with Colonel Pollock, Camp Lejeune, August 8, 2008.
53. Fletcher, "Fighting Back."
54. Discussion with Brigadier General David Reist, CNA, Alexandria, Virginia, April 22, 2009. Colonel Peter Devlin and Major General Walter Gaskin, commander of II Marine Expeditionary Force, both cite this as a major factor. Jim Michaels, *A Chance in Hell: The Men Who Triumphed Over Iraq's Deadliest City and Turned the Tide of War* (New York: St. Martin's Press, 2010), 93, 98.
55. Discussion with Task Force 1-172, Camp Ramadi, March 14, 2006.
56. Michael Totten, "The Liberation of Karmah, Part II, April 1, 2008. See blog responses at www.commentarymagazine.com/blogs/index.php/totten/3153, accessed June 19, 2009.

57. Discussion with Task Force 1-172, Camp Ramadi, March 14, 2006. The exact date of the death of Sittar's father is somewhat unclear. There are reports it occurred in November 2004. Michaels, *A Chance in Hell*, 93.
58. Discussion with Brigadier General David Reist, CNA, Alexandria, Virginia, April 22, 2009. Discussion with Colonel Adam Strickland, former foreign area officer for Anbar, August 21, 2016.
59. Discussion with Brigadier General David Reist, CNA, Alexandria, Virginia, April 22, 2009.
60. Discussion with 1-506 IN, Camp Corregidor, Ramadi, June 4, 2006. Meeting with 1st Brigade, 1st Iraqi Division, Combat Outpost, Ramadi, July 10, 2006. Discussion with 1-506 IN, Camp Corregidor, Ramadi, July 10, 2006.
61. Meetings with Khalef al-Aliyan, Baghdad, June 17, 2006.
62. Numerous reports have come out about a group called "Thawra al-Anbar" or "al-Anbar Revolutionaries" that was supposedly conducting an assassination campaign around Ramadi during this time. Stories about the group are very confusing and often contradictory. I have chosen to write about the specific leaders and tribes involved in attacks on AQI rather than group them under one name. Staff Brigadier General Nuri al-Din Abd al-Kareem Mukhlif al-Fahadawi, Colonel Said Mohammed Muad al-Fahadawi, and Staff Major General Khadim Mohammed Faris al-Fahadawi in *Al-Anbar Awakening, Volume II: Iraqi Perspectives*, 197–199, 206–207, 265–266.
63. Discussion with Lieutenant Colonel Walrath, Commanding Officer, 1st Battalion, 6th Infantry Regiment, Camp Blue Diamond, Ramadi, July 8, 2006. Colonel Gronski and his officers had also been aware of the Albu Thiyab and Albu Risha activities and had met with them.
64. Discussion with 1st Battalion, 6th Infantry Regiment, Camp Blue Diamond, Ramadi, July 8, 2006. Discussion with 4th Civil Affairs Group, US Navy Yard, Washington DC, June 7, 2008. Lieutenant Colonel John Tien, Task Force Commanders Assessment of TF 2-37 Area of Operations, January 25, 2007.
65. Comments by Colonel Sean MacFarland, provincial security meeting, government center, Ramadi, August 6, 2006. Discussion with 1st Battalion, 6th Infantry Regiment, Camp Blue Diamond, Ramadi, July 8, 2006.
66. Michaels, *A Chance in Hell*, 116.

67. Sheikh Wissam Abd-al-Ibrahim al-Hardan al-Aethawi in *Al-Anbar Awakening, Volume II: Iraqi Perspectives*, 55.
68. Marine Corps Historical Center, Marine Corps Historian Interview with Colonel Sean MacFarland, 1st Brigade, 1st Armored Division, December 13, 2006.
69. Ahmad al-Rishawi in *Al-Anbar Awakening, Volume II: Iraqi Perspectives*, 46–47.
70. Michaels, *A Chance in Hell*, 95–97, 104–108.
71. Khalid al-Ansary and Ali Adeeb, "Most Tribes in Anbar Agree to Unite Against Insurgents," *New York Times*, September 18, 2006.
72. Michael Totten, "The Liberation of Karmah, Part II," April 1, 2008. See blog responses at www.commentarymagazine.com/blogs/index.php/totten/3153, accessed June 19, 2009.
73. Al-Iraqiyya Broadcast, September 26, 2006.
74. Thomas Ricks, "Situation Called Dire in West Iraq," *Washington Post*, September 11, 2006.

Chapter 5

1. The Albu Aetha, a small tribe, are sometimes mentioned as part of the initial awakening. Wissam Hardan al-Aethawi, one of their tribal leaders, indeed joined the movement early on. But there was no significant participation of his tribesmen in the early police forces or in setting up their own neighborhood watches at this point. The tribe was then aligned with AQI. A faction of the Albu Faraj also assigned thirty or forty of their tribesmen to the police at this point but did not yet fully stand up. According to Lieutenant Colonel Adnan, commander of the Jazirah police station, the Albu Faraj were deeply infiltrated by AQI. Meeting with Lieutenant Colonel Adnan al-Thiyabi, Jazirah police station, Ramadi, July 28, 2006.
2. Jassim had contributed three police to the August recruitment drive and had a handful of men defending his home. Discussion with 1-506 IN, Camp Corregidor, Ramadi, August 11, 2011.
3. Thiebauld Malterre, "Ramadi: Defended by Insurgents Turned Police," *AFP*, December 2, 2006.
4. Discussion with police, Jazirah Police Station, Ramadi, July 28, 2006.
5. Benjamin Bahney, Howard Shatz, Carroll Ganier, Renny McPherson, and Barbara Sude, "An Economic Analysis of the Financial Records of al-Qa'ida in Iraq," RAND Corporation research study (Santa Monica: RAND Corporation, 2010), 40–45.

6. Richard Tapper, "Anthropologists, Historians, and Tribespeople on Tribe and State Formation in the Middle East," *Tribes and State Formation in the Middle East*, ed. Philip Khoury and Joseph Kostiner (Berkeley: University of California Press, 1990), 65.
7. Discussion with police, Jazirah Police Station, Ramadi, July 28, 2006.
8. Major General Tariq Yusef Mohammad al-Thiyabi in *Al-Anbar Awakening, Volume II: Iraqi Perspectives*, Eds. Gary Montgomery and Timothy McWilliams (Quantico: Marine Corps University Press, 2009), 185.
9. Discussion with 1st Battalion, 6th Infantry Regiment, Camp Blue Diamond, Ramadi, July 8, 2006.
10. Discussion with Brigadier General David Reist, CNA, Alexandria, Virginia, April 22, 2009.
11. A common accusation has been that the staff of the I Marine Expeditionary Force wanted to work with the head tribal leaders in Jordan, who supposedly derided Sittar. In my experience, the Marine leadership was pretty skeptical about the potential of a Jordan-based solution.
12. Discussion with Brigadier General David Reist, CNA, Alexandria, Virginia, April 22, 2009.
13. Some number of weapons captured from the insurgency were donated to the police affiliated with the awakening movement too. Jim Michaels, *A Chance in Hell: The Men Who Triumphed Over Iraq's Deadliest City and Turned the Tide of War* (New York: St. Martin's Press, 2010), 143.
14. Discussion with 4th Civil Affairs Group, US Navy Yard, Washington DC, June 7, 2008.
15. Discussion with civil affairs team leader, 1st Battalion, 6th Infantry Regiment and Task Force 2-37 (his tour crossed over both battalions), Pentagon, May 5, 2009.
16. Ibid.
17. Michelle Tan, "Civil Affairs Troops Help Open New School," *Army Times*, January 25, 2007.
18. Discussion with 4th Civil Affairs Group, US Navy Yard, Washington, DC, June 7, 2008; Department of Defense News Briefing with Colonel Sean MacFarland, September 29, 2006, www.defenselink.mil, accessed April 18, 2009.
19. Interview with civil affairs team leader, 1st Battalion, 6th Infantry Regiment and Task Force 2-37 (2006–2007), Pentagon, May 5, 2009.

20. Sheikh Ahmad Bezia Fteikhan al-Rishawi in *Al-Anbar Awakening, Volume II: Iraqi Perspectives*, 48.
21. Discussion with 4th Civil Affairs Group, US Navy Yard, Washington, DC, June 7, 2008.
22. Interview with civil affairs team leader, 1st Battalion, 6th Infantry Regiment and Task Force 2-37 (2006–2007), Pentagon, May 5, 2009. Thomas Ricks, *The Gamble* (New York: The Penguin Press, 2009), 64.
23. Niel Smith and Sean MacFarland, "Anbar Awakens: The Tipping Point," *Military Review* (March–April 2008): 43.
24. Dan Murphy, "How Al Qaeda Views a Long Iraq War," *Christian Science Monitor*, October 5, 2006. Michael Scheuer, "Al Qaeda's Top Ideologues Release New Statements on the Global Jihad," *Terrorism Focus* 3, no. 38 (2006): www.jamestown.org.
25. Khalid Al Ansary and Ali Adeeb, "Most Tribes in Anbar Agree to Unite against Insurgents," *New York Times*, September 18, 2006.
26. Ibid.
27. Thiebauld Malterre, "Ramadi: Defended by Insurgents Turned Police," *AFP*, December 2, 2006.
28. Interview with civil affairs team leader, 1st Battalion, 6th Infantry Regiment and Task Force 2-37 (2006–2007), Pentagon, May 5, 2009.
29. This is one of the occasions in which "Thawra al-Anbar" appears as the name of a raid force in Anbar. The ties between the different occurrences of the name are unclear.
30. Mussab al Khairalli, "Sunni Chiefs Offer al-Maliki Help in War on Militants," *Washington Times*, September 28, 2006. Ellen Knickmeyer and Muhammed Saif Adin, "Families Flee Iraqi River Towns on 4th Day of Sectarian Warfare," *Washington Post*, October 17, 2006.
31. Discussion with police, Jazirah Police Station, Ramadi, July 28, 2006.
32. Discussion with Brigadier General David Reist, CNA, Alexandria, Virginia, April 22, 2009.
33. Abu al-Waleed al-Salafi, "An Account of Abu Bakr al-Baghdadi and Islamic State Succession Lines," trans. Aymenn Jawad Al-Tamimi, Aymenn Jawad Al-Tamimi's Blog, January 24, 2016, www.aymen-njawad.org. Aymenn Jawad Al-Tamimi, "2006—Announcement of the Caliphate?," December 9, 2015, www.aymennjawad.org.
34. Muhammed al-'Ubaydi, Nelly Lahoud, Daniel Milton, and Bryan Price, "The Group That Calls Itself a State: Understanding the Evolution and Challenges of the Islamic State," The Combating

Terrorism Center at West Point, December 2014, 15–16, www.ctc.usma.edu. Aymenn Jawad Al-Tamimi, "2006—Announcement of the Caliphate?," December 9, 2015, www.aymennjawad.org.

35. Abu al-Waleed al-Salafi, "An Account of Abu Bakr al-Baghdadi and Islamic State Succession Lines."
36. William McCants, *The ISIS Apocalypse: The History, Strategy, and Doomsday Vision of the Islamic State* (New York: St. Martin's, 2015), 31–41. al-'Ubaydi, Lahoud, Milton, and Price, "The Group That Calls Itself a State," 14.
37. Miriam Karouny, "Gunmen in Iraq's Ramadi Announce Sunni Emirate," *Reuters*, October 18, 2006.
38. Combating Terrorism Center, "Analysis of the State of ISI, 2006–2007," translated document, 2007, https://www.ctc.usma.edu/posts/analysis-of-the-state-of-isi-english-translation, 24–25.
39. Sudarsan Raghavan, "Sunni Factions Split with Al Qaeda Group," *Washington Post*, April 14, 2007.
40. Mussab al Khairalli, "Sunni Chiefs Offer al-Maliki Help in War on Militants," *Washington Times*, September 28, 2006.
41. Discussion with Brigadier General David Reist, CNA, Alexandria, Virginia, April 22, 2009. Sheikh Wissam Abd-al-Ibrahim al-Hardan al-Aethawi in *Al-Anbar Awakening, Volume II: Iraqi Perspectives*, 59. "Maliki: Iraq Able to Keep Security After U.S. Exit," *Associated Press*, July 14, 2007.
42. Discussion with Matt Sherman, former political advisor to 1st Cavalry Division in Baghdad, September 2006 to September 2007, September 21, 2016.
43. Joshua Partlow, "Sheiks Help Curb Violence in Iraq's West, U.S. Says," *Washington Post*, January 27, 2007.
44. Peter Beaumont, "Iraqi Tribes Launch Battle to Drive al Qaeda out of Troubled Province," *The Guardian*, October 3, 2006.
45. Marine Corps Historical Center, Marine Corps historian interview with Colonel Mark Econie, provincial police advisor, December 14, 2006.
46. Mark Kukis, "Turning Iraq's Tribes Against Al Qaeda," *Time*, December 26, 2006.
47. These were later known as provincial security forces (PSF). Marine Corps Historical Center, Marine Corps historian interview with Lieutenant Colonel James Lechner, deputy commanding officer, 1st Brigade, 1st Armored Division, December 15, 2006.

48. Discussion with Brigadier General David Reist, CNA, Alexandria, Virginia, April 22, 2009; Discussion with Major General Robert Neller, Camp Courtney, Okinawa, June 2009.
49. Marine Corps Historical Center, Marine Corps historian interview with Colonel Mark Econie, provincial police advisor, December 14, 2006.
50. Discussion with Major General Robert Neller, Camp Courtney, Okinawa, June 15, 2009. Colonel John Charlton press conference from Ramadi, Pentagon Press Corps, March 15, 2008.
51. Linda Robinson, *Tell Me How This Ends: General David Petraeus and the Search for a Way Out of Iraq* (New York: Public Affairs, 2008), 152–153.
52. Al-Iraqiyya TV interview with Shaykh Moayad al-Hmayshi, Spokesman for Sahawa al-Anbar, October 1, 2006.
53. Discussion with Brigadier General David Reist, CNA, Alexandria, Virginia, April 22, 2009; Discussion with Lieutenant General Richard Zilmer, Camp Hansen, Okinawa, June 14, 2009.
54. Bing West, *The Strongest Tribe* (New York: Random House, 2008), 209.
55. Interview with civil affairs team leader, 1st Battalion, 6th Infantry Regiment and Task Force 2-37 (2006–2007), Pentagon, May 5, 2009. Discussion with Colonel Adam Strickland, former foreign area officer in Anbar, August 22, 2016.
56. Marine Corps Historical Center, Marine Corps historian interview with Lieutenant Colonel William Jurney, 1st Battalion, 6th Marine Regiment, February 17, 2007.
57. Discussion with Abdul Salaam, Al-Anbar provincial police chief, Quantico, July 2007.
58. Ibid.
59. Interview with civil affairs team leader, 1st Battalion, 6th Infantry Regiment and Task Force 2-37 (2006–2007), Pentagon, May 5, 2009.
60. Discussion with police, Jazirah Police Station, Ramadi, July 28, 2006.
61. Marine Corps Historical Center, Interview with Sergeant Paul Lindberg, July 30, 2007.
62. Discussion with Abdul Salaam, al-Anbar Provincial Police Chief, Quantico, July 2007.
63. Martin Fletcher, "Fighting Back," *London Times*, 20 November 2006.
64. Michaels, *A Chance in Hell*, 170.
65. Jassim claimed ninety insurgents were killed, but these figures are unverified and likely understandable exaggerations. Smith and

MacFarland, "Anbar Awakens," 43; Correspondence with Major Niel Smith, 2007. Sheikh Jassim Muhammad Saleh al-Suwadawi and Sheikh Abdul Rahman al-Janabi in *Al-Anbar Awakening, Volume II: Iraqi Perspectives*, 68–69.

66. Sarah Childress, "Retaking Ramadi: All the Sheik's Men," *Newsweek*, December 12, 2006.
67. Marine Corps Historical Center Interview: Lieutenant Colonel James Lechner, Camp Ramadi, December 15, 2006.
68. Ibid.
69. Discussion with Abdul Salaam, al-Anbar Provincial Police Chief, Quantico, July 2007.
70. There are conflicting accounts of Masri's presence on the battlefield. US forces did receive intelligence reports, of unknown quality, that Masri was sometimes forward in Ramadi, once planning an attack in July, and possibly later in November planning the battle of Sufiya. If true, Masri was closer to the battlefield than his chief judge claimed. McCants, *The ISIS Apocalypse*, 34–35. Michaels, *A Chance in Hell*, 79–80, 170.
71. Sam Dagher, "Sunni Muslim Sheikhs Join US in Fighting Al Qaeda," *Christian Science Monitor*, May 3, 2007.
72. Lieutenant Colonel John Tien, Task Force Commanders Assessment of TF 2-37 Area of Operations, January 25, 2007. Task Force 2-37 Brief, January 31, 2007, provided by Lieutenant Colonel John Tien, May 31, 2009. Interview with Civil Affairs Team Leader, 1st Battalion, 6th Infantry Regiment and Task Force 2-37 (2006–2007), Pentagon, May 5, 2009. Megan McCloskey, "Battling Violence in the Heart of Darkness," *Stars and Stripes*, January 14, 2007.
73. West, *The Strongest Tribe*, 213.
74. Marine Corps Historical Center: Interview with Major Daniel Whisnant.
75. Discussion with Regimental Combat Team 5, Camp Pendleton, April 1, 2007.
76. Ricks, *The Gamble*, 122.
77. Discussion with Major Rodrick McHaty, Quantico, January 3, 2008.
78. Correspondence with Captain Rodrick McHaty, March 2007.
79. Discussion with Brigadier General David Reist, CNA, Alexandria, Virginia, April 22, 2009.
80. Discussion with 5th Marine Regiment, Camp Pendleton, June 2007.
81. Discussion with Brigadier General Robert Neller, Camp Courtney, Okinawa, June 15, 2009.

82. Lieutenant Colonel John Tien, Task Force Commanders Assessment of TF 2-37 Area of Operations, January 25, 2007. Interview with Civil Affairs Team Leader, 1st Battalion, 6th Infantry Regiment and Task Force 2-37 (2006–2007), Pentagon, May 5, 2009.
83. Sudarsan Raghavan, "Sunni Factions Split with Al Qaeda Group," *Washington Post*, April 14, 2007.
84. Discussion with Colonel Adam Strickland, former foreign area officer for Anbar, August 21, 2016.
85. There are reports that Faris and the tribal leaders "swore allegiance" to Sittar. Swearing allegiance would have gone beyond traditional tribal norms and would have signified submission. Thus, "alignment" is more likely what occurred. Discussion with Colonel John Shook, advisor to 1st Iraqi Division, Camp Courtney, Okinawa, June 15, 2009.
86. Carter Malkasian, Working papers on impact of police, Center for Naval Analyses, December 2006 to July 2007.
87. Jonathan Schroden, "Measures for Security in a Counterinsurgency," *Journal of Strategic Studies* 32, no. 5 (October 2009): 722.
88. Combating Terrorism Center, Analysis of the State of ISI, 2006–2007, translated document, Combating Terrorism Center, www.ctc.usma.edu, 2007.
89. Ibid., 5, 22–23.
90. Ibid., 22–23.
91. Amit Paley, "Shift in Tactics Aims to Revive Struggling Insurgency," *Washington Post*, February 8, 2008. "The Al Qaeda Diaries," *Jane's Terrorism and Security Monitor*, March 4, 2008.
92. Combating Terrorism Center, Analysis of the State of ISI, 2006–2007, 5–7.
93. Schroden, "Measures for Security in a Counterinsurgency," 722.
94. Amit Paley, "Shift in Tactics Aims to Revive Struggling Insurgency," *Washington Post*, February 8, 2008.
95. Combating Terrorism Center, Analysis of the State of ISI, 2006–2007, 20–21.
96. Ibid., 24.

Chapter 6

1. Stephen Biddle, Jeffrey Friedman, and Jacob Shapiro, "Testing the Surge: Why Did Violence Decline in Iraq in 2007?," *International Security* 37, no. 1 (Summer 2012): 24.

2. Shaykh Ali Hatim Abd al-Razzaq Ali al-Sulayman al-Assafi in *Al-Anbar Awakening, Volume II: Iraqi Perspectives*, Eds. Gary Montgomery and Timothy McWilliams (Quantico: Marine Corps University Press, 2009), 117.
3. Major General John Allen in *Al-Anbar Awakening, Volume I: American Perspectives*, 231.
4. Sheikh Ahmad Bezia Fteikhan al-Rishawi in *Al-Anbar Awakening, Volume II: Iraqi Perspectives*, 48.
5. Brigadier General Martin Post in *Al-Anbar Awakening, Volume I: American Perspectives*,263.
6. Department of Defense News Briefing with Major General John Kelly, March 10, 2008.
7. Major General John Kelly in *Al-Anbar Awakening, Volume I: American Perspectives*, 248–249.
8. Anthony Shadid, "Iraq Election Highlights Ascendancy of Tribes," *Washington Post*, January 25, 2009.
9. Gary Langersept, "What They're Saying in Anbar Province," *New York Times*, September 16, 2007.
10. Anthony Shadid, "In Anbar, U.S.-Allied Tribal Chiefs Feel Deep Sense of Abandonment," *Washington Post*, October 3, 2009. Sam Dagher, "In Anbar Province, New Leadership, but Old Problems Persist," *New York Times*, September 12, 2009.
11. Adeed Dawisha, *Iraq: A Political History from Independence to Occupation* (Princeton, NJ: Princeton University Press, 2009), 270.
12. Correspondence with Dr. Ben Connable, August 18, 2016.
13. Joel Rayburn, *Iraq After America: Strongmen, Sectarians, Resistance* (Palo Alto, CA: Hoover Institution Press, 2014), 221.
14. "Make or Break: Iraq's Sunnis and the State," International Crisis Group report, August 14, 2013, 15.
15. Ibid., 15, 17.
16. Ibid., 30.
17. Discussion with key Albu Nimr tribal leader, Amman, Jordan, 9 March 2017. "Iraq: Falluja's Faustian Bargain," Crisis Group Middle East Report, April 28, 2014.
18. Visit to CTS training facility, Baghdad, January 7, 2016. Discussion with United Nations Development Program officer, July 30, 2016.
19. "Make or Break: Iraq's Sunnis and the State," 15.
20. Liz Sly, "Arab Spring-Style Protests Take Hold in Iraq," *Washington Post*, February 8, 2013. Daveed Gartenstein-Ross and Sterling

Jensen, "The Role of Iraqi Tribes after the Islamic State's Ascendance," *Military Review* (July–August 2015): 106.

21. "Make or Break: Iraq's Sunnis and the State," 17.
22. Priyanka Boghani, "In Their Own Words: Sunnis on the Treatment in Maliki's Iraq," PBS News Hour transcript, October 28, 2014.
23. Discussion with leading Albu Fahad tribal leader, Amman, Jordan, 9 March 2017. Boghani, "In Their Own Words."
24. Ned Parker, "Why Iraq's Most Violent Province Is a War Zone Again," *Time*, January 4, 2014. Rayburn, *Iraq After America*, 238.
25. Sterling Jensen, "The Fall of Iraq's Anbar Province," *Middle East Quarterly* (Winter 2016).
26. Rick Brennan, "Withdrawal Symptoms: The Bungling of the Iraq Exit," *Foreign Affairs* 93, no. 6 (November/December 2014): 25.
27. "Iraqi Sheiks Take the Fight to Al Qaeda in Fallujah, *The Daily Beast*, January 4, 2014.
28. Brian Fishman, "Dysfunction and Decline: Lessons Learned from Inside Al Qa'ida In Iraq," monograph, Combating Terrorism Center at West Point, March 1, 2009, 9–15.
29. Daniel Byman, "Understanding the Islamic State—A Review Essay," *International Security* 40, no. 4 (Spring 2016): 127.
30. Sam Dagher, "In Anbar Province, New Leadership, but Old Problems Persist," *New York Times*, September 12, 2009.
31. Will McCants argues the pair were ineffective. William McCants, *The ISIS Apocalypse: The History, Strategy, and Doomsday Vision of the Islamic State* (New York: St. Martin's, 2015), 31–41. Muhammed al-'Ubaydi, Nelly Lahoud, Daniel Milton, and Bryan Price, "The Group That Calls Itself a State: Understanding the Evolution and Challenges of the Islamic State," The Combating Terrorism Center at West Point, www.ctc.usma.edu, December 2014, 14.
32. "Loose Ends: Iraq's Security Forces Between U.S. Drawdown and Withdrawal," International Crisis Group report, October 26, 2010, 2, 4.
33. McCants, *The ISIS Apocalypse*, 75.
34. Ibid., 79–82.
35. Aymenn Jawad Al-Tamimi, "The Islamic State of Iraq and Al-Sham," *Middle East Review of International Affairs* 17, no. 3 (Fall 2013): 21.
36. Ibid.
37. Mushreq Abbas, "Has al-Qaeda found Zarqawi's successor?," *Al-Monitor*, January 15, 2014, www.al-monitor.com/pulse/originals/2014/01/iraq-isis-shaker-wahib-zarqawi.html.

38. Aymenn Jawad Al-Tamimi, "2006—Announcement of the Caliphate?," December 9, 2015, www.aymennjawad.org.
39. Khalil al-Anani, "The ISIS-ification of Islamist politics," *Washington Post*, January 30, 2015, 37.
40. Michael Weiss and Hassan Hassan, *ISIS: Inside the Army of Terror* (New York: Regan Arts, 2015), 160–161.
41. Anani, "The ISIS-ification of Islamist Politics," 37.
42. Vicken Cheterian, "ISIS and the Killing Fields of the Middle East," *Survival* 57, no. 2 (April–May 2015): 113, 115.
43. Weiss and Hassan, *ISIS: Inside the Army of Terror*, 98.
44. "Iraq: Falluja's Faustian Bargain." "Make or Break: Iraq's Sunnis and the State," 33.
45. Discussion with US military advisors, al-Asad airbase, al-Anbar province, January 8, 2016.
46. Gartenstein-Ross and Jensen, "The Role of Iraqi Tribes after the Islamic State's Ascendance," 106. Liz Sly, "Arab Spring-Style Protests Take Hold in Iraq," *Washington Post*, February 8, 2013.
47. Discussion with key Albu Nimr tribal leader, Amman, Jordan, 9 March 2017. Rayburn, *Iraq After America*, 236.
48. Discussion with US generals, Irbil, Iraq, October 20, 2015. Discussion with Marine command, Kuwait, August 24, 2015. Discussion with Albu Fahad tribal leader, Baghdad, April 3, 2017.
49. Correspondence with Dr. Ben Connable, August 17, 2016.
50. Boghani, "In Their Own Words," PBS News Hour transcript, October 28, 2014.
51. Ibid.
52. Discussion with key Albu Nimr tribal leader, Amman, Jordan, 9 March 2017. Gartenstein-Ross and Jensen, "The Role of Iraqi Tribes after the Islamic State's Ascendance," 106–107, 108. Discussion with leading Albu Fahad tribal leader, Amman, Jordan, 9 March 2017.
53. Suadad Al-Salhy, "Al Qaeda Tightens Grip on Western Iraq in Bid for Islamic State," *Reuters*, December 11, 2013.
54. Michael Knights, "The ISIL's Stand in the Ramadi-Falluja Corridor," *CTC Sentinel*, May 29, 2014.
55. Yasir Ghazi, "Deadly Clashes between Iraqi Forces and Tribal Fighters in Anbar," *New York Times*, December 30, 2013. "Al Qaeda Seizes Partial Control of 2 Cities in Western Iraq," *The Long War Journal* (blog), January 2, 2014, www.longwarjournal.org/archives/2014/01/al_qaeda_seizes_cont.php. Knights, "The ISIL's Stand in the Ramadi-Falluja Corridor."

56. Liz Sly, "Al-Qaeda Force Captures Fallujah Amid Rise in Violence in Iraq," *Washington Post*, January 3, 2014.
57. Knights, "The ISIL's Stand in the Ramadi-Falluja Corridor."
58. Sly, "Al-Qaeda Force Captures Fallujah Amid Rise in Violence in Iraq."
59. Yasir Ghazi and Tim Arango, "Qaeda-Linked Militants in Iraq Secure Nearly Full Control of Falluja," *New York Times*, January 4, 2014.
60. Ahmed Ali, "Iraq Update," *Institute for the Study of War* (blog), January 2014, iswresearch.blogspot.com/2014/01/iraq-update-2014-9-anbar-standoff.html .
61. Juan Cole, "Iraq's Sunni Civil War," *Informed Comment* (blog), January 4, 2014. "Iraqi Sheiks Take the Fight to Al Qaeda in Fallujah," *The Daily Beast*, January 4, 2014.
62. Sly, "Al-Qaeda Force Captures Fallujah Amid Rise in Violence in Iraq."
63. Discussion with Special Marine Air-Ground Task Force, Kuwait, August 25, 2015.
64. Erin Banco, "Sunni Tribesmen Helped ISIS Take Control of Ramadi, Leaders Say," *International Business Times*, May 22, 2015. Gartenstein-Ross and Jensen, "The Role of Iraqi Tribes after the Islamic State's Ascendance," 107. Robert Tollast, "Civil Wars of Iraq's Sunni Tribes: Fault Lines within 8 Sunni tribes and Sub-tribes, 2003–2016," *Iraqi Thoughts* (website), March 28, 2016, 1001iraqithoughts.com/. . ./the-civil-wars-of-iraqs-sunni-tribes-fault-lines-within-8-sunni-tribes-and-sub-tribes-2003-2016/.
65. "Iraq: Falluja's Faustian Bargain."
66. Yasir Ghazi and Tim Arango, "Qaeda-Linked Militants in Iraq Secure Nearly Full Control of Falluja." Suadad Al-Salhy, "Iraq Army, Tribes Join Forces against al Qaeda," *Reuters*, January 3, 2014. Ned Parker, "Why Iraq's Most Violent Province Is a War Zone Again," *Time*, January 4, 2014.
67. Michael Knights, "The ISIL's Stand in the Ramadi-Falluja Corridor," *CTC Sentinel*, May 29, 2014. "Iraq: Falluja's Faustian Bargain."
68. Aymenn Jawad Al-Tamimi, "Brief Note on Fighting in Fallujah and the Periphery," September 18, 2014, www.aymennjawad.org. "Iraq: Falluja's Faustian Bargain."
69. Yasir Ghazi and Tim Arango, "Iraq Fighters, Qaeda Allies, Claim Falluja as New State," *New York Times*, January 3, 2014.
70. Sly, "Al-Qaeda Force Captures Fallujah Amid Rise in Violence in Iraq." Ghazi and Arango, "Iraq Fighters, Qaeda Allies, Claim Falluja as New State."

71. "Iraq: Falluja's Faustian Bargain."
72. Mushreq Abbas, "Has al-Qaeda Found Zarqawi's Successor?," *Al-Monitor* web-site, January 15, 2014.
73. Correspondence with Colonel Adam Strickland, former foreign area officer for Anbar, August 28, 2016.
74. Discussion with leading Albu Fahad tribal leader, Amman, Jordan, 9 March 2017. al-'Ubaydi, Lahoud, Milton, and Price, "The Group That Calls Itself a State: Understanding the Evolution and Challenges of the Islamic State," 23–24. Knights, "The ISIL's Stand in the Ramadi-Falluja Corridor."
75. Discussion with UNDP, Baghdad, July 29, 2016.
76. Discussion with US military advisors, al-Asad airbase, Anbar province, January 8, 2016. Discussion with Marine command, Kuwait, August 24, 2015.
77. Discussion with US generals, Irbil, Iraq, October 20, 2015. Discussion with key Albu Nimr tribal leader, Amman, Jordan, 9 March 2017.
78. Deputy Assistant Secretary Brett McGurk, Senate Foreign Relations Committee Hearing: Iraq at a Crossroads, Washington, DC, July 24, 2014.
79. David Gartenstein-Ross, "ISIL vs. the World," *War on the Rocks* (website), October 15, 2014.
80. Anand Gopal, "The Hell after ISIS," *The Atlantic Monthly*, May 2016. Gartenstein-Ross and Jensen, "The Role of Iraqi Tribes after the Islamic State's Ascendance," 103.
81. Discussion with Larissa Mihalisko, United Nations Development Program, Arlington, May 18, 2016. Eli Lake, "The Rise and Fall of America's Favorite Iraqi Sheik," *Bloomberg View*, www.bloomberg.com, June 11, 2015. Jennifer Janisch, "Iraqi Sheikh Asks U.S. for Weapons, but Obstacles Remain," CBS News, February 13, 2015.
82. Boghani, "In their Own Words," *PBS News Hour* transcript, October 28, 2014.
83. Tariq had been promoted to major general and served as provincial police chief from 2007 to 2009. Discussion with leading Albu Fahad tribal leader, Amman, Jordan, 9 March 2017.
84. Discussion with key Albu Nimr tribal leader, Amman, Jordan, 9 March 2017. Discussion with leading Albu Fahad tribal leader, Amman, Jordan, 9 March 2017. Discussion with Marine advisors, al-Asad airbase, al-Anbar province, January 8, 2016.
85. Discussion with United National Development Program, Baghdad, July 29, 2016.

86. Erin Banco, "Sunni Tribesmen Helped ISIS Take Control of Ramadi, Leaders Say," *International Business Times*, May 22, 2015. Daveed Gartenstein-Ross, "The Islamic State's Anbar Offensive and Abu Umar al-Shishani," *War on the Rocks* (website), October 9, 2014. Caleb Weiss, "Islamic State Launches Assault on Ramadi," *The Long War Journal* (blog), November 21, 2014.
87. "Call for Reinforcements from Aleppo Province to Anbar and Salah ad-Din Provinces," trans. Aymenn Jawad Al-Tamimi, Aymenn Jawad Al-Tamimi's blog, www.aymennjawad.org, April 27, 2015.
88. Correspondence with Adam Strickland, former foreign area officer in Anbar, August 28, 2016.
89. Discussion with leading Albu Fahad tribal leader, Amman, Jordan, 9 March 2017. Kevin Rawlinson, "ISIS Takes Iraqi City of Ramadi," *The Guardian*, May 18, 2015. Margaret Coker, "How the Islamic State's Win in Ramadi Reveals New Weapons, Tactical Sophistication, and Prowess," *Wall Street Journal*, May 25, 2015. Ayman Oghanna, "Anbar Tribes Look On as Iran Takes Fight to Jihadists," *The Times*, June 22, 2015.
90. Jane Arraf, "How Iraqi Forces Drove ISIS from Ramadi," *Newsweek*, March 4, 2016.
91. Discussion with Marine command, Kuwait, August 24, 2015.
92. Discussion with Larissa Mihalisko, UNDP, Arlington, May 18, 2016. Mihalisko traveled to Ramadi after the battle.
93. Discussion with Lieutenant General Sean MacFarland, Irbil, Iraq, October 20, 2015. Discussion with CJTF and Lieutenant General Sean MacFarland, Baghdad, January 7, 2016. Visit to CTS training facility, Baghdad, January 7, 2016. Meeting with Iraqi defense staff, Baghdad, January 7, 2016.
94. Discussion with US military advisors, al-Asad airbase, al-Anbar province, January 8, 2016.

Chapter 7

1. John Bagot Glubb, longtime military advisor to the Kingdom of Jordan and leader of the Arab Legion, spent the 1920s as a political advisor in Ramadi and fighting with tribes in southern Iraq against Wahhabi raids out of Saudi Arabia. John Bagot Glubb, *Arabian Adventures* (London: Cassell, 1978), 26.
2. In theoretical terms, I am arguing that cohesion and esprit de corps were together an immediate cause of the awakening. The

presence of US forces and the tribal power struggle with AQI were intermediate and longer-standing causes. All three are necessary conditions, yet of different weight. It is possible that without the cohesion and esprit de corps of the initial awakening tribes another intervening variable or another set of equally capable tribesmen would have emerged and started their own awakening. For those reasons, cohesion and esprit de corps hold less weight than US presence and the tribal power struggle with AQI as necessary conditions for the success of the awakening.

3. Steven Caton, "Anthropological Theories of Tribe and State Formation in the Middle East: Ideology and the Semiotics of Power," *Tribes and State Formation in the Middle East*, ed. Philip Khoury and Joseph Kostiner (Berkeley: University of California Press, 1990), 86.
4. "State of the Insurgency in al-Anbar," I MEF G-2, August 17, 2006, printed in Thomas Ricks, *The Gamble: General David Petraeus and the American Military Adventure in Iraq, 2006–2008* (New York: Penguin, 2009), 331.

Bibliography

Abbas, Mushreq. "Has al-Qaeda Found Zarqawi's Successor?" *Al-Monitor* (website). January 15, 2014.

Abdul-Jabar, Faleh. *Ayatollahs, Sufis, and Ideologues*. London: Saqi, 2002.

Abdul-Jabar, Faleh, and Hosham Dawod. *Tribes and Power: Nationalism and Ethnicity in the Middle East*. London: Saqi, 2003.

Al-Anani, Khalil. "The ISIS-ification of Islamist politics." *Washington Post*, January 30, 2015.

Al-Ansary, Khalid, and Ali Adeeb. "Most Tribes in Anbar Agree to Unite against Insurgents." *New York Times*. September 18, 2006.

Al Khairalli, Mussab. "Sunni Chiefs Offer al-Maliki Help in War on Militants." *Washington Times*. September 28, 2006.

Al-Salhy, Suadad. "Al Qaeda Tightens Grip on Western Iraq in Bid for Islamic State." *Reuters*. December 11, 2013.

Al-Salhy, Suadad. "Iraq Army, Tribes Join Forces against al Qaeda." *Reuters*. January 3, 2014.

Al-Tamimi, Aymenn Jawad. "The Islamic State of Iraq and Al-Sham." *Middle East Review of International Affairs* 17, no. 3 (Fall 2013): 19–42.

Al-Tamimi, Aymenn Jawad. "Brief Note on Fighting in Fallujah and the Periphery." www.aymennjawad.org. September 18, 2014.

Al-Tamimi, Aymenn Jawad. "2006—Announcement of the Caliphate?" www.aymennjawad.org. December 9, 2015.

Al-'Ubaydi, Muhammed, Nelly Lahoud, Daniel Milton, and Bryan Price. "The Group That Calls Itself a State: Understanding the Evolution and Challenges of the Islamic State." The Combating Terrorism Center at West Point. www.ctc.usma.edu. December 2014.

Allam, Hannah, and Mohammed al Dulaimy. "Iraqis Lament Call for Help." *Philadelphia Inquirer*. May 17, 2005.

Arraf, Jane. "How Iraqi Forces Drove ISIS from Ramadi." *Newsweek*. March 4, 2016.

Asfura-Heim, Patricio. "'No Security without Us': Tribes and Tribalism in Al Anbar Province, Iraq." CNA Research Memorandum. June 2014.

Bahney, Benjamin, Howard Shatz, Carroll Ganier, Renny McPherson, and Barbara Sude. "An Economic Analysis of the Financial Records of al-Qa'ida in Iraq." RAND Corporation research study. Santa Monica, CA: RAND Corporation, 2010.

Banco, Erin. "Sunni Tribesmen Helped ISIS Take Control of Ramadi, Leaders Say." *International Business Times*. May 22, 2015.

Barfield, Thomas. *Afghanistan: A Cultural and Political History*. Princeton, NJ: Princeton University Press, 2010.

Batatu, Hanna. *The Old Social Classes and the Revolutionary Movements of Iraq: A Study of Iraq's Old Landed and Commercial Classes and of its Communists, Ba'thists and Free Officers*. London: Saqi, 2004.

Beaumont, Peter. "Iraqi Tribes Launch Battle to Drive al Qaeda out of Troubled Province," *The Guardian*. October 3, 2006.

Bell, Gertrude. *The Arab of Mesopotamia*. Edited by Paul Rich. New York: Lexington Books, 2001.

Biddle, Stephen, Jeffrey Friedman, and Jacob Shapiro. "Testing the Surge: Why Did Violence Decline in Iraq in 2007?" *International Security* 37, no. 1 (Summer 2012): 7–40.

Bloom, Mia. *Dying to Kill: The Allure of Suicide Terror.* New York: Columbia University Press, 2005.

Boghani, Priyanka. "In Their Own Words: Sunnis on Their Treatment in Maliki's Iraq." PBS News Hour transcript. October 28, 2014.

Bremer, Paul. *My Year in Iraq*. New York: Simon and Schuster, 2006.

Brennan, Rick. "Withdrawal Symptoms: The Bungling of the Iraq Exit." *Foreign Affairs* 93, no. 6 (November/December 2014): 25–36.

Bulliet, Richard. *Islam: The View from the Edge.* New York: Columbia University Press, 1994.

Byman, Daniel. "Understanding the Islamic State—A Review Essay." *International Security* 40, no. 4 (Spring 2016): 127–165.

Casey, George. *Strategic Reflections: Operation Iraqi Freedom, July 2004–February 2007.* CreateSpace Independent Publishing, 2015.

Cheterian, Vicken. "ISIS and the Killing Fields of the Middle East." *Survival* 57, no. 2 (April–May 2015): 105–118.

Childress, Sarah. "Retaking Ramadi: All the Sheik's Men." *Newsweek*, December 12, 2006.

Clover, Charles. "Smiles and Shrugs Speak Volumes about Nature of Attacks on American Troops." *London Financial Times.* September 25, 2003.

Coker, Margaret. "How the Islamic State's Win in Ramadi Reveals New Weapons, Tactical Sophistication, and Prowess." *Wall Street Journal.* May 25, 2015.

Connable, Ben. "Warrior-Maverick Culture: Evolution of Adaptability in the U.S. Marine Corps." Doctoral dissertation, King's College London, 2016.

Dagher, Sam. "Sunni Muslim Sheikhs Join US in Fighting Al Qaeda." *Christian Science Monitor.* May 3, 2007.

Dagher, Sam. "In Anbar Province, New Leadership, but Old Problems Persist." *New York Times.* September 12, 2009.

Daraghi, Borzou. "Death's at the Door in Iraq." *Los Angeles Times.* July 23, 2006.

Dawisha, Adeed. *Iraq: A Political History from Independence to Occupation.* Princeton, NJ: Princeton University Press, 2009.

DeYoung, Karen. "Pakistan Will Give Arms to Tribal Militias." *Washington Post.* October 23, 2008.

Dodge, Toby. *Inventing Iraq: The Failure of Nation Building and a History Denied.* New York: Columbia University Press, 2003.

Fishman, Brian. "Dysfunction and Decline: Lessons Learned from Inside Al Qa'ida in Iraq." Monograph. Combating Terrorism Center at West Point. March 1, 2009.

Fletcher, Martin. "Fighting Back." *London Times.* November 20, 2006.

Gartenstein-Ross, Daveed. "The Islamic State's Anbar Offensive and Abu Umar al-Shishani." *War on the Rocks* (blog). October 9, 2014, https://warontherocks.com/.../the-islamic-states-anbar-offensive-and-abu-umar-al-shishani/.

Gartenstein-Ross, David. "ISIL vs. the World." *War on the Rocks* (blog). October 15, 2014, https://warontherocks.com/2014/10/the-fight-goes-on-in-anbar-isil-vs-the-world/.

Gartenstein-Ross, Daveed, and Sterling Jensen. "The Role of Iraqi Tribes after the Islamic State's Ascendance." *Military Review* (July–August 2015): 102–110.

Ghazi, Yasir. "Deadly Clashes between Iraqi Forces and Tribal Fighters in Anbar." *New York Times.* December 30, 2013.

Ghazi, Yasir, and Tim Arango. "Iraq Fighters, Qaeda Allies, Claim Falluja as New State." *New York Times.* January 3, 2014.

Ghazi, Yasir, and Tim Arango. "Qaeda-Linked Militants in Iraq Secure Nearly Full Control of Falluja." *New York Times.* January 4, 2014.

Ghosh, Bobby. "In Iraq's Old Battlefields: Two Kinds of Americans." *Time*. October 8, 2010. www.content.time.com.

Glubb, John Bagot. *Arabian Adventures*. London: Cassell, 1978.

Gopal, Anand. "The Hell after ISIS." *The Atlantic Monthly*. May 2016.

Graham, Bradley. "Top Iraq Rebels Elude Intensified U.S. Raids." *Washington Post*. February 15, 2005.

Haddad, Fanar. *Sectarianism in Iraq: Antagonistic Visions of Unity*. New York: Columbia University Press, 2011.

Hafez, Mohammed. *Suicide Bombers in Iraq: The Strategy and Ideology of Martyrdom*. Washington, DC: US Institute for Peace Press, 2007.

Hashim, Ahmed. "The Insurgency in Iraq." *Small Wars and Insurgencies* 14, no. 3 (August 2003): 1–22.

Hashim, Ahmed. *Iraq's Sunni Insurgency*. International Institute for Strategic Studies Adelphi Paper 402. February 2009.

Innocent, Malou. "A Model for Modern Counterinsurgency." *Armed Forces Journal*. August 2008.

"Iraq: Falluja's Faustian Bargain." Crisis Group Middle East Report. April 28, 2014.

"Iraqi Sheiks Take the Fight to Al Qaeda in Fallujah. *The Daily Beast*. January 4, 2014.

Isser, Deborah, ed., *Customary Justice and the Rule of Law in War-Torn Societies*. Washington, DC: US Institute for Peace Press, 2011.

Janisch, Jennifer. "Iraqi Sheikh Asks U.S. for Weapons, but Obstacles Remain." CBS News. February 13, 2015.

Jaffe, Greg. "Tribal Connections." *Wall Street Journal*. August 8, 2007.

Jensen, Sterling. "The Fall of Iraq's Anbar Province." *Middle East Quarterly* (Winter 2016): 1–7.

Jervis, Rick. "Police in Iraq See Jump in Recruits." *USA Today*. January 15, 2007.

Kagan, Frederick. "The Gettysburg of This War." *National Review*. September 3, 2007.

Karouny, Miriam. "Gunmen in Iraq's Ramadi Announce Sunni Emirate." *Reuters*. October 18, 2006.

Keegan, John. *The Face of Battle*. New York: Penguin, 1976.

Khalil, Lydia. "Anbar Revenge Brigade Makes Progress in the Fight against al-Qaeda." *Terrorism Focus*, vol. 3, no. 12 (March, 28 2006).

Khoury, Philip, and Joseph Kostiner, eds. *Tribes and State Formation in the Middle East*. Berkeley: University of California Press, 1990.

Khuri, Fuad. *Imams and Emirs: State, Religion, and Sects in Islam*. London: Saqi, 2006.

Kilcullen, David. *The Accidental Guerrilla: Fighting Small Wars in the Midst of a Big One*. New York: Oxford University Press, 2009.

Knickmeyer, Ellen. "Ramadi Insurgents Flaunt Threat." *Washington Post*. December 2, 2005.

Knickmeyer, Ellen, and Jonathan Finer. "Insurgents Assert Control over Town Near Syrian Border." *Washington Post*. September 6, 2005.

Knickmeyer, Ellen, and Muhammed Saif Adin. "Families Flee Iraqi River Towns on 4th Day of Sectarian Warfare." *Washington Post*. October 17, 2006.

Knights, Michael. "The ISIL's Stand in the Ramadi-Falluja Corridor." *CTC Sentinel* 29 (May 2014).

Kukis, Mark. "Turning Iraq's Tribes against Al Qaeda." *Time*. December 26, 2006.

Kukis, Mark. *Voices from Iraq: A People's History, 2003–2009*. New York: Columbia University Press, 2011.

Langersept, Gary. "What They're Saying in Anbar Province." *New York Times*. September 16, 2007.

Long, Austin. "The Anbar Awakening." *Survival* 50, no. 2 (April/May 2008): 67–94.

"Loose Ends: Iraq's Security Forces between U.S. Drawdown and Withdrawal." International Crisis Group report. October 26, 2010.

Lynch, Marc. "Explaining the Awakening: Engagement, Publicity, and the Transformation of Iraqi Sunni Political Attitudes." *Security Studies* 20 (2011): 36–72.

"Make or Break: Iraq's Sunnis and the State." International Crisis Group report. August 14, 2013.

Malterre, Thiebauld. "Ramadi: Defended by Insurgents Turned Police." *Agence France-Presse* 2 (December 2006).

Marr, Phebe. *The Modern History of Iraq*. 3rd edition. Boulder, CO: Westview, 2011.

McCary, John. "The Anbar Awakening: An Alliance of Incentives." *The Washington Quarterly* 32, no. 1 (January 2009): 43–59.

McCants, William. *The ISIS Apocalypse: The History, Strategy, and Doomsday Vision of the Islamic State*. New York: St. Martin's, 2015.

McCloskey, Megan. "Battling Violence in the Heart of Darkness." *Stars and Stripes*, January 14, 2007.

Michaels, Jim. *A Chance in Hell: The Men Who Triumphed Over Iraq's Deadliest City and Turned the Tide of War*. New York: St. Martin's, 2010.

Montgomery, Gary, and Timothy McWilliams, eds. *Al-Anbar Awakening, Volume I: American Perspectives.* Quantico, VA: Marine Corps University Press, 2009.

Montgomery, Gary, and Timothy McWilliams, eds. *Al-Anbar Awakening, Volume II: Iraqi Perspectives.* Quantico, VA: Marine Corps University Press, 2009.

Murphy, Dan. "How Al Qaeda Views a Long Iraq War." *Christian Science Monitor.* October 5, 2006.

O'Hanlon, Michael, and David Petraeus. "America's Awesome Military." *Foreign Affairs* 95, no. 5 (September/October 2016): 10–17.

Oghanna, Ayman. "Anbar Tribes Look On as Iran Takes Fight to Jihadists." *The Times.* June 22, 2015.

Paley, Amit. "Shift in Tactics Aims to Revive Struggling Insurgency." *Washington Post.* February 8, 2008.

Parker, Ned. "Why Iraq's Most Violent Province Is a War Zone Again." *Time.* January 4, 2014.

Partlow, Joshua. "Sheiks Help Curb Violence in Iraq's West, U.S. Says." *Washington Post.* January 27, 2007.

Pirnie, Bruce, and Edward O'Connell. *Counterinsurgency in Iraq (2003–2006).* Santa Monica, CA: RAND Corporation, 2008.

Raghavan, Sudarsan. "Sunni Factions Split with Al Qaeda Group." *Washington Post* April 14, 2007.

Rawlinson, Kevin. "ISIS Takes Iraqi City of Ramadi." *The Guardian.* May 18, 2015.

Rayburn, Joel. *Iraq After America: Strongmen, Sectarians, Resistance.* Palo Alto, CA: Hoover Institution Press, 2014.

Ricks, Thomas. "Situation Called Dire in West Iraq." *Washington Post.* September 11, 2006.

Ricks, Thomas. *The Gamble: General David Petraeus and the American Military Adventure in Iraq, 2006–2008.* New York: Penguin, 2009.

Robinson, Linda. *Tell Me How This Ends: General David Petraeus and the Search for a Way Out of Iraq.* New York: Public Affairs, 2008.

Robinson, Linda. "What Petraeus Understands." www.foreignpolicy.com. September 2008.

Sattler, John, and Daniel Wilson. "Operation Al Fajr: The Battle of Fallujah–Part II." *Marine Corps Gazette.* July 2005.

Scheuer, Michael. "Al Qaeda's Top Ideologues Release New Statements on the Global Jihad." *Terrorism Focus* 3, no. 38 (October 2006), www.jamestown.org.

Schroden, Jonathan. "Measures for Security in a Counterinsurgency." *Journal of Strategic Studies* 32, no. 5 (October 2009): 715–744.

Schultz, Richard. *The Marines Take Anbar: The Four Year Fight against Al Qaeda* (Annapolis: Naval Institute Press, 2013).

Shadid, Anthony. "In Anbar, U.S.-Allied Tribal Chiefs Feel Deep Sense of Abandonment." *Washington Post*. October 3, 2009.

Shadid, Anthony. *Night Draws Near: Iraq's People in the Shadow of America's War*. New York: Henry Holt, 2005.

Shadid, Anthony. "Iraq Election Highlights Ascendancy of Tribes." *Washington Post*. January 25, 2009.

Sly, Liz. "Arab Spring-Style Protests Take Hold in Iraq." *Washington Post*. February 8, 2013.

Sly, Liz. "Al-Qaeda Force Captures Fallujah Amid Rise in Violence in Iraq." *Washington Post*. January 3, 2014.

Smith, Niel, and Sean MacFarland. "Anbar Awakens: The Tipping Point." *Military Review*. March–April 2008.

Tan, Michelle. "Civil affairs Troops Help Open New School." *Army Times*. January 25, 2007.

Tavernise, Sabrina, and Dexter Filkins. "Local Insurgents Tell of Clashes with Al Qaeda's Forces in Iraq." *New York Times*. January 12, 2006.

"The Al Qaeda Diaries." *Jane's Terrorism and Security Monitor*. March 4, 2008.

"The Secret Letter from Iraq." *Time*. October 6, 2006.

Todd, Lin. "Iraqi Tribal Study—Al Anbar Governorate." Quantum Research International. June 18, 2006.

Weiss, Michael, and Hassan Hassan. *ISIS: Inside the Army of Terror*. New York: Regan Arts, 2015.

West, Bing. *No True Glory: A Frontline Account of the Battle for Fallujah*. New York: Bantam Books, 2005.

West, Bing. *The Strongest Tribe: War, Politics, and the Endgame in Iraq*. New York: Random House, 2008.

Weston, J. Kael. *The Mirror Test: America at War in Iraq and Afghanistan*. New York: Knopf, 2016.

Woodward, Bob. "Why Did Violence Plummet? It Wasn't Just the Surge." *Washington Post*. September 8, 2008.

Index

www.ingramcontent.com/pod-product-compliance
Ingram Content Group UK Ltd.
Pitfield, Milton Keynes, MK11 3LW, UK
UKHW020554200726
13851UKWH00027B/20

9 780190 659424